AS WE WERE
The Story of Old Elizabethtown

Governor Jonathan Belcher. Courtesy E. J. Grassmann.

AS WE WERE

The Story of Old Elizabethtown

by

THEODORE THAYER

Published for
The New Jersey Historical Society
by
The Grassmann Publishing Company, Inc.
Elizabeth, New Jersey

The Collections of
THE NEW JERSEY HISTORICAL SOCIETY

This is Volume XIII in the Collections.
Copyright 1964 by Theodore Thayer.
Library of Congress Catalogue Card Number: 64-21662
Printed in the United States of America
by
Quinn & Boden Company, Inc.,
Rahway, New Jersey.

Preface

Elizabethtown, founded in 1665, was the first English settlement in New Jersey. For that reason alone it is deserving of special attention. Its importance, however, did not diminish after the town was founded. During the whole colonial period it was the center of a bitter controversy with the Proprietors over land rights. In this long contest, wherein the town generally won out, Elizabethtown learned to battle vested interests and to keep alive what they considered to be their rights and privileges as freeborn Englishmen. Schooled in the Proprietary conflict, Elizabethtonians were bold in upholding the principles of liberty during the American Revolution.

After the Revolution, Elizabethtown became the principal stronghold of Federalism in New Jersey. Communities such as Elizabethtown with an aristocratic character backed the policies of Washington and Hamilton whereby the Federal Republic was successfully launched and carried through perilous times. After 1800, Elizabethtown gradually swung to the Jeffersonian party and thereby continued to play a recognizable role in national and state affairs.

Significant too was Elizabethtown's social and cultural history. One of its ministers founded the College of New Jersey in Elizabethtown; another led a Millennial movement predicting the end of the world; others were prominent in the Sunday Schools, public education, and other movements of the nineteenth century. During the 1790's Elizabethtown became the haven for over one hundred French, fleeing the massacres in the West Indies and the guillotine in Paris. Although most of them did not stay in America, their manners and customs had a lasting influence on Elizabethtonians as well as the nation at large.

Elizabethtown became a city in 1854, nearly two hundred years after its founding. During all this time it kept its quasi-rural character with houses and mansions on large plots surrounded by shade trees, orchards and gardens. On the outskirts of the town were fields for farming. With the coming of the railroad in 1836 a great transformation began. Soon whole districts were occupied by factories and crowded housing for the workers. Only the last chapter of this book deals with the transition between 1836 and 1854. The story as a whole is concerned with Elizabethtown before the advent of the industrial revolution. In this setting, so common in early American towns, Elizabethtown played its part in the history of New Jersey and the new nation.

I wish to thank Edward J. Grassmann whose knowledge and understanding of Elizabethtown history has been most helpful in writing this book. I want also to thank Mrs. John Kean and George J. Miller, for their aid and encouragement. In addition I am indebted to many people at the libraries I have used. Among these are Donald A. Sinclair and Anthony Nicolosi of the Department of Special Collections, Rutgers University; Robert M. Lunny, Mrs. Gerald L. May, and Howard W. Wiseman of the New Jersey Historical Society; Alexander Clark and Miss Julie Hudson of the Manuscript Division, Princeton University; and Wilmer R. Leech of the Manuscript Division, New York Historical Society.

THEODORE THAYER

Chatham, New Jersey, 1964

Introduction

When I was a boy there was still much in Elizabeth to remind one of the olden days when Elizabethtown was a small and picturesque American town. There were many old mansions with gardens and orchards as in former times. Along Elizabeth River there were tremendous willows quite as large as the giant elms on Jersey Street. Elizabeth Avenue and part of Broad Street likewise had many fine houses and shade trees. Some of the Broad Street stores, as in the old days, had wooden sheds that reached to the curb, affording protection in winter and summer. In truth, the town still merited the comment of a Revolutionary traveler who wrote: "We came to a very pretty place opposite Staten Island called Elizabethtown."

After graduating from the Battin High School, I served a three-year apprenticeship in the old Meyer office, a surveying firm taken over by Ernest L. Meyer in 1851. Mr. Meyer, who had studied at Heidelberg and Göttingen, became very interested in American history. He gathered together many documents and papers of old Elizabethtown in addition to those that came down with the business which was reputed to date from 1720. Fortunately these papers have been preserved and were of use in the writing of this book.

Our title researching in connection with salt meadow surveys involved examination of records in the court houses and in the Surveyor General's office in Perth Amboy. In this way I developed an interest in our early history. My interest grew as I came in contact with many old timers who filled me with tales and anecdotes of the "good old times." Later when I took over the business and cleared meadow titles in Newark and Elizabeth, it was necessary to renew and enlarge on old friendships to secure family history and records.

After the depression set in, it became a sad and familiar sight to see many of the old buildings torn down and destroyed. But with no money available no one could attempt to save them. Sage old Julian Kean, however, assured us that we only had to live long enough and things would change. Fortunately his prediction has come true and most of the remaining old houses in Elizabeth are being saved for posterity. The Belcher House is one of these.

Having decided to undertake some publishing, I am happy that Dr. Thayer has been willing to carry out my forty-year-old plan of putting in writing the story of old Elizabethtown and its people— people who lived out their lives without the benefit of gas, electricity, running water, and a host of other modern conveniences. By working long hours, often under great hardship, they laid the foundations and did their part in making America great. This, I think is the central theme in the story to follow.

EJG

Contents

Illustrations

AS WE WERE
The Story of Old Elizabethtown

I

The Belcher House

It was with a certain feeling of nostalgia that Aaron Ogden in 1797 purchased the old mansion in Elizabethtown known today as the Belcher House in honor of Governor Belcher who once lived there. Located at the corner of East Jersey and Catherine streets, the house stands on land which was awarded as a town-lot, to John Ogden, Jr., when Elizabethtown was first settled in 1665.

Aaron Ogden, the new owner, was not of the line of John Ogden, Jr. He was a descendant of John Ogden's brother, Jonathan, also a founder of Elizabethtown. However, since the days when the house was built on the old townlot early in the eighteenth century, possibly earlier, members of the Ogden family had occupied it until a few years before Aaron was born in 1756. Aaron could very well remember the house with its carefully cultivated gardens and orchards as it appeared in his boyhood days. At that time it was owned by the wealthy and distinguished William Peartree Smith. Presumably some of the beautiful furnishings in the mansion, as Aaron remembered it, had been acquired by Smith from Governor Jonathan Belcher who lived in the house from the time he moved to Elizabethtown in 1751 until his death six years later.

Quite naturally Colonel Ogden, as he was usually called, was proud of his new home and of its family and historic associations. In a way, too, its acquisition signified that he had made his mark in the world. With a distinguished record behind him as an officer in the Revolution, he was now at the age of forty-one a prominent member of the New Jersey bar and a leading politician in the state. As such, he had acquired financial means befitting the owner of one of the finest mansions in town.

In becoming the home of Colonel Ogden, the old Belcher

1

House acquired new importance. Aaron Ogden's heroic career in the American Revolution was enough to give luster to any house. However, the most notable years of his life still lay ahead when he purchased the Belcher House. As a leader of the Federalist party in New Jersey, he was destined to become the war-time governor in 1812. Following his governorship he became an outstanding promoter of steamboating and as such was soon locked in a steamboat war out of which would come the case of Gibbons *vs.* Ogden with its basic principles for Federal control of interstate commerce and navigation.

The new owner of the Belcher House looked the part he was to play during his long and stirring career. Tall, broad-shouldered, and muscular, Ogden could be as rough as a bear when occasion demanded. Otherwise he was gentle, kind, and considerate. His acquiline nose and rugged features under a shock of straw-colored hair, cut in bangs, complemented a set of keen blue eyes that appeared to take the measure of all that came before them. His ability to size up a situation and act accordingly made him a bold soldier, a resourceful lawyer, an enterprising business man, and a dynamic war-time governor of New Jersey.

When purchased by Colonel Ogden, the old brick mansion with its barns, outbuildings, and five or six acres of orchards and gardens, looked much as it did in Governor Belcher's day, a half-century before. The scars of war, suffered during the Revolution, were gone or hidden under new paint and finishings. Like all the houses in Elizabethtown, the premises were enclosed by a sturdy wooden fence daubed with whitewash. In the yard, back of the kitchen, was a well with the customary grey sandstone collar carved from the solid rock at a nearby quarry. Above the well rose the familiar well-sweep with its long pole tilted at an angle to lift the water from the cool but shallow well. Set off by several ancient trees which seemed to frame the old building, the Belcher House had acquired a certain enchantment so often found in the houses of that era.

After purchasing the Belcher House, Colonel Ogden added a frame wing to the western side for an office. This made the house more attractive by balancing the frame section, used as a kitchen, at the eastern end of the house. He also laid out much

Governor Aaron Ogden. Courtesy New York Historical Society.

Belcher House about 1870.

West Room, first floor of the Belcher House.

East Room, first floor of the Belcher House.

Governor Belcher's Bedroom, second floor.

East Room, second floor of the Belcher House.

money for redecorating and making changes in the interior of the house, befitting the prevailing style of the Adams or Federal period. The east room, off the entrance hall, formerly Governor Belcher's dining room and retained by Ogden for the same purpose, was redone in a motif predominately French. The ceiling and panels under the windows were embellished with elliptical moldings in white plaster. From the center of the inner ellipse on the ceiling hung an ornate chandelier in bronze and glass. A French mantle, done in white plaster, made the fireplace match the ceilings and panels and added charm to the room. The walls, painted a soft lemon, conveyed a cheery, airy feeling. The new brass coal grate, with its iron basket purchased for the fireplace, made heating less difficult than in Belcher's time when the only improvement over the open fireplace was the none-too-successful Franklin stove.

It may be that Aaron Ogden did not know the age of the section of the house he had remodeled for his dining room. He knew, nonetheless, that this and the adjoining structure, used as a kitchen, were the oldest parts of the house. Originally it had but one story. Now it had a second floor; and to the right of the center hall was a whole new wing added in 1751 when Governor Belcher came to stay. Clearly defined from the old single story section, with its larger bricks, were the newer sections in Flemish bond with distinctive checker-board-like patterns of glazed and unglazed bricks.

The question of the age of the oldest section of the Belcher House is intriguing. One can virtually rule out any possibility that the single story brick section was the original house built by John Ogden, Jr., after his arrival on the shores of Achter Kull. Conceivably the frame section, long used as a kitchen but no longer standing,* could have been the house Ogden erected on his townlot in 1665, but this is not very likely. So far as is known, all of the little houses or huts built by the founders were along the main highways bordering the river.

It is entirely possible that the orange brick section of the Belcher House dates back as far as 1680 and that it was one of the first brick buildings in Elizabethtown. In the year 1680, it is known, a large brick mansion, called the Second Government

* The kitchen was rebuilt in 1963-64.

House, was built for Governor Carteret. Since all of the Ogdens were bricklayers, most likely one or more of them had a hand in constructing the Governor's house; clearly the construction had demanded the services of the best craftsmen in town. Certainly the old brick section could have been built about the same time as the Second Government House. Its wide orange bricks apparently were made in Elizabethtown, where bricks were made as early as 1679. That year the German traveler, Jasper Danckaerts, saw a boat loading bricks at Elizabethtown for delivery at New York. Quite likely John Ogden, Sr., owned the brickyard, since he was a brickmaker as well as a man of many other skills.

Although there is good reason to believe that the Belcher House goes back to about 1680, the earliest record of the house bears the date of 1722. In that year Benjamin Ogden, son of John, the founder, willed the property to his sons and spoke of the house as the one where son John then lived.

Solidly constructed, the Belcher House was built to last for centuries. Today it stands as a reminder of colonial Elizabethtown, the first English settlement in New Jersey. Its restoration brings to mind the stirring times during the first century or more of its existence when Elizabethtown saw the long struggle with the Proprietors, the upheavals of the War for Independence, and the great changes wrought during the years following the Revolution.

In 1854, the Borough of Elizabethtown finally became the City of Elizabeth. Already the stage was set for the revolutionary changes of an industrial society. With increasing momentum the once familiar landmarks of old Elizabethtown were swept away as swarms of new people flocked into the city to live in crowded housing and work in the mushrooming factories of the Elizabethport area. This, however, is another story, for the narrative about to unfold is confined to the days of Elizabethtown when the Belcher House was a mansion of more than ordinary distinction. From the voices of the distant past, the stirring drama of old Elizabethtown will be told. The story first turns upon how the colonizers came to purchase land from the Indians and how they then made a home for themselves in the primeval forest.

II

The Elizabethtown Purchase

The Elizabethtown purchase of 1664 marked the first step in the colonizing of New Jersey by the English. At the time only a few Dutch plantations at Hoboken, Bayonne, Hackensack, and nearby points broke the solitude of the surrounding wilderness. In southern New Jersey, the population was slightly greater; there Swedes were located at Salem and several other tiny settlements. Pennsylvania still remained unsettled; it would be nearly twenty years before Philadelphia was planted by the Quakers.

As early as 1641, the Dutch, who had founded New Amsterdam in 1614, had established a few plantations in northern New Jersey. Harsh treatment of the Indians, however, caused the savages to kill or drive away all the settlers in 1643 and again in 1655. It was not until 1660, when the Indians seemed pacified, that the Dutch once more undertook to plant settlements on the New Jersey side of the Hudson.

About the time the Dutch were returning to New Jersey, some Englishmen living within the borders of New Netherlands decided to approach the Dutch government with a scheme for planting a settlement of their own in New Jersey. At this time the Dutch appeared well-entrenched in America, having strengthened their holdings along the Hudson and "conquered" the Swedes without bloodshed in Delaware and southern New Jersey. At the eastern end of Long Island the English retained a bond with Connecticut, but their countrymen who had taken land at Jamaica and other places near the center of Dutch power had accepted the fact that they were Dutch citizens and that New Jersey was Dutch territory.

The first proposal of English-speaking people for settling New Jersey came in February, 1660. It came in the form of a petition to Governor Petrus Stuyvesant from John Strickland, spokesman for interested parties in Huntington and Jamaica. In the quaint language of the time, the letter asked "whither or no that place upon the mayne land which is called Arther Cull be free from any engagement: secondly if free, then whither or no he will be pleased to grant it to a Company of honest men that may decide to sit doune ther to make a plantation under his government—." In answer, Governor Stuyvesant invited the petitioners to come and view the land. After that, they were assured, the Dutch would be pleased to entertain a proposal for colonization.[1]

About the time John Strickland received his answer from the Dutch, intense interest in colonizing New Jersey also arose in the New Haven colony. The people of New Haven had learned that Hartford had sent Governor John Winthrop, Jr., to England for a new charter to include the towns of southern Connecticut. This was not welcomed by the New Haveners, who were Puritans of a much stricter sort than those at Hartford. Consequently many were in favor of moving out, especially if they could obtain a grant to virgin country with all its economic opportunities. Soon a delegation, led by Robert Treat of Milford, made a trip to New Amsterdam where they earnestly discussed with the Dutch the possibilities of settling in New Jersey.

After hearing the proposal, Governor Stuyvesant replied that he would gladly grant the petitioners a liberal franchise with religious freedom and control over local affairs. But no agreement was reached. On reflection, the Connecticut men (as did John Strickland and the Long Island English) concluded that the Dutch land titles were defective. Furthermore, they feared for their safety against the Indians under the Dutch, who did not care to take measures that might injure their fur trade. Neither did they like the thought of the Dutch having appellate jurisdiction over causes arising in the local courts of New Jersey. The petitioners objected also to an assessment of one-tenth of all they produced by the Dutch West India Company, the proprietors of New Netherlands. Clearly the English yeomen in the New World were jealous of their liberties as well as watchful of their economic interests.

The next year the Connecticut people again tried unsuccessfully to persuade the Dutch to allow them to colonize New Jersey on their own terms. The Dutch were disappointed, too, for they very much desired the colonization of New Jersey as a "bulwark to our nation against the savages on the Raritan and Minisink." Finally Stuyvesant placed the question before the Directors of the Dutch West India Company in Amsterdam. In reply, he was empowered to make any concession necessary to induce the petitioners to colonize. No progress, however, was made during the short time remaining before the English conquered New Netherlands.

One other attempt was made by Englishmen to colonize New Jersey before the surrender occurred. Late in 1663, a score or more of Long Island adventurers from Jamaica, Flushing, and Gravesend sailed to the mouth of the Raritan to buy land from the Indians without consulting the Dutch. Apparently these were the men represented by John Strickland three years before. However, they were speedily expelled with their mission unfulfilled when Governor Stuyvesant sent over an armed force to squelch the enterprise.

Only a few months after this episode, there occurred an event as dramatic as it was far-reaching in its consequences. In March, 1664, King Charles II granted to his brother, the Duke of York, all lands from the west bank of the Connecticut River to the eastern shores of the Delaware. All New Jersey, by the stroke of the pen, thereby became the property of the Duke of York. The English based their claim to the territory to be seized from the Dutch on John Cabot's discovery and exploration of the eastern coast of North America in 1498. To expel the Dutch, who in the eyes of the English were but interlopers, the Duke of York, as Lord High Admiral of the King's Navy, fitted out four warships under the command of Sir Robert Carr. All this was part of a deep-laid plan of the English to take over as much as possible of the lucrative Dutch trade and possessions throughout the world. Altogether three wars were fought before the English triumphed over their rivals. At New Amsterdam, however, the English won a bloodless victory at the outset.

Upon arriving in New York, Sir Robert Carr sent Governor Stuyvesant a demand for the surrender of the colony. Since the Dutch were no match for the English, surrender was inevitable. Early in September, therefore, after a few days of negotiations, Stuyvesant with bowed head hobbled out of the fort on his wooden leg and capitulated. New Amsterdam now became New York—after its new owner, the Duke of York.

With Sir Robert Carr was Colonel Richard Nicolls, the Duke of York's deputy governor for the conquered province. Nicolls, who was to lose his life in a naval battle with the Dutch eight years later, had barely time to get himself established as deputy governor of New York before he was waited upon by a delegation from Jamaica, Long Island. The men were John Bailey, Daniel and Nathaniel Denton, Thomas Benedick, John Foster, and Luke Watson. They represented an association formed for carrying out the long-cherished colonizing of Albania (as Governor Nicolls called New Jersey in honor of James who was the Duke of York and Albany). Certainly some, if not all, of the men who waited upon the Governor were among those so recently expelled from New Jersey by Governor Stuyvesant.

On being admitted to the Governor's presence, the men from Long Island presented a petition, dated September 26, 1664. In it they described how they had tried repeatedly to obtain permission from the Dutch to colonize New Jersey. They had nearly given up hope and were on the point of moving elsewhere, when Colonel Nicolls appeared to change the outlook of all Englishmen seeking to colonize New Jersey. In conclusion, they asked permission to purchase from the Indians Achter Kol, as the land west of Staten Island was called. Nicolls had orders to colonize as swiftly as possible. He, therefore, immediately granted the request of the petitioners. "I do consent unto the proposals," he wrote, "and shall give the undertakers all due encouragement in so good a work." [2]

Upon receiving the Governor's answer, the Associators lost no time in getting started. Within a month several of them made their way to the wigwam of Mattano on Staten Island and bought what became known as the Elizabethtown Purchase. The deed, signed by Mattano and two other sachems, was dated October 28, 1664. In the name of the Associators the deed was made out to John Bailey, Daniel Denton, and Luke Watson. The purchasers bound themselves to pay the Indians, upon entry, twenty fathoms * of trading cloth, two coats, two guns, two kettles, ten bars of lead, and twenty handsful of powder. One year after entry

* A fathom measures six feet.

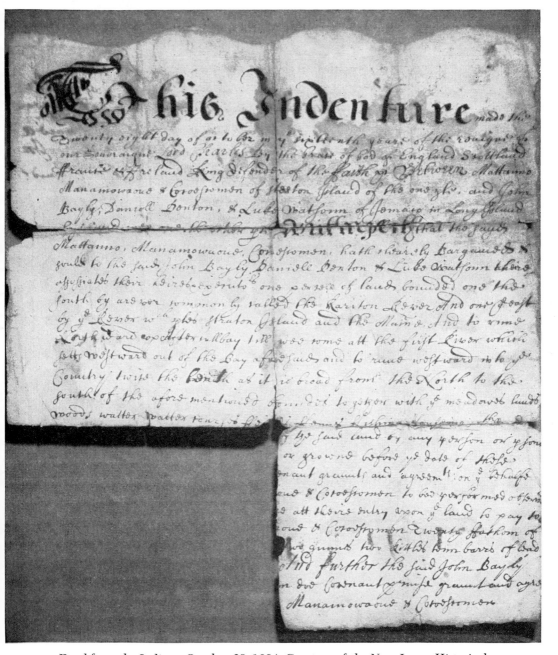

Deed from the Indians, October 28, 1664. Courtesy of the New Jersey Historical Society.

Lenape Indian painted by Gustavus Hesslius. Courtesy of the Historical Society of Pennsylvania.

upon the land, the colonists were to pay the Indians four hundred fathoms of white wampum.[3] The total cost came to about £154. What a bargain for a purchase of approximately five hundred thousand acres!

One may wonder about the thoughts that went through the minds of the Indians when they made their marks signing away the lands they had occupied so long. At this time there were only about two thousand Indians living in New Jersey. Most of them lived inland and came down to the seacoast during the summer in search of seafood. They were the Lenni-Lenapi, a branch of the Algonquin family who had occupied New Jersey far back into prehistoric times. Those who lived on Staten Island and the region west of the waters of Achter Kull are known as the Raritans. They were a rather stout people, described by David De Vries, the Dutch colonizer, as "very foul and dirty."

Mattano's wigwam on Staten Island, where the deed for the Elizabethtown Purchase was signed, was a typical Indian dwelling. These huts were usually about fifteen feet long, half as wide, and seven or eight feet high. They were covered with bark (commonly from the large chestnut trees of the area) over which was draped overlapping sheets of deerskin. Within were low couches against the sides. Rush mats were spread upon the ground. In the center was a fire pit from which smoke escaped through a hole in the roof. Hanging from notches were tom-toms, hunting and fishing equipment, and other artifacts used by the Indians in pursuit of the necessities of life.

As it was autumn when the purchase was made, weather-beaten women and statuesque girls were seen busying themselves outside the wigwams caring for the harvest which must carry them through the long winter ahead. The women wore their hair loose flowing, with a band of bead work to keep it in place. Most of them wore jackets and skirts well embroidered with wampum and beads. Dark paint around their eyes gave them an evil look to the white men come to strike a bargain with their men.

On entering the village, around which ran naked children and playful puppies, the one as carefree as the other, the visitors noticed the cornfields, now stripped of their golden harvest. In the fields stood platforms where boys during the summer were stationed with drums to scare off the birds which would, if left to their own devices, have made short shrift of the ripening corn. In the village skulked mean-looking creatures, half-wolf and half-dog. They were the ones that killed the woodchucks and other rodents to save the fields of corn, and gardens of beans, peas, squash, and other vegetables.

Mattano and the sachems who welcomed the visitors were men of the native dignity for which their race has long been known. They had, with their loosely-wrapped mantles of furs, not a little the appearance of Roman senators about to enter upon some business of state. All were manifestly good-looking men with active, muscular bodies, though most were well past middle-age. On their chests and arms, left partly bare by the loose draping of furs, were tattooes denoting their clan. On their cheeks and temples were streaks of white and red paint. From their hair, shaved into scalp locks, hung one or more eagle or turkey feathers. All had pendants of some kind in their ear lobes and on their arms were bracelets of copper or silver. From a cord around the neck hung the customary tobacco pouch embroidered with bright colored beads and shells. As it was late October, the men wore fringed leggings over breech clouts, their only summer wear.

When all were seated in the wigwam, Mattano lighted a long ceremonial pipe of yellow copper. After taking a few puffs, he started it around the circle for all to smoke. During the conference, the Indians spoke very slowly, one at a time, while the rest listened without once interrupting the speaker. After the business was completed and the deed signed, Indian girls served food which had been cooking outside. After dinner the white men took joyously to their boat and sailed for New York to acquaint the Governor of their success. Whether or not the Indians ever realized how much land they had deeded away is not known. In any event they never contested the boundaries of the purchase. Rather it would be the Proprietors who would endeavor to have it appear that the Indians never intended to sell but a fraction of the land claimed by Elizabethtown.[4]

On December 1, only a month after the purchase, Deputy Governor Nicolls confirmed the Associators' title to the Elizabethtown Purchase. Men from eastern Long Island had now joined the company; the name of John Ogden, Sr., of Northampton, appears in the grant with John Bailey, Luke Watson, and John

Baker, the interpreter during the conference with the Indians. The document confirming the deed repeated the boundaries of the purchase as contained in the Indian indenture. From the mouth of the Raritan, the line followed the shores of Achter Kull and Newark Bay to a small stream which emptied into the Passaic at its mouth. This was seventeen miles north of the starting point at the Raritan. From here it ran directly westward for thirty-four miles. It then turned south to the Raritan River, which it followed to the starting point at the mouth of the river. The grant included all of the present-day Union County and much of Morris and Somerset counties.[5]

So that the people would be encouraged to colonize, Governor Nicolls next proclaimed what was tantamount to a charter of liberties for New Jersey. In general the people were to enjoy all the freedoms and rights bestowed upon any of his Majesty's subjects in America. Specifically, besides freedom of religion, town government was sanctioned with a free choice of officers, both civil and military. All except servants and hired laborers were entitled to townlots, with the right to vote and hold office. No property would be taxed by the Duke's government for five years; then it would be taxed only according to the customary rates imposed upon other subjects under his jurisdiction.[6] Admittedly, Governor Nicolls deserves honor for conferring upon the infant colony the blessings of a free government. But it must be remembered that it was the pioneers, themselves, who had insisted all along on having New Jersey founded upon republican principles of government. It is therefore primarily to them that we owe the foundation of liberty upon which the future was to rest.

III

The Founding Fathers

Men had waited long for an opportunity to settle New Jersey. With the way now open through the Elizabethtown Purchase, no time, it appears, was lost in taking advantage of the opportunity. However, in view of all the necessary preparations and with winter coming on, most Associators chose to wait until spring before migrating. But a few intrepid souls, it would seem, would not be detained. Presumably, therefore, within a month after the purchase in October, 1664, entry upon the land was made by some of the Associators. Perhaps they were led by Luke Watson, a true pioneer and one of the principal stockholders at Jamaica. Or it could have been John Ogden, who came with some of his neighbors from eastern Long Island. Conceivably, all of the principal stockholders—Watson, Ogden, John Bailey, and John Baker—were there to take possession of their purchase. Sailing into Achter Kull, as the waters between Staten Island and New Jersey were called, the men presumably landed on November 24, 1664. Huts were built, perhaps at Luke Watson's Point or perhaps at the head of navigation of the Elizabeth River at the site of the future town.*

That the first settlers landed within the bounds of Elizabethtown in November, 1664, seems a fairly valid conclusion. One year later, the Elizabethtown Associators, in obedience to the terms of the purchase, made their final payment to the Indians. According to the agreement, the final payment was to be made one year from the date of entry. Since there was no reason for the Associators to make the final payment in advance, the conclusion

---

* Luke Watson's claim to one hundred acres at Luke Watson's Point on the Achter Kull may have rested upon his landing there in November, 1664.

12

appears well-founded that the first settlement of Elizabethtown took place on November 24, 1664.*

It is not at all surprising that some of the Associators were anxious to get on the land regardless of the season of the year. Lumber would be needed in the spring for building houses, and the winter could be profitably spent felling trees, working the logs into beams and planks, and getting them partially seasoned. Land cleared would be ready for early planting. Another compelling reason for coming in the fall was the opportunity it afforded for trading with the Indians who ordinarily took their furs to the Dutch.

As the Elizabethtown pioneers surveyed the wide expanse of meadows and the dense forest rising like a wall to the westward, a great thrill must have seized the heart of everyone. It was truly a land of boundless promise—for them, for their children, and for generations to come. Now that it was autumn, the pioneers saw the waters alive with ducks, geese, and other varieties of water birds. Almost everywhere along the shore, bushels of clams, oysters, and scallops could be gathered in an amazingly short time. The streams and the salt waters teemed with fish, large and small. Perched in the tallest trees or circling aloft, hawks and eagles were having a final feast before flying off to warmer climes. On penetrating the forest, the men came upon great numbers of wild turkey, grouse, and other game birds. In the spring would come immense flocks of song birds from the south as well as clouds of passenger pigeons, so thick in the sky as fairly to obscure the light of the sun.

In many places the forest was an open park-like expanse of giant oaks and chestnuts. At other places, especially along the borders of the bays and in the inland swamps, dense growths of white cedar, spruce, and pines were found. In the forest the pioneers found herds of deer drawn together for protection against the cold and the beasts of prey. Occasionally they saw the lordly elk. Until winter set in, bears, racoons, and other hibernating animals were common. When winter did come, they

* The Indians did receive a payment in advance of one hundred fathoms of white wampum in August, 1665, but the final payment of three hundred fathoms was made on November 24, 1665.

could hear the howling of the wolf packs back in the forest and occasionally could glimpse the slinking panther.

It was doubtlessly early spring when the first families arrived and were greeted by the men who had wintered at Achter Kol. The site for the town was selected at a point about two and a half miles from Achter Kull (Arthur Kill) where enough fall was provided for erecting a mill dam. Up to this point, too, ships of thirty or forty tons burden could dock at high tide. The spot selected for the town rose up from the river to elevations of twenty to thirty feet or more. Here the soil was a rich sandy loam, highly suitable for farming.

From widely scattered areas, the colonizers came in boatloads from western and eastern Long Island and from embarcation points along the shores of Connecticut. All the boats were loaded high with everything needed to make a start in a new country. Live stock and tools had a priority, although room was found for some choice articles of furniture brought from England years before. Since sloops could navigate the Elizabeth River as far as the site chosen for the town, the pioneers unloaded their belongings on the spot selected for their future home.

The largest party of settlers came from eastern Long Island, which already was considered over-populated. Heavily represented were the towns of Southampton, Easthampton, and Southold. Fifty-six-year-old John Ogden, Sr., was the leader of the "East Enders"—as the people of eastern Long Island were called. Upon his arrival at Achter Kol (soon to be named Elizabethtown), the leadership of the whole community fell to him. Soon after the purchase in October, Ogden and John Baker, the interpreter, had purchased the shares belonging to Thomas Benedick and the two Dentons. Ogden's purchase signified that a large number of "East Enders" had decided to join in the enterprise and move to Achter Kol. The principals whose names appeared on the deed and on the confirmation of title by the Governor may have advanced all the funds for acquiring the land, but, in any event, it was understood that any freeman was entitled to purchase a share and become an associator until a quota of about eighty was reached.

Accompanying John Ogden was his wife, Jane, the sister of Robert Bond, a prominent citizen of Easthampton who also came with the "East Enders" to Elizabethtown. With John Ogden also came his five sons, ranging in age from about twelve to twenty-six. No doubt most of the "East Enders" came together with Captain Thomas Young, a Southold mariner whose ocean-going ship was capable of transporting a goodly number of settlers.

John Ogden was a man well-suited to lead the Elizabethtown Associators. Born at Bradley Plains, England, in 1609, he came to America and settled at Southampton in 1640. By this time, Jane, whom he married three years before, already had borne him three sons, John and the twins David and Jonathan. His other two sons, Joseph and Benjamin, were born in America. After living at Southampton for about two years, Ogden took his family to live at Stamford, Connecticut, where he was given ten acres in return for building a dam for the town.

John Ogden's fame as a bricklayer and stonemason soon spread beyond the borders of the English settlements. Hearing of his work, Governor Willem Kieft, in 1642, hired John and his brother Richard to build a large stone church within the walls of the little fort at New Amsterdam. St. Nicholas, as the church was named, was finished in 1645. For their services the Ogdens received what amounted to about one thousand dollars in beaver pelts, merchandise, and cash. After finishing the church, John Ogden joined a group consisting of John Strickland and other Englishmen in founding the town of Hempstead on land procured from the Dutch. Not long after, he moved back to Southampton having become dissatisfied with the Dutch treatment of the Indians.

So far John Ogden had done a great deal of moving about, a trait common among the English colonizers. This time, however, he and his family settled down for a long stay. Eastern Long Island became their home for nearly twenty years. By the time Ogden moved back to Southampton, he had accumulated considerable wealth as well as a reputation for leadership. At Southampton he soon became a magistrate, a town treasurer, and on many occasions a commissioner for treating with the Indians. For five years from 1656, he represented Southampton in the General Assembly at Hartford, in spite of the protests of the Dutch who claimed all of Long Island. Following his services in the Assembly, he was a delegate to the Upper House. In this capacity his name appears in Connecticut's new charter secured from Charles II.[1]

A natural-born promoter, John Ogden was not long at Southampton before he was heading a group that settled Northampton, a harbor for Southampton on Peconic Bay. Here his friend, Wyandanch, a Shinnecock or Montauk sachem, deeded him 324 acres (retaining only hunting and fishing rights) for a yearly rent of twenty-five shillings.[2] A little later, Ogden organized a whaling company with a monopoly for off-shore whaling, by order of the Town of Southampton. This is thought to have been the first whaling company in America.[3]

Having decided to throw in his lot with the Elizabethtown Associators, John Ogden sold his property at Northampton. After buying what amounted to about a fourth interest in the Elizabethtown Purchase, he sold shares in turn to his neighbors of eastern Long Island. A share cost four pounds, payable ordinarily in beaver pelts, a common form of exchange in the colonies. Years later one Josiah Lettin remembered how he had helped carry the goods purchased by the Associators and used for payment when Achter Kol was bought from the Indians in 1664.[4]

It has long been claimed by certain writers that there were but four families, if that many, at Elizabethtown when Governor Carteret arrived. This assumption is based upon but one source: that of a statement made thirty years after the town was founded. Quite likely the witness confused the settling of the town with the purchase of the land wherein the names of the four buyers appear in the deed.[*]

Logic as well as some evidence favors the assumption that a considerable number of Associators had arrived and were in the process of building a town when the Governor arrived early in August, 1665. A month before Carteret arrived, Governor Nicolls wrote from New York that a town was "beginning" at Achter Kol. This statement and the fact that we know that John Ogden and

---

[*] In 1747 in the famous *Bill in the Chancery of New Jersey* (New York, 1747), James Alexander made the most of the argument that there were only four families in Elizabethtown when the Governor arrived. W. A. Whitehead in his *East Jersey under the Proprietary Governments* (Newark, 1875), agrees with Alexander. Hatfield as well as A. Van Doren Honeyman in his *History of Union County, New Jersey* (2 vols., New York, 1923), wrote that the town was settled and laid out before Carteret arrived.

a few other key figures were at Achter Kol during the last half of the year 1665 is about all there is to go by in drawing a conclusion. John Ogden was there at least as early as July, 1665. Luke Watson also must have been there for sometime since the Indians were billed for killing his oxen in November, 1665. John Dickinson of Southold and Jeremiah Osborne of Easthampton were witnesses to the final payment of the Indians in November. All were leaders who would attract others. For reasons of safety alone, they would have come in numbers sufficient to defend themselves in case of attack.

Although it appears that many families had arrived and were building their homes at Achter Kol when the Governor arrived, the quota of eighty families was nonetheless far from filled. Believing that a full town was needed for protection, if nothing else, Carteret issued a proclamation promising all pioneers who settled at Achter Kol before January 1, 1666, more land than those who came later. Whether or not the Governor's offer brought settlers to Achter Kol is hard to answer. Some writers have thought that because there were sixty-five men in the colony by February 9, 1666, that the offer was effective in bringing settlers who might not otherwise have joined the colony. On the other hand, it seems doubtful that the Governor's offer could have borne much fruit in so short a time. It seems more plausible that the settlers arriving during the latter part of 1665 had been planning to come all along and had just been able to get under way late that year. All of the settlers from Long Island and Connecticut came as Associators. As stockholders in the enterprise, they were entitled to their full share in the division of land. All of them understood this. It was a system long practiced in New England and Long Island. This was really all the incentive the people needed to have them move to Achter Kol.

The conduct of the settlers after they arrived also supports the view that they colonized as Associators and without any particular inducement from the Governor or the proprietary "Concessions and Agreements," as the instrument for governing the colony was called. From the beginning the Associators acted as independent colonizers without owing any particular obligation to the Proprietors. The Associators had purchased the land from the Indians; they had received confirmation of the grant from

Governor Nicolls. They therefore looked upon the land as their very own. Even Governor Carteret was obliged to purchase his share and become an Associator to procure land within the township.

It is impossible to determine when the Associators undertook to make the first surveys and create the townlots. This had to be done, however, quite early so that the pioneers could get busy developing their land and building their houses. Probably the first surveys were made in the spring of 1665 after a sufficient number of people had arrived to warrant calling a town meeting. As was customary among English colonizers, rules were made in town meeting for laying out the town. Next a committee was chosen for carrying out the resolutions of the meeting. That John Ogden headed the committee can hardly be questioned. Furthermore, as it was common for migrating groups to give their leaders first choice in the selection of townlots, Ogden, it would appear, was the recipient of this favor. His townlot was the most centrally located in town at the head of navigation where a dam could be built for mills.*

With the exception perhaps of John Bailey and Luke Watson, the rest of the Associators drew lots for their town plots. The first townlots to be laid out started on either side of the river and went back twelve to fifteen chains (790 to 990 feet). The frontage was ordinarily four chains (264 feet). John Ogden, Jr., age twenty-six, received a strip four by nine chains, extending from the King's Highway (Elizabeth Avenue) to what became East Jersey Street. Two more acres between the highway and the river gave him the customary six acres. The Ogden twins, David and Jonathan, also were the recipients of townlots.

Townlots of other settlers were distributed along the King's Highway, formerly a section of the old Dutch trail leading to the Delaware. Nearest the bridge on the King's Highway and opposite John Ogden's lot was the townlot of Abraham Shotwell. Other lots along the King's Highway were granted to John Brackett, John Woodruff, Leonard Headly, Jonathan Ogden, and

---

* John Ogden's homestead was recorded in 1691 as "Bounded South by a highway, West by Mill River, North by lands of the said Elizabethtowne for a place of burial." *NJA*, XXI, 187; W. O. Wheeler, *The Ogden Family, Elizabeth Branch* (Philadelphia, 1909), p. 42.

John Ogden, Jr. At the bend in the river (Spring Street), the village ended and the meadows began.

On the west side of the river more of the owners of the town-lots can be identified. The lots began at Crane's Brook (north of Grand Street) and extended southward along what is now Cherry and Pearl streets to the meadows. Since this is considerably longer than the occupied area along the King's Highway, the majority of the settlers apparently lived on the west side of the river. Starting at Crane's Brook and going southward were to be found, among others, the lots of Stephen Crane, William Trotter, Peter and Robert Morse (Moss), Nathaniel Tuttle, Barnabas Wines, William Cramer, Thomas Thompson (Tomson), Jeffery Jones, Evan Salisbury, and David Ogden. All but three of these were "East Enders" who came with or followed John Ogden.

The first town meeting on record at Elizabethtown was held on February 19, 1666. At this meeting sixty-five men took the oath of allegiance to King Charles the Second and swore to be "true and faithful to the Lords Proprietors." In addition to the oath, other important business was transacted. All Associators who had not yet arrived were warned to be on their land by April 15 or forfeit their rights. It was also determined that no land could be sold for three years. Thereafter Associators were to be given the first opportunity to buy. No one would be admitted as a settler without the consent of the town. For the present, it was decided to limit the number of Associators to eighty men. Sometime later, twenty more would be admitted.[5]

At the February meeting the townsmen ruled on the highly important question of how much land each Associator should have. Three classes were established. Those with the smallest investment were called First Right Men. Each of these would receive, in addition to a townlot, a minimum of sixty or seventy acres of land. The next group, the Second Lot Men, who had invested about twice as much as the First Lot Men, would get a double portion of land. The Third Lot Men, with the largest investment, would receive three times as much as the First Lot men. John Ogden, Sr., John Baker, Luke Watson, Thomas Young, Philip Cartwright, John Woodruff, Benjamin Price, and about a dozen others were Third Lot Men. Townlots, regardless of investment, were all of about the same size.[6]

By the time of the February town meeting, the little colony bordering the Elizabeth River had received its name. No longer was it simply known as the settlement at Achter Kol. It was now Elizabethtown, named in honor of Elizabeth Carteret, the wife of Sir George Carteret, the Proprietor. The name undoubtedly was given by Governor Philip Carteret.[7] Nothing much is known of Elizabeth Carteret except that she was a puritanical old lady, a formidable kill-joy in the eyes of the pleasure-loving court of Charles the Second. "She cries out the vices of the Court, and how they are going to set up plays already," Samuel Pepys recorded in his diary. Her portrait was painted by Sir Peter Lely, court painter for Charles the Second. It hangs at Carteret Castle, St. Ouen, on the Isle of Jersey.

Most of the Elizabethtown pioneers were young and strong. They plunged into the work of building their homes in the wilderness with characteristic zeal and within a remarkably short time had a roof over their heads and the necessary facilities for pioneer living. In building the men had to rely on the broadax, adz, and handsaw, since there was no sawmill until later. Pegs were used for the larger timbers while wrought-iron nails, which they had brought along, were used as sparingly as possible for the boarding and shingles.

All the houses were small, Governor Lawrie noted in 1683, and made of planks set on end with the butts anchored in the ground and the tops fastened to risers. All were a story or a story and a half, with eaves barely six feet from the ground. Because of low foundations, the doors opened nearly on a level with the street. The massive stone chimney (the first of which were usually made of clay and timber) covered almost one end of the house. At first some of the pioneers may have made thatched roofs from the coarse meadow grass, as was done in New England. Just outside the back door was a rain barrel kept filled with water for washing and for fire protection.

Inside the house, the large eight or ten foot fireplace dominated the main room, which served as a kitchen, dining room, and living quarters. All the houses had plastered walls made with a mixture of clay and ground seashells. To conserve heat the ceilings were very low and the windows small. A trap door in the main room or kitchen led down into a small cellar used for storing vegetables and other commodities requiring cold storage.

After the house was built, one of the most pressing needs was fencing. Gardens and fruit trees required protection against both wild and domestic animals and before long all the lots up and down the streets were surrounded by tight fences or "palisades" made of poles set in the ground. In the early days, towns had an officer known as the "Fence Viewer," whose duty it was to see that both private and public fencing was properly maintained. Cattle or hogs that broke through the fences were caught by an officer known as the "Cattle Reeve" or "Hog Reeve" who drove stray animals to the village pound where they could be ransomed by their owners. That the pioneers managed to get their fences up and fruit trees planted early is attested to by the good fruit harvested in less than fifteen years. Elizabethtown apples, like those of Newark, produced cider famous throughout America.

After the houses were built and the town lots fenced, the pioneers cleared their outfields for grain. Oats, wheat, rye, corn, and buckwheat were the standard crops. Buckwheat was highly prized. From it came buckwheat flour for griddle cakes, buckwheat honey, and straw for livestock forage.

Within a year after Elizabethtown was founded, a great transformation had taken place. Acres of land that so recently had been covered by woods was cleared for houselots and highways. Dotting the roads which paralleled the river were forty or fifty little houses with smoke curling from their chimneys. The fences, woodpiles, wells, and sheds that became part of the setting bore witness to how busy the townspeople had been since their arrival.

Naturally much attention was given to the care of the livestock. At night, until the dangers from wild animals and Indians subsided, the cattle were usually driven into a well-fenced common within the borders of the town. Sheep were not plentiful in the early days since they had to be carefully watched lest they fall prey to the wolves. Consequently sheep were pastured in the yards and streets of the town. In the fall, hogs which could take care of themselves in the woods, grew fat feeding on the chestnuts and acorns that covered the ground in many places. As on Long Island and in New England, the cattle and horses were branded since they were pastured and herded together.

The branding was performed by the Town Brander who kept a record of each earmark (made by cutting the animal's ear) and received a small fee for his services. Later, when cattle grazed over a wide area, brands were necessary to mark the cattle belonging to Newark, Woodbridge, or Elizabethtown. By 1680 some prosperous pioneers had twenty or thirty cattle, eight or ten oxen, as well as seven or eight slaves or indentured servants to help with the work.[8]

Oxen and milch cows naturally received more care than ordinary cattle. The sheds which sheltered them in winter were bedded with salt hay gathered from the meadows. Salt hay manure, which the farmers spread upon their gardens in the spring, became a feature of Elizabethtown farming. Families too poor to own oxen, hired teams for plowing and paid for the service by working for the owner. Highly prized as oxen were in pioneer days, it is no wonder that Luke Watson became very angry when his oxen were killed by the Indians. Perhaps the Indians thought they had discovered a new breed of elk or buffalo. In any event, they paid for the oxen when the loss was deducted at the final payment on the Elizabethtown Purchase.

While the men and older boys were busily engaged in town building, the women and girls were not idle. With them had come their spinning wheels, looms, candle molds, kettles, and tubs. Soon all were put to use. There was endless fireplace cooking, washing by the river, and preserving food for the winter. At times a child was obliged to stand at the fireplace for hours twisting a roast suspended above the fire until it was "done to a turn." Soap-making, sewing, knitting, candle-making, spinning and weaving were chores always waiting when the other work was done. Children were kept busy with innumerable chores. They fetched the wood, swept the chimney, herded the cattle, gathered nuts and berries and plants from the fields and forest.

Since Elizabethtown was in great need of a sawmill, John Ogden lost no time in utilizing his skill as a stonemason. First he constructed a dam, a major project in itself in a new country. Often towns chose to assist in so expensive an undertaking. In Newark the town meeting ordered the men to help the miller build the dam and saw timber for the mill. Probably John Ogden received similar aid from Elizabethtown. Nevertheless, before the year 1666 had ended, he apparently had his dam built and a sawmill in operation. In time more sawmills were built. By 1683, it was reported that Elizabethtown had another sawmill on Thompson's Creek and one or two more under construction.

John Ogden had in mind more than just a sawmill for his dam across the Elizabeth River. Fully as much as a sawmill, the town needed a corn or grist mill for grinding grain. This, however, would take more time to build and would require Ogden's best engineering skill.* Nonetheless, indefatigable John Ogden had a "Corn mill" in operation within two years after the dam was finished. It stood on the east bank of the river near the bridge and about two hundred yards below the dam. The sawmill was presumably on the other side of the river. Ogden probably hired a miller to run his grist mill as did Robert Treat in Newark. The men and boys who came to the mill never became tired of watching the miller, covered with flour dust, as he stood by the chute and tested with his thumb the fineness of the flour as it flowed from the grinding stones.

Leather was another commodity in great demand in pioneer communities; and again it was John Ogden who first met the need in Elizabethtown by constructing a tanyard on his property by the river. He was a tanner of long experience. Hard heavy leather was made for boots and shoes, while soft, pliable buckskin was produced for work clothes to be worn by the men in their daily round of hard labor. Soon there were other tanneries in Elizabethtown. By 1690 it was recognized as one of the leading leather centers in the colonies. The Ogdens, themselves, continued to carry on the business generation after generation. In 1797, when Colonel Ogden moved into the Belcher House, he could remember the hours spent working in his father's tanyard in the days before the War for Independence.

Few towns have had a founder more versatile than John Ogden. Before he had his corn mill completed, he was busy organizing a whaling company like the one he had started at Southampton twenty years before. A license issued by Governor Carteret, in 1669, created a company that gave Ogden and twenty others exclusive whaling rights in the waters from Sandy Hook to Bar-

* Parts for the first grist mill in Pennsylvania were brought over from England.

nagate Bay. Whales were at this time so common in the Atlantic that they were seen almost daily in New York Bay. "It is not possible to describe how this bay swarms with fish, both large and small, whales, tunnies and porpoises," wrote Jasper Danckaerts in 1679.[9] No doubt Ogden made money in whaling but with so many business ventures taxing his resources, he was compelled to mortgage his corn mill to a New York merchant for £191.

As suggested earlier, considering his knowledge of the art of brick-making and his great capacity for tackling almost anything, John Ogden most likely was the man engaged in brick-making in Elizabethtown as early as 1679. But he and his sons were not the only craftsmen who migrated to Elizabethtown. In Yankee fashion, the average pioneer was in practice a Jack-of-all-trades. He could make his own furniture, build his own house, make and repair the family's shoes, turn out his own tools, or make almost anything needed in his home or on his farm. Often, however, when he wanted something a little better than his own make, he would go to one of his neighbors better trained in one of the other crafts. Thus the Ogdens were considered tanners, brick-makers, and stonemasons. Francis Barber and William Cramer were carpenters, while John Hinds was a cooper by trade and therefore one who could make excellent tubs for the busy housewives. He could also make smooth-running spinning wheels or almost anything of wood requiring more than ordinary skill. William Hill and the two Whiteheads were cordwainers (cobblers) who went from house to house as well as town to town plying their trade.* For those who could afford to buy cloth, the town had two professional weavers, Matthias Hatfield and John Winans. It also could boast of a tailor in the person of John Painter and a clothier (cloth merchant), Benjamin Wade.

There were also other men with specialties. One was Peter Wolversen, a Dutchman of old New Amsterdam and a brewer of long experience. He came with the first wave of settlers, yet before six months had elapsed he had a tavern and brewery in operation. Taverns were considered almost a necessity in pioneer days and

---

* The upper parts of shoes were often made by members of the family leaving the soles to be attached by the cobbler.

Wolversen received every encouragement.* Governor Carteret, who saw the need of a public house where strangers could stay, loaned Wolversen money for his enterprise and took a mortgage on the tavern for security.[10]

Other taverns were soon to be found in Elizabethtown. Pierre Jardine, a Frenchman, kept an inn as early as 1679 at Elizabethtown Point, on land belonging to George and Philip Carteret. Accommodation was miserable but still it was a place to stay if nothing better were available. Travelers had to sleep on hay on the floor; in summer they were pestered by swarms of mosquitoes. Often the proprietor had no food to offer.[11] By 1679 there was another tavern in Elizabethtown kept by Jonas Wood.

As a good part of the livelihood of the pioneers came from nature's bounty, much time was spent in hunting, fishing, and gathering cranberries, huckleberries, wild honey, and innumerable edibles from the fields and forest. In the spring great quantities of shad were salted and put in barrels for the winter. Oysters were pickled and stored in casks. Wild geese and ducks, which had been shot or trapped, helped out the larder and furnished feathers and down for the fluffy feather beds used by the early settlers. From walnuts, butternuts, and sumac, the women made dyes for coloring cloth after the spinning and weaving were done. Each house had a dyeing pot carved from the trunk of a gumwood tree. It stood by the fireplace with a cover so that it could be used as a seat. In the fall and winter men and boys trapped for furs, which were sold at a ready market in New York.

For the most part, the pioneers were their own doctors. Many kinds of roots and plants were gathered for medicinal purposes. Among the most common were partridge berries, thoroughwort, wild mandrakes, blue flag, sassafras roots, bloodwort, ginseng, and pennyroyal. After they had been dried from the rafters, what concoctions were brewed from these wondrous herbs! Certain members of the community with a reputation for skill in making medicines and curing the sick, were usually the nearest thing to a doctor in town. When an epidemic struck, the whole town took alarm and turned to these healers for help. The first severe wave

---

* A New Jersey law of 1668 required all towns to have a tavern for the entertainment of strangers. Another law of 1677 fixed the prices at taverns for lodging, meals, liquor, and the care of horses.

of sickness came in 1668 when many died from the "noxious fevers." By 1687, to be sure, Elizabethtown had a professional doctor, one Edward Gay, but nothing is known of him other than that he was usually on hand to witness the wills, presumably of his dying patients. After Gay, it was apparently a long time before another doctor came to town.

Most of the recreation of the early pioneers was tied in with earning a livelihood. For the men and boys, hunting wolves which preyed on livestock was an exciting adventure. The town placed a bounty on wolves, whose ears customarily decorated a post in the center of the town to show the progress against the enemy. So far as possible bounties were paid only for the wolves killed within the boundaries of the town. Wolves never were dangerous unless an unarmed person was caught out alone in the forest by a hungry pack. But the pioneers had to be forever on the alert against poisonous reptiles, mainly rattlesnakes. In the fields the men habitually carried clubs to kill the snakes whenever discovered. Bears were seldom dangerous but they enjoyed killing hogs, and were considered at best poor neighbors. The pioneers had uses for the bear's grease but they were chiefly sought after for their furry hides, which provided an excellent cover for the wide pine-board floors of the colonial houses.

Keeping the fireplace going in winter was a task requiring much labor. Great stacks of cordwood had to be accumulated to feed the devouring flames. Sometimes a huge backlog was hauled into the kitchen by an ox or horse and rolled into the fireplace to keep the fire going until morning. With such heavy demands on timber, frontier towns soon passed ordinances against illegal cutting of trees. As early as June, 1666, Governor Carteret was moved to announce that any person discovered cutting trees on land not his own would be prosecuted by officers of the law.[12]

Like the Indians before them, the pioneers burned over the woods and fields in the spring or fall. Both had the same end in view. The fire consumed the low undergrowth but did not harm the trees. In this way the woods and fields were kept clear of brush and weeds, thus allowing the grass to grow under the great oaks and chestnuts in the park-like areas of the forest. The burning was supervised by town officials. All men and boys were required to turn out to help. While some saw to the burning, others were posted to shoot game as the frightened animals sped away.

It was two or three years after the founding of Elizabethtown before the people built a church, called a meetinghouse after the Puritan manner. Previously, religious worship was held out of doors or in private homes; deacons led the service before the town had a minister. Quite possibly Governor Carteret opened his large house for this purpose. Elizabethtown's first meetinghouse, on the site of the present-day First Presbyterian Church, was no doubt fashioned after the prevailing Puritan or Congregational churches of the period. These buildings were ordinarily about thirty-six feet square with windows and doors at the gable ends.[13] Since it was the intention to have the meetinghouse serve also as a fort, the windows were small and high off the ground. A cupola from the center of the roof served as a lookout tower. The inside was as drab as the outside. A high pulpit looked down on rows of rough-hewn benches of heavy timber. The flooring was of heavy planking of chestnut or oak. No heat was provided but the parishioners were permitted to bring foot-warmers during the cold weather. During the weighty sermons, which often consumed several hours, the minister would customarily announce a recess to allow the congregation to repair to a nearby tavern or house to get warm.

Townspeople were called to church by the beat of the drum as the drummer boy made his rounds through the streets early in the morning. Usually the whole family walked to church, but after the town began to spread out, farmers living some distance from the meetinghouse often brought their families in ox carts. At the meetinghouse door, public notices were posted advertising sales, town meetings, or whatever was of interest to the community. Inside were ushers whose duty it was to keep the boys quiet in their section and to see that none of the congregation fell asleep. A knob on one end of a pole was used to rap the heads of male offenders, while a squirrel's tail on the other end served as a more gentle reminder to the fair sex.

Most of the people who settled Elizabethtown were Puritans of more moderate views than those who founded Newark. Unlike Newark, where only church members could vote before 1677, Elizabethtown had no religious test for voting or holding office.

Robert Barclay, the Quaker governor, noted in 1684 that the inhabitants of Elizabethtown were religious but not zealous. However, Elizabethtown upheld the Puritan Sabbath by prohibiting all unnecessary traveling and labor on the Lord's day. From early childhood Puritans were taught to hold their ministers in esteem. Men and women stood aside bowing low whenever they met the minister on the street. Children stopped their play and stood quietly by the side of the road until he had passed. Everyone at this time was more or less imbued with ideas of witchcraft but fortunately New Jersey escaped any serious manifestation of the delusion.* In 1680, the appearance of a "dreadful comet-star" with its fiery tail frightened every last sinner in Elizabethtown into attending church regularly for a long time to come. Epidemics were also a powerful incentive for people to mend their ways.

Elizabethtown's first minister was the Reverend Jeremiah Peck. After graduating from Harvard, Peck alternately preached and taught school in Connecticut. In 1666, he came with the first settlers to Newark where he stayed for about three years before moving to Elizabethtown. Installed as pastor of the congregation in 1668, he remained ten years before moving on to a pastorate at Greenwich, Connecticut. In Elizabethtown his houselot, on the corner of Broad and West Jersey streets, extended to the river. A rather strict Puritan, Peck was strongly opposed to persons becoming church members who could not testify that they had experienced a true conversion. How this was received by his Elizabethtown parishioners is not known but it got him into trouble at Greenwich and he was forced to leave after preaching there for twelve years.†

The Elizabethtown pioneers, people of Puritan extraction, were concerned for the education of their children. Ordinarily they tried to give them enough schooling to enable them to read the Bible, write a little, and handle simple arithmetic. If no one in the immediate family could do the teaching, other means were found. For a small fee a housewife often conducted a "Dame

* While John Ogden lived at Southampton several witchcraft cases arose in eastern Long Island. *Documentary History of the State of New York* (Albany, 1849), I, 683.
† Peck opposed the "Half-Way Covenant" which allowed the baptism of children of parents who had not experienced the Puritan conversion and become numbered among the "Elect."

School" in her kitchen; here the ABC's were taught. Since ministers generally supplemented their income by teaching, the Reverend Peck probably taught the few boys whose parents desired them to learn some Greek and Latin. As early as 1681, however, Elizabethtown had a regular schoolmaster in the person of John Inquehart, a Quaker. He probably taught boys in his home at any level, including Greek and Latin, since he was college-bred, presumably at Edinburgh.

By the time Inquehart had begun school-teaching in Elizabethtown, the Reverend Peck had left and the pulpit was filled by the Reverend Seth Fletcher, another Harvard man. The new minister, who came from the church at Southampton, was in some ways not so strict a Puritan as his predecessor. Years before, in Maine, he had been released from the pulpit for "laxness in his views on the sanctification of the Sabbath." He was not one, however, passively to allow the Quakers, who were beginning to settle in New Jersey, to undermine his flock.

It was not long before the Reverend Fletcher found himself at loggerheads with the Quaker schoolmaster, Inquehart. Among other things Fletcher told his people that a Quaker could not be saved. At a meeting in which he explained the fallacies of Quakerism, Inquehart and his followers made their appearance and caused as much disturbance as possible. In a letter to the Reverend Increase Mather, Fletcher told his story: "I in every argument demanded what part of the Arguments they would deny but instead of answer there was railing and threatening mee that my destruction was nigh at hand. To prove the Minor, I continually produced their owne authors and several things out of their Rabbie's books, which so exceedingly gauled them that they set themselves to Huming, singing, reeling, their Heads and bodies (Antique like) whereby both to disturb mee and to take off the people from attending to what I had to say for maintaining the Assertion." [14] Within about a year after his brush with the Quakers, the Reverend Seth Fletcher died. Recognized as a scholar, he owned what was no doubt the first library of any size in Elizabethtown. Since suitable clergymen were hard to find, Elizabethtown was left without a minister for five years.

Because the town records were lost at an early date, most of the names of the early officials are unknown. Shoemaker Isaac

Whitehead, however, is known to have held the office of town clerk during the first twenty-six years of the town's existence. Other men who held various offices were John Ogden, Sr., Luke Watson, William Meeker, and John Woodruff. The offices to be filled at town meeting were those of tax collector, treasurer, surveyor of highways, assessor, fence viewer, branding master, keeper of the pound, town watch, and a few other posts of local importance. The offices of justice of the peace, constable, and town surveyor, were by appointment of the governor. Besides the town tax, there was after 1668 a small New Jersey tax which the local collector gathered and turned over to the provincial treasurer. The town tax included a levy for the minister's salary. Most, if not all, of the town tax was paid in produce or in services. Winter wheat was receivable for taxes at the rate of five shillings per bushel; summer wheat at four shillings, six pence; peas at three shillings, six pence; rye at four shillings; and beef at two pence per pound. Service included working on the roads, ditching the meadows, building and repairing bridges, and constructing public buildings and fences.

As the years passed, town ordinances tended to increase, thus reflecting the needs of the community. From the beginning, a householder was required to own a ladder and a pail for fire fighting. He also must have had his chimney swept at least once a month during the winter. Other ordinances pertained to the use of the commons, the curfew, to fencing, and so on. Naturally, more trouble and litigation arose over fencing and trespassing than over all other causes combined.

Besides the town ordinances, there were the provincial laws requiring observance. When the first English settlements were founded in New Jersey, Governor Nicolls proclaimed the "Duke's Laws," made at Hempstead, Long Island, as binding upon both New York and New Jersey. In 1668, the New Jersey legislature formally adopted this code, essentially the laws enacted by Connecticut a few years earlier. Some of the acts were identical to the harsh Levitical laws of the Old Testament. Capital offenses were as many as thirteen. The harsh treatment prescribed for children guilty of wrong-doing, however, was apparently never enforced in New Jersey. According to law, stocks were erected in all towns so that the inhabitants could gaze upon drunkards and other misdemeanants. Elizabethtown's stocks stood for many years in front of the first Court House, which was erected about 1682. Among the laws of New Jersey none were more important than those regulating the services and treatment of bond servants. Not long after the founding of Elizabethtown, a flurry of excitement occurred when a "hue and cry" went out for Robert Gray, a servant of Luke Watson who had stolen something and run away with another bondsman. Other provincial laws regulated the trade with the Indians, prescribed standards for weights and measures, as well as the value of wampum, and erected courts of law. By order of the Crown, no colonial laws could be contrary to those in England.

By 1680, fifteen years after the founding of Elizabethtown, East New Jersey had attained a population of about three thousand. Seven towns had been established. The largest was Elizabethtown itself, with a population of about seven hundred and an area extending back as far as thirty-four miles, if the town could realize its full claim under the Nicolls' grant. The other towns were Woodbridge and Piscataway (purchased from Elizabethtown) and the towns of Newark, Middletown, Shrewsbury, and Bergen.* During this period, Elizabethtown was the capital of New Jersey and the center of provincial politics. The County Court House, however, was located in Newark after Essex County was created in 1682.

Not long after Elizabethtown and Newark were founded, a question arose as to the location of the boundary between the towns. To settle the question, John Ogden, Sr., Luke Watson, Robert Bond, and Jeffery Jones were chosen by Elizabethtown. Those of Newark were Robert Treat and five others. Many of the negotiators from the two towns were old friends whose paths had crossed at one time or another. Years later, Robert Treat paid tribute to the arbitrators for the Christian way in which the question was settled. The boundary, it was decided, would start at an old oak tree, on a knoll called Divident Hill (near Weequahic Lake), and extend in a northwestern direction. After the

---

* Philip Carteret, John Ogden, and Luke Watson sold the land between the Rahway and the Raritan rivers in December, 1666, to Woodbridge Associates. Piscataway was purchased from Woodbridge. See Stevens MSS. #2884; Whitehead, pp. 41-42.

boundary was settled (the date was January 20, 1668), "Mr. Ogden (being one of the first purchasers) prayed among the people, and returned thanks for their loving agreement." [15]

When Governor Philip Carteret arrived at Elizabethtown in August, 1665, the New Jersey settlers suddenly found themselves confronted with a governmental authority they had not counted upon. Until then, Governor Richard Nicolls was governor of New Jersey as well as of New York. He had, however, abdicated most of his authority when as an inducement to colonize he gave the settlers what amounted to home rule in New Jersey. Now the situation was much altered. Governor Carteret came as governor for the new proprietors, Sir George Carteret and Lord John Berkeley. The full meaning of the change, however, could not be foreseen by the Elizabethtown pioneers. Nevertheless, there must have been some apprehension when the news arrived that henceforth New Jersey would be owned by proprietors in far-away England and would be ruled by a governor of their choosing.

IV

The Struggle for Town Rights

Philip Carteret sailed from England in April, 1665, just as the great plague was sweeping over the land leaving an appalling toll of death. He had been detained from sailing by the outbreak of a war with the Dutch, but finally, after a long and exhausting voyage, he arrived at New York late in July. A few days later, he crossed the bay and landed at Achter Kol amid the cheering of all the townsfolk gathered at the landing. Since word of the transfer of New Jersey to the Proprietors had preceded him, everyone was anxious to see and hear the Governor.

Exactly what happened when Philip Carteret met the town fathers at the landing rests upon tradition. After the greetings and introductions, he read the commission naming him governor of "Nova Caesarea or New Jersey." Then he explained how New Jersey had been granted to Lord John Berkeley and Sir George Carteret by the Duke of York. To consummate the grant, the Proprietors had paid ten shillings and had given a promise of an annual rent of one peppercorn, if demanded by the Duke. The Proprietors, Philip continued, had been pleased to grant the inhabitants of New Jersey a liberal charter, called "The Concessions and Agreements," which conferred upon them the rights customarily belonging to freemen of the English nation. The Governor's words met with a favorable response from the pioneers, who listened intently.*

After Philip Carteret had explained the Proprietary role in the new colony, John Ogden stepped forth to present the interests of the Associators. He described how they had purchased the land from the Indians, and showed Philip the deed signed by the sachems. He then presented Governor Nicolls' confirmation of

* The "Landing of Carteret," painted by Howard Pyle, hangs in the Essex County Court House, Newark, N.J.

the deed in the form of a grant to the Associators. Carteret no doubt pointed out that the Proprietary grant from the Duke of York, dated June 20, 1664, preceded the Nicolls' patent by nearly five months. Governor Carteret, nonetheless, acknowledged the rights of the Associators and signified his desire to buy a share and become a planter. To dramatize his dual role of planter and governor, tradition tells that he took a hoe and placing it on his shoulder marched up to the village with the whole town trooping along behind him. About a month later, he fulfilled his promise to become an Associator by buying the rights of John Bailey, who had decided not to settle in Elizabethtown.[1]

Not long after his arrival, everyone in New Jersey knew all about the Carterets, who had so suddenly entered their lives for good or ill. Philip, they learned, was a distant cousin of Sir George Carteret, the life-long friend and favorite of the Stuart kings. During the Civil War, Sir George had defended the Isle of Jersey against the Cromwellians, only to be compelled to flee to Europe for safety. At the Restoration, Sir George had accompanied Charles II triumphantly to London. Thereafter he served as a Privy Councillor and as Vice Chancellor and Treasurer of the Royal Navy in which he had been an officer in his younger days.

Upon his arrival, Philip Carteret made a good impression on the pioneers. He was twenty-six, handsome and congenial. However, the period of his good graces with the inhabitants would not last more than two or three years. When the interests of the Proprietors and the Associators finally began to clash, Philip's popularity disappeared like smoke. As shall be seen, after he had intermittently served as governor for sixteen years, the fortunes of politics ebbing and flowing, he ended his career universally disliked and condemned for his policies.

For some unknown reason, the Proprietors failed to make James Carteret, son of Sir George, governor of New Jersey. Perhaps they saw in Philip more of the qualities necessary for a man governing a colony in the New World. Philip, to be sure, was a man of strong will and determination, one who would look after the interests of the Proprietors and not be easily discouraged. Son of Helier de Carteret, and fourth cousin of Sir George, he had no prospect of ever inheriting an interest in the colony. This in itself may have weighed heavily in favor of his appointment since it presumably would make him more acceptable to the colonists. Philip, it may be noted, accumulated no more than four thousand acres of land in New Jersey, all of which was obtained by purchase or special grants.

In Devon, England, Philip left a sweetheart, Mistress Penelope, who he hoped would follow him to New Jersey and become his wife. "Since I left you far away in Devon," he wrote soon after arriving in Elizabethtown, "not a day hath past in which your face doth not appear before me." But Penelope never came to America and finally, after sixteen years, Philip married Elizabeth Lawrence, a wealthy widow of New York.

With Carteret came a party of about thirty men and women from the Isle of Jersey. Eighteen were servants of one kind or another who were looked upon as socially inferior by the yeomen from New England and Long Island. Some of the servants had been solicited for their skill in salt-making, since Sir George had purchased a device for the manufacture of salt which he planned to send to New Jersey where he hoped the industry would take hold. No salt-making, however, was ever attempted by the bondsmen from the Isle of Jersey and nothing further is heard of the project. Most of the people from the Isle of Jersey were Catholic, all presumably supporters of the Stuarts, unsympathetic to the Puritan tradition, dear to the hearts of the New Englanders.

Foremost among the gentlemen accompanying Philip Carteret was Robert Vauquellin, a native of Caen, sometimes known as Sieur des Praries. With his wife, Vauquellin traveled to London with Philip Carteret to see the Proprietors before sailing to America. While there, the Proprietors appointed him surveyor general for New Jersey, a position of great importance in a new colony with vast tracts of land awaiting disposal. Vauquellin proved to be a loyal and devoted servant of the Proprietors, thereby earning the enmity of the people of New Jersey. In return for his services, he became the recipient of numerous grants of land from Governor Carteret.

While the work of clearing the land and building a town was going on, Governor Carteret took an active part in town affairs. Since he was the most distinguished Associator, he (or in his absence his secretary, James Bollen) was given the honor of presiding at town meetings.

James Bollen had come with Colonel Nicolls and with the fleet in 1664. After the surrender of the Dutch, he served as Commissary of Ammunition at New York. Like Vauquellin, in the eyes of the Associators he soon became one of the Governor's puppets. When Carteret appointed a Council to serve as his advisor as well as an upper house of the legislature, Bollen and Vauquellin were appointed to the Council and became its leading members.

As soon as Carteret had an opportunity to look around after arriving, he became alarmed in fear of an attack by the Indians. To aggravate the situation, certain men in New York, who probably traded with the Indians, secretly desired to see the new colony fail, so Carteret believed. It was "one of their greatest hopes that the Indians would not suffer us to inhabit here," he wrote a few weeks after his arrival. The envious ones, he declared, had even refused to sell him ammunition or give assurance that they would help defend New Jersey against the Indians.[2]

But the Indians remained friendly, though they caused the Elizabethtown pioneers minor disturbances from time to time. In the spring of 1666, Oratan and his Hackensack Indians troubled the Newark settlers but, after Carteret interceded, the colonizers were allowed to occupy peacefully the land to be purchased.[3] Fear of the Indians, nonetheless, kept the New Jersey pioneers huddled together in their towns for over a decade.

Soon after Philip Carteret had arrived, he took occasion to explain to the Associators that one-seventh of all land within any settlement was to be reserved for the Proprietors. From the start, however, he found the settlers altogether opposed to parting with any land within the village. To Berkeley and Carteret, he wrote in August that notwithstanding the provision in the Concessions for the one-seventh allotment, he found it impossible to execute the provision with the people "in General against it for the Present." Carteret explained to the Proprietors that since it was expedient to live close together, it seemed unreasonable to insist upon having these lots set aside for the Proprietors. He thought, moreover, that the Proprietors would be compensated in part by the quitrents derived from a rapid settlement of the towns. Outside the village, however, Philip was able to reserve land for the Proprietors. This perhaps took the form of a compromise with the Associators. As early as July, 1666, Carteret set aside land at Elizabethtown Point for the Proprietors.[4]

When Philip wrote to the Proprietors in August, 1666, he seemed to think that the Associators would not object to paying the half penny per acre quitrent, stipulated in the Concessions. The first payment was due in March, 1670. At the appointed time, Newark, which was purchased and settled after Philip arrived with the Concessions, went about gathering wheat to pay the quitrent to the Proprietors. But whatever encouragement Philip had for thinking that Elizabethtown and the other towns settled under the Nicolls' patents would pay was abruptly dissolved. When the date for the payment arrived, Elizabethtown, Woodbridge, Piscataway, Shrewsbury, and Middletown refused to pay because the Nicolls' patents, which antedated the arrival of Carteret, contained no provision for quitrents. This was the first major clash between the interests of the Proprietors and the Associators. It would soon widen into so deep-seated controversy over the Nicolls' patents, that it would follow Carteret throughout the remainder of his life.[5]

In 1670, when the dispute over the quitrents came to a head, the honeymoon which marked Carteret's early years in Elizabethtown had ended. By this time, with the colony five years old and well-established, he had much less reason for being conciliatory. Indeed, as Philip matured in years and grew to savor authority, the autocratic nature inherent in his Stuart background came increasingly to the fore.

The controversy over quitrents was enough to strain severely the relations between the Associators and the Governor. Nevertheless it was less disruptive than Philip's mounting encroachment upon the powers of the town meeting. Although, out of courtesy, the Associators allowed him to preside at town meetings, they had no intention of allowing him to dominate the meetings or assume control of town affairs. New Associators, by the rules of the organization, could be admitted only by majority vote in town meeting. Likewise, the Associators insisted that all town land must be appropriated by the voters in town meeting.

By 1670, Philip Carteret was ready to lock horns with the townspeople by disregarding the claims of the Associators and the powers of the town meeting. Shortly before the quitrents became due, he sold a houselot he had purchased to Claude Vallot, one of his servants from the Isle of Jersey. This action made Vallot a Third Lot man without the consent of the town. When the Associators protested, Philip answered that the Concessions conferred upon the Governor and Council all power over the disposition of land and the conferring of freemanship.

That Carteret would use his official powers to coerce anyone daring to take issue with him was soon revealed. Most of the local officers were chosen by town meeting but Luke Watson and John Woodruff, as militia officers, were appointed by the Governor and subject to his control. Since Watson and Woodruff were leaders who had openly opposed Carteret's invasion of town rights, Philip removed them from office and threatened them with death if they dared call out the militia for training. This order came at a time when there was some fear of the Indians who had been causing trouble in New England and Virginia. That New Jersey had a real autocrat in the governor's seat was the general opinion. By his depriving the town of the means of defense, no greater proof of misuse of power could be found, the people declared.[6]

The dispute over the invasion of town rights came to a head not long after the dismissal of Watson and Woodruff. Another servant from the Isle of Jersey, Richard Michell, was given a townlot by the Governor. Feeling that Carteret must be stopped or all power over the disposal of land would be lost, a town meeting was called on June 19, 1671, to consider the question. The men who gathered at the beat of the drum were in no mood to be trifled with. Michell, everyone agreed, had no right to the lot received from Carteret since the town had not been consulted. Drastic measures were demanded to show the Governor that the disposition of land did not rest with him.

Early the next morning, several men were seen approaching Michell's lot—not far from his house. At the moment, Michell was smoking his pipe with several neighbors belonging to the Governor's party. As the men approached, Michell recognized them as William Meeker, his son Joseph, John Ogden, Jr., and Hur Thompson. When the four got to his fence they began throwing it down as fast as possible. Soon they were joined by Luke Watson and some others.

Michell shouted to the men to stop, but they paid not the

slightest attention. In a few minutes William Pardon, a justice of the peace and a member of the Governor's Council, appeared. "Have you come to help pull down the fence?" young Ogden asked. Pardon replied that he had not and that he was there only to witness what happened. Ogden stopped long enough in his work at the fence to let Pardon know that they did not care "if a hundred such fellows" took notice of what they were doing. Pardon then observed that Luke Watson was only an onlooker like himself. "Not at all," replied Watson, who promptly went over and "heaved one log from the fence." After pulling down half the fence, the men decided that they had proved their point and left for the morning chores.

Michell, however, was in for more trouble. Not long after the others had left, Robert Morse and Stephen Crane knocked at William Lett's door and asked for a drink. Since he had none to offer, they presently left and went across the road to Michell's house and began pulling off the clapboards. Next they began to knock down the "palisade" around his garden. Within two hours the hogs which roamed the streets found the opening and rooted up most of the garden.[7]

Any pretense of good feeling between the townspeople and the Governor and his clique had completely evaporated. In March 1672, a Court of Oyer and Terminer, of which four out of six judges were members of the Governor's Council, ordered a trial of the men involved in the Michell affair. Indictments for rioting were issued and a jury selected. When the trial took place, the newly-erected Court House on the ground between Ogden's Mill and the meetinghouse was jammed with people.

Everyone in Elizabethtown knew that the Governor had the jury as well as the Court picked for the trial. Captain John Berry, William Pardon, Robert Vauquellin, and Samuel Edsall of the Council comprised the Court. No members of the jury were from Elizabethtown or Newark. Consequently the accused made no answer when asked if they were guilty of the charges against them. All eight were found guilty. William Meeker, accused of being the ringleader, was fined five pounds. The others were each fined three pounds.

Never before had Elizabethtown been in such an uproar. According to law, the Marshall of the Court was to distrain the goods of offenders who refused to pay the fines, but he dared not act. People in Newark and other towns were as incensed as the Elizabethtown Associators. If the Governor could lord it over Elizabethtown, he could do it everywhere in New Jersey. In Newark, a town meeting selected Robert Treat and Lieutenant Swain to talk with John Ogden and other leaders in Elizabethtown about the threat to town rights in the province.[8]

By the time of the Michell affair, Elizabethtown was not the only town involved in a quarrel with Governor Carteret. In 1668, Middletown and Shrewsbury had instructed their delegates to the first General Assembly not to vote for any law infringing upon the liberties of their Monmouth patent. When the action of the two towns caused their delegates to be disqualified by the Assembly, Middletown and Shrewsbury refused to pay their share of the provincial tax.[9]

Bad feeling between the colonists and the Governor was also excited when Carteret quarreled with the delegates at the first meeting of the General Assembly in May, 1668, over matters of legislative procedure. Most irritating to the Assembly was the Governor's refusal to allow his Council to sit jointly with the Assembly. On this point, because the Concessions were not very clear, both sides insisted that they were in the right. In the end, with legislative practice as well as the powers of government on the side of the Governor, the Assembly was compelled to sit alone.

By the spring of 1672, with nearly all towns on bad terms with Governor Carteret, it is not surprising that a conspiracy developed to rid the province of their unwanted chief executive. It happened that James Carteret, son of Sir George, the Proprietor, had come to America and for several months had been living in Elizabethtown. The townspeople liked James, who took their side against Philip. James perhaps was motivated by resentment against Philip for being favored by his father and Lord Berkeley. In any event, James was fully prepared to conspire with the Elizabethtown Associators against Philip.

In May, 1668, when the Assembly convened, the delegates launched a savage attack on the Governor's invasion of town rights by the court action in Elizabethtown. Resolutions were passed in support of town rights. Then the Assembly adjourned. Later in the month the Assembly met again without "writts from the Governor or without the knowledge, approbation or Consent of the Governor and Council." Without sufficient force at his command, all Philip could do was to condemn the proceedings as a wanton and illegal invasion of the powers of government. This, however, was just what the Assembly wanted him to do. Without waiting any longer, the Assembly elected James Carteret "president" of New Jersey. They had a right, it was said, to make James the chief executive inasmuch as he was the son of Sir George Carteret. As for Philip, his wanton disregard of the rights of the people and the welfare of the province, had caused him to forfeit the governorship.[10]

James Carteret accepted his new post without hesitation. Although he was supposedly on his way to Carolina to be one of the landgraves in that complicated government worked out by John Locke for the Proprietors, he seemed in no hurry to leave Elizabethtown. Said to have been a natural son of Sir George, James was a sea captain with a good record in the King's Navy. The battle royal raging in New Jersey seemed just the thing to amuse this rover of the ocean waves.

Since William Pardon refused to hand over the provincial records upon the election of James Carteret, an order was issued for his arrest. Alarmed for their safety amid the rising tide of resentment, Philip and his Council fled to Bergen. From there he issued an order for the rebels to submit in ten days or be proceeded against as mutineers.

Using all the power at his command to stem the tide of revolt, Philip made concessions to the towns of Middletown and Shrewsbury to secure their support. In particular, they were granted "full Power, License, and Authority to dispose of the said Lands expressed in the said (Monmouth) Patent, as to them shall seem meet."[11] The rest of the towns, however, could not be bought and continued to defy the Governor. In June, when William Pardon braved the wrath of the people by appearing in Elizabethtown to read Philip's proclamation declaring the town in rebellion, he was seized by Constable William Meeker. After suffering numerous insults, Pardon succeeded in escaping and returned to the Governor in Bergen.

The day following Pardon's escape, Justice of the Peace John Ogden, the elder, issued a warrant for the Constable to attach the movables on Pardon's property. As charged in the warrant, Pardon's offense was disobeying James Carteret's order to produce the provincial records. Constable Meeker acted promptly. Accompanied by several deputies, he entered Pardon's house, removed the furniture, and sent all the papers found there to James Carteret. This was not all. Five acres of peas were confiscated and the Secretary's livestock driven away to be sold.

Believing that it was hopeless to contend against the uprising without help from England, Philip presently left America and sailed for the homeland. With him went his loyal supporters: James Bollen, Robert Vauquellin, William Pardon and one or two others. Meanwhile Captain James Carteret moved into the Governor's house on the King's Highway in Elizabethtown and made himself at home. Later he married Frances Delavall, daughter of a New York merchant, and brought her to live in his new home.

About the time that James Carteret took a wife, Bollen and Pardon returned from England. They came armed with a battery of papers from the Duke of York and from the Proprietors asserting that Philip was the legitimate governor and that James must go. Pardon also had orders for John Berry, named deputy governor of New Jersey until Philip returned. One order commanded Berry to see that Pardon was indemnified for all losses suffered at the hands of the rebels. Berry acted promptly by issuing a proclamation forbidding anyone from buying property from Constable Meeker or his deputies. This was accompanied by another order demanding all who had participated in the revolt to come to Bergen and seek the pardon of the governing authorities.

Determined to get at the root of the trouble by putting an end to the land claims of Elizabethtown, Woodbridge, and Piscataway under the Nicolls' patent, Berry was ordered by the Proprietors to set a time limit for all colonizers to have their land surveyed and patented by proprietary officials. Whoever should neglect to apply for a warrant of survey and have his land duly registered would "forfeit such lands as they are settled upon and pretend unto." So read the ominous proclamation.[12]

Confronted by the authority vested in the Deputy Governor as well as by a letter from Sir George, his father, instructing him to be on his way to Carolina, James Carteret decided that the little revolution in New Jersey was ended. The people, too, realized that they must submit or be branded as rebels in England as well as America.

Berry moved fast. In June, Meeker and his deputies were arrested and brought to trial in a court properly fixed for the work at hand. Meeker had his estate confiscated; the others were fined ten pounds each. All that the towns could do in the grip of the iron hand of executive authority was to draw up petitions and send them to the Proprietors; but help from an altogether unexpected source was at hand.

In July, when the sloop bearing Captain James Carteret and his wife was nearing the capes of Virginia, it was presently surrounded by a powerful Dutch fleet of five vessels. The Dutch were prowling the coast of North America in the wake of the outbreak of another war with England. On board the sloop, the Dutch found Samuel Hopkins, one of the ringleaders in the recent revolt at Elizabethtown. Hopkins told the Dutch not to listen to the Captain of the sloop. Instead of being strongly defended as the Captain maintained that it was, New York was in truth quite defenseless; so Hopkins assured Cornelius Evertsen, Jr., and Jacob Benckes in command of the Dutch fleet. To the delight of Hopkins, who relished the thought of witnessing the upset of the Proprietaries, Evertsen took his advice and sailed for New York. Finding himself no match for the Dutch, Governor Francis Lovelace surrendered New York after little resistance. Not long afterward, Samuel Hopkins saw Deputy Governor Berry at New York surrender New Jersey to the Dutch.

Most of the people of New Jersey were as pleased as Samuel Hopkins with the turn of events. Just as they thought they were hopelessly caught in the vice prepared by the Proprietors, all was changed. Three days after the surrender, John Ogden, Sr., and deputies of several other towns petitioned the Dutch officers for an audience. As a special favor they asked that Captain Berry not be given an audience until they had a chance to be heard.[13]

In reply the Dutch asked the towns of Elizabethtown, Newark, Woodbridge, and Piscataway to send delegates to New Orange (New York had been renamed in honor of William of Orange). The towns friendly to the Proprietors, Middletown and Shrewsbury, were told to have representatives there also or be subdued by "force of arms."

When John Ogden and his friends reached New Orange, they were cordially received by the Dutch conquerors. The New Jersey towns, they were assured, would have all the privileges enjoyed by any Dutch towns. The New Jersey men were then instructed in the way they should set up local government under the Dutch. Each town was to choose six men out of whom the Dutch would select three for town schepens (magistrates). The towns would also choose two men to form a committee for nominating three candidates for the office of schout and three for that of secretary. All candidates were to be the wealthiest and most intelligent men available.

From the slate proposed by Elizabethtown (where seventy-six men took the oath of allegiance to the Dutch) John Ogden, Samuel Hopkins, and Jacob Melyn were made schepens. From the nominees for schout, an office tantamount to that of governor of New Jersey, the Dutch chose John Ogden. Samuel Hopkins became the secretary for the province. Jacob Melyn, an Elizabethtown Dutchman, was selected by Anthony Colve, the Dutch governor general, to be captain of the local militia.[14]

As schout, John Ogden had the responsibility of laying out highways, building bridges, and erecting public buildings in the province. To him also fell the duty of laying out land to qualified applicants. By orders from the Dutch, he was to permit only the services of the Dutch Reformed Church. This directive apparently did not bother the people of Elizabethtown since the Dutch Reformed Church was Calvinistic, like their own. Moreover it was clear that the Dutch did not intend to be strict in the matter of religion, since their instruction carried notice that office holders should be of the Dutch Reformed Church or persons "at least well affected thereunto."

With political power now firmly in their hands, the Elizabethtown Associators, with John Ogden at their head, turned to righting matters with the Proprietary minions. For not delivering to Ogden some property taken from the Governor's house, Robert Vauquellin (who had returned from England) was called to New Orange at the instance of Elizabethtown officials and found guilty of sedition. His sentence was banishment from the Dutch colonies.[15] Proceedings were also started for reversing the recent action against William Meeker and his deputies. Samuel Moore, the Marshall under Berry, was compelled by Ogden to turn in Meeker's and Thompson's bail bonds. If the Dutch rule had continued longer this would have been the beginning of the end for the troubles of Meeker and his men. But it was not to be. After a rule of about six months, New York and New Jersey were restored to the English when the Dutch lost the war and made a treaty dictated by the conquerors.

Not long after New York and New Jersey became English again, Philip Carteret returned after an absence of two years. With his return, Elizabethtown Associators found themselves altogether at the mercy of Proprietary authority. Sir George Carteret had become sole owner of the northern section of the colony, known as East New Jersey. Lord Berkeley had sold out and the Duke of York had divided the province between Carteret and the new Proprietors, who were given the southern part called West New Jersey.

From the Duke, Sir George received a new patent which, besides defining the boundaries of East New Jersey, strengthened his hand in the governing of the colony. The Concessions consequently were remodeled by Sir George to give the Governor greater authority, especially over the legislative Assembly. Fortified with his amplified powers, Philip Carteret arrived at Bergen in the autumn of 1674 to pick up the reins of government from Captain Berry. Soon he was back in Elizabethtown, settled once more in his "Government House" and attended by his servants and all his officials.

Philip Carteret first of all moved to put an end to the Elizabethtown patent, long considered by Sir George the most vexing source of trouble in New Jersey. Philip's instructions, dated July 31, 1674, were very explicit. "For such as pretend to a right of propriety to land and government within our Province, by virtue of any patents from Governor Colonel Richard Nichols, as they ignorantly assert, we utterly disown any such thing," declared the Proprietor. The instructions stated that the inhabitants would be given just one year to obtain warrants and have their land patented by the Governor. After that, all lands not registered as prescribed would be confiscated and sold by the Proprietor.[16]

As was expected, Governor Carteret commanded Samuel Moore, the Marshal, to collect the fines against William Meeker and others convicted of wrongs committed against Richard Michell and William Pardon. This time, with no escape possible, the fines and penalties were reluctantly paid. For his part, William Meeker forfeited everything he owned in the defense of town rights. His friends, however, came to his rescue with a collection from Elizabethtown and Newark which partially compensated him for his losses.[17] Intent upon silencing all opposition, Carteret again put the courts to his use by obtaining an order for the confiscation of the Elizabethtown property of Abraham Shotwell, accused of using abusive language against the Governor.[18] Shotwell's lot, extending from where St. John's Church now stands to the River, was purchased by Thomas Blumfield who sold it to Philip Carteret in 1675.

Confronted by an intransigent and powerful overlord, the people of Elizabethtown decided to try to make a deal with the Governor. In town meeting, a decision was made to offer the Proprietor a yearly sum of twenty pounds in exchange for a charter granting the Associators exclusive rights in a township of eight square miles.[19] Philip Carteret, however, would make no concession. His only answer was that the inhabitants would have to obey the proprietary order and register their land or suffer the consequences. Land thus registered became subject to the annual payment of quitrents.

In spite of the threats of the Governor, the deadline for registering lands came and went with the people of Elizabethtown still holding out. Sentiment, however, was changing. Registering their land, they reasoned, would not necessarily mean that they were abandoning town rights guaranteed by the Nicolls' patent or their claims to the land by virtue of the Indian deed of 1664. Although there still was no rush to get warrants, applications for them were finally made. The requests were made over a period of three years; old John Ogden was the last to make his claim.[20]

Considering the volatile nature of New Jersey's colonial politics, it is not surprising that Philip Carteret's day of ruling with a high and mighty hand was not a long one. His adversary this time was not the people. It was rather another autocrat in the person of the cold and calculating Edmund Andros, Governor of New York.

Colonel Andros had come over on the ship which brought Philip back to America. On board, the relations between the two men, who were kinsmen, were cordial enough. Carteret may have known that Andros carried a commission which named him governor of all the territory between the Connecticut and the Delaware rivers. In any event he did not let that trouble him, and the men parted on good terms. Carteret may have felt that as his papers made him governor of New Jersey in contradiction to Andros' commission, he had no cause to worry. However, it was known that the Duke of York wished to abolish proprietary rule in New Jersey and that the terms of Andros' commission could not be construed as merely a mistake on the part of a secretary. In any event, Andros was at first too preoccupied with New York affairs to concern himself with New Jersey, and Carteret was not troubled for some time.[21]

The question which finally brought Andros to decide to assert his authority over New Jersey arose over the control of navigation. Most annoying to him was Carteret's insistence that New Jersey was not bound by New York's ruling that all ships entering or leaving New York Bay must pay duty at New York. From the beginning Carteret had insisted that New Jersey was not bound by New York's pretension to exclusive control of the Hudson. Writing to the Proprietors in August, 1666, Carteret had vigorously voiced his objections to the New York ruling. Plagued by the New York laws, he finally fined a New England ship, which had paid tolls at New York, for not registering and paying duty at Woodbridge. This happened before Andros became governor. However, within two years after Andros arrived on the scene, Carteret issued an order making Elizabethtown a port of entry with duties five percent lower than those at New York. Undercutting such as this was the very reason for New York's insistence upon controlling Hudson River navigation.[22]

When Carteret refused to bow to the claims of New York or recognize its jurisdiction over the province of New Jersey, Andros resolved to go to England to place the matter before the Duke of York. Before leaving, however, he came over to Elizabethtown and had a long and seemingly friendly talk with Carteret. If he had not known it before, he now became thoroughly convinced that it would require all the weight that could be brought to bear from England to make Carteret give up governing New Jersey.

After his trip to England, where he was knighted, Andros returned to America early in 1680, armed with a mandate to govern New Jersey as well as New York. The capture of New York and New Jersey by the Dutch a few years before, Andros announced when he landed, had voided the proprietary grant, causing New Jersey once again to become the domain of the Duke of York. The Duke consequently, he declared, had made him the governor of both colonies. Philip's claim to the governorship was further weakened by the death of Sir George Carteret just before Andros sailed for America.

Sir Edmund Andros did not wait long after his arrival at New York before starting his campaign against Governor Carteret. Philip was sent a note restating Andros' right to govern New Jersey. To assert his authority, Andros announced that New York would presently build a fort at Sandy Point (Sandy Hook) on the New Jersey shore. Five days later he wrote again commanding Philip to cease exercising the powers of government.

Upon receiving the notes, Philip answered that he would defend his right to govern New Jersey to the last extremity. He asked Sir Edmund, however, to refrain from any act of hostility, pending a settlement of the dispute by the proper authorities in England.

For once the people of New Jersey sided with Carteret. Although both Andros and Carteret were much alike, Philip was indeed much the more likeable. Andros was forty-three, only two years older than Philip. Both were from old feudal families from islands in the English Channel. Andros came from the Isle of Guernsey, only about twenty miles from Carteret's home on the Isle of Jersey. Both families were staunch supporters of the Stuarts. Andros had seen service as a major in the army, fighting the Dutch in the West Indies. This experience stimulated his natural autocratic and overbearing disposition. In New Jersey, Newark echoed the prevailing sentiment toward Sir Edmund when it declared that inasmuch as the town had taken an oath "to the present government," it would continue to recognize Carteret as governor until his Majesty directed otherwise.[23]

With the approval of his Council, Andros presently decided to go to Elizabethtown again to try to persuade Philip to recognize his authority. After crossing the bay in a brisk wind on a cool day in early April, 1680, he landed with a party of governing officials on Staten Island, directly opposite Elizabethtown Point. Here he sent two embassaries to inform Carteret that he had come in peace and would like a conference. The next morning the messengers returned with word that Philip would be pleased to see him.

Andros and his party at once left for Elizabethtown. After crossing the narrow waters between Staten Island and the mainland, they sailed up the Elizabeth River and landed at Samuel Hopkins' wharf, some few lots below the Governor's house. Walking up the King's Highway, they crossed the brook in the low marshy hollow and ascended the slight grade to the Governor's house. Surrounding the house was a strong stockade recently erected for defense against Andros. Outside the stockade stood a throng of armed men who allowed Andros and his party to pass. Inside the gate, the New Yorkers found Philip Carteret surrounded by another group of armed men. As Andros approached, Philip stepped forward smiling and bowing to his cousin with every mark of courtesy.

Carteret ushered Sir Edmund and his companions into the council room, explaining how happy he was to find that Andros wished to settle the dispute amicably. Encouraged by his reception, Andros began reading his commission and instructions from the Duke of York. Since there was a great throng endeavoring to crowd into the room, he suggested that they repair to a nearby field where everyone could hear. This was agreed upon, and he read his papers and stated his claim to the whole town assembled in the open air.

When he had finished, Carteret invited his visitors to return to the house. Here Carteret read his commission and instructions from Sir George Carteret. In response, Andros stated that his papers were derived from a higher source and that Carteret's were consequently invalid. Philip vehemently denied this. When he finished speaking, the room resounded with applause and Captain Berry and others declared that New Jersey would support Philip to the last. Sensing that further discussion was useless, Andros closed the conference by saying that he was sorry that his visit had failed to open the eyes of the people of New Jersey to their mistake. After partaking of a sumptuous dinner, he and his companions were escorted to the wharf by Philip and all his men. On parting each side fired a salute.

Although he did not show it, Sir Edmund was incensed by his reception at Elizabethtown. Back in New York he quickly swore out a warrant for Philip's arrest. Soon all was ready, and on a dark night a party of soldiers sailed for Elizabethtown with orders to bring Philip back, dead or alive. Landing not far from the Governor's house, the soldiers silently made their way to the house without causing alarm. After getting within the stockade, they broke into the house, seized Philip, and dragged him off. "In the dead of night," wrote Philip, "they broke open my doors and most barbarously and inhumanly and violently hauled me out of bed." The episode was related more graphically by the German traveler, Jasper Danckaerts: "They entered the house, I know not how at midnight, seized him naked, dragged him through the window, struck and kicked him terribly, and even injured him internally. They threw him, all naked as he was, into a canoe— and carried him in that condition to New York, where they furnished him clothes and shoes and stockings, and then conducted him to the fort and put him immediately in prison." [24]

About five weeks after his imprisonment, Carteret was brought to trial on the charge of illegally exercising the office of governor of New Jersey. In defense, he produced his commission from the late Proprietor, Sir George Carteret. To Sir Edmund's surprise, the jury for the Special Court of Assizes brought in a verdict of "Not Guilty." Extremely vexed, Andros tried to browbeat the jury by sending it out several times with new charges. Each time the jury returned with the verdict, "Not Guilty." In rendering the decision, however, the judges appended this note: "Capt. Carteret shall go to New Jersey, he should give security or engagement not to assume any authority or jurisdiction there, civil or military." Believing he had no alternative, Philip accepted the ruling of the Court.

After the trial, Sir Edmund, accompanied by a great throng of ladies and gentlemen, escorted Philip back to Elizabethtown in "great pomp." Upon his return, he kept his promise not to assume the powers of government. Instead he busied himself improving his estate, and supervising the building of his new brick mansion on a lot purchased from Captain Bollen just to the east of the First Government House. Soon he married Elizabeth Lawrence, a widow of a wealthy planter of Flushing, Long Island, mother of seven children.

Following Carteret's release, Andros proceeded to take over the government of New Jersey. He soon convened an Assembly and came to Elizabethtown accompanied by his wife and the usual entourage of ladies and gentlemen. His reception was civil enough, but as he presently fell to disputing matters of legislative procedure, nothing was accomplished. Although most people held their tongues and made no move to offend the Governor, there were some who could not be restrained. One "Doctor" William Taylor, from parts unknown, took it upon himself to harangue anyone in the taverns who would listen to his diatribes on the iniquities of Sir Edmund. Taylor became so offensive that Andros had him seized and carried to New York, where he was found guilty of slander. Since nothing would be gained by punishing him, Taylor was freed after promising to hold his tongue in the future.

When they had time to think it over, many citizens of Elizabethtown were inclined to favor Andros over Carteret. Andros was found to be sympathetic to the claims of the Associators, a most compelling reason in itself for a change in sentiment. William Meeker was one of those who saw in Andros an opportunity for the Associators to reassert their claims and press for recovery of losses at the hands of the Proprietary faction.

William Meeker soon started an action against William Pardon for recovering his losses—estimated at three hundred pounds. Next we find him in New York conferring with Andros, who seemed not at all displeased with the possibility of making more trouble for Carteret and his friends. When the case was tried, the Court ordered Pardon to return Meeker's property and pay twenty pounds damages and the court costs. When Pardon refused to comply, Andros was asked to have the Marshal proceed against the delinquent. No further record of the dispute has survived. Apparently, since Sir Edmund was presently recalled to answer charges of maladministration, Meeker never recovered anything. William Pardon soon moved away and appears no more in the annals of Elizabethtown.[25]

When Sir Edmund left New York for England in the spring of 1681, Philip Carteret at once resumed the powers of government in New Jersey. One of the first things he did was to advise all who had suffered losses during the Andros regime to file suits for recovery. Sick and irritable, Carteret, however, was fast losing his sense of proportion. Having called an Assembly, he engaged in a stormy and protracted dispute over legislative powers and over questions involving the provincial courts. He also plunged into a heated controversy with New York over the ownership of Staten Island. When Carteret's career as governor of New Jersey was finally terminated by the appointment of a successor, few lamented his retirement. It was truly a happy day when Thomas Rudyard arrived in November, 1682, to take over the reins of government.

Philip Carteret lived only about a month after his retirement. No doubt his death at the age of forty-four resulted from the injuries received at the hands of Andros' soldiers two years before. All of Philip's property in America, consisting of the brick house and several thousand acres of land, went to his wife, Elizabeth. This good lady soon married Colonel Richard Townley, a gentleman who had recently come to America with Lord Effingham, Governor of Virginia.* In his will Carteret remembered to free his faithful Negro servant, Black Jack.

With the death of Philip Carteret and the purchase of East New Jersey by a group of proprietors in Great Britain, one phase of the history of Elizabethtown passed away and another began. The new proprietors and their governors sought to avoid the mistakes and pitfalls encountered by their predecessors by seeking an understanding with the people and an avoidance of disputes. Their attempt, however, ended in failure. Soon the old issues of land rights and quitrents reappeared and before long the contest was more bitter than in the days of Philip Carteret. As before, Elizabethtown became the center of the conflict.

* Elizabeth Townley had a long contest with the new proprietors over the ownership of the Second Government House. Finally the court found in her favor.

The Clinker Lot Right Men

Soon after East New Jersey was purchased from Lady Carteret for £3,400, in 1682, the number of proprietors was enlarged from twelve to twenty-four. Later the stock was fractionalized, and the number of proprietors was greatly enlarged. Not long after the new organization was founded, Robert Barclay, a Scottish Quaker—wealthy, enterprising, and young—became the leading spirit in the organization which in the beginning was composed primarily of Quakers. A friend of the house of Stuarts, he was made governor of New Jersey for life at the instance of Charles the Second. Highly respected among Quakers for his religious writings and a close friend of William Penn, he enjoyed the prestige befitting his office. More than anything, New Jersey is indebted to him for the sturdy Scottish immigrants, both Quaker and Presbyterian, whom he helped send to America. Having decided against residing in New Jersey, Barclay appointed Thomas Rudyard, a capable London Quaker lawyer, to the office of deputy governor.

Imbued with a deep humanitarianism, Barclay hoped that the differences of the past in New Jersey could be resolved and that the relationship between the Proprietors and the people would become marked by harmony and goodwill. In Thomas Rudyard, Barclay made an admirable choice for implementing his benevolent policies. Rudyard was pleasant and courteous, always tactful in his dealings with people. Having nothing of the haughtiness of the Cavalier class with their fancy dress and dangling swords, he made a favorable impression on the plain New Jersey yeomanry.

To signify that he desired to rule by the consent of the people, Rudyard appointed townsmen like Benjamin Price of Elizabethtown to his Council. This was a noticeable departure from the policy of Philip Carteret, who had surrounded himself with court favorites to the exclusion of town leaders. Moreover the Carteret faction—Vauquellin, Robert Vicars, Henry Greenland, Samuel Edsall, and others who had abused their power, especially during the final period of Philip's rule—were made to answer for their misdeeds.

As one of the Proprietors, William Penn visited Elizabethtown in 1683. His "inoffensive carriage" won the hearts of the inhabitants and helped smooth the path for Governor Rudyard. While in Elizabethtown, Penn bought out the holdings of Luke Watson, who had moved to Delaware. He also offered to buy John Baker's share in the Elizabethtown Purchase. No wonder that Penn became the subject of some criticism by fellow proprietors who could not understand why he should want to become an Associator.

At the start, Governor Rudyard pleased the Elizabethtown Associators on the occasion when some of the leaders came to him and asked for a town meeting for the purpose of recording land allotments since 1666. In answer, Rudyard told them that they could have town meetings as often as they pleased. This indeed was a departure from anything the townspeople had experienced under Philip Carteret.[1]

But as much as Rudyard might please New Jerseyans, his tenure lasted only ten short months. Barclay and the Proprietors heard that he was manipulating land warrants for his own benefit and lost no time in dismissing him and appointing a successor. The new deputy governor was Gawen Lawrie, a London Quaker merchant who arrived at Elizabethtown with his daughter and son-in-law, William Haige, whom he had made surveyor general.

Lawrie carried instructions from Barclay for putting an end to the claims under the Nicolls' patents and for collecting the quitrents. During Rudyard's term, the Proprietors had found that the Associators in the several towns had indicated no intention of abandoning their claims under the Nicolls' patents. Even Robert Vicars, Carteret's last provincial secretary, was accused of stirring up the Elizabethtown Associators to assert their claims now that the proprietaryship had changed hands. Vicars, possibly, had a part in Elizabethtown's recent request for a town meeting for investigating land titles. In any event, Barclay brought the issue to the fore by sending an open letter to all Associators in New

Jersey. "But we find you lay stress upon your Purchase from the Indians," he wrote, "which it will never bear, for we would have you informed, that thereby you have acquired no right but what is duly confirmed by us, or our legal predecessors."

All Associators, Barclay explained, must have their land properly registered and pay quitrents as prescribed by law. As in the early days when Carteret demanded payment of quitrents, the erosion of good relations between the people and the Proprietors at once began to be felt. Lawrie, however, like Rudyard, was considerate of and even ingratiating toward the people, and thus postponed a severe break with the Proprietors for a time. The Elizabethtown Associators, nonetheless, were alarmed. Presently they came to Lawrie with a proposal for a town charter in exchange for a nominal quitrent. The Governor, however, felt obliged to turn the offer down as one not attractive enough to the Proprietors. But he was too good a politician to close the door on the possibility of an accommodation.[2]

Notwithstanding his order from Barclay to terminate the claims under the Nicolls' patents in one way or another, Lawrie made no effort to carry out his instructions. Quite the contrary, he saw fit to participate in the affairs of the Elizabethtown Associates in such a way as to all but recognize the legitimacy of their claims. This happened when Lawrie asked Town Clerk Isaac Whitehead and Captain John Baker who, since the death of John Ogden and the removal of Luke Watson, was the only one left of the 1664 patentees, to describe the boundaries of the town. Lawrie wanted the information, he said, because he wished to purchase land from the Indians west of the Elizabethtown boundary.

With a governor as accommodating as Lawrie, the Elizabethtown Associators jumped at the opportunity to mark out a boundary—one that would be far enough to the west to give all shareholders a generous slice of new land. Soon Captain Baker, the old interpreter, held a conference in his house, which was attended by leaders of the Association, by several Indians, and by Governor Lawrie. After discussing the boundary, they decided that Captain Baker would conduct a party to mark out the western boundaries of the town. On a July day in 1684 he set out to explore the wilderness with some Associators and several Indians, includ-

ing the old sachem, Wewanapo. As soon as the explorers returned, Elizabethtown paid the Indians for a tract of land extending from the settlements back to the first range of the Watchung
Mountains.* Apparently the Associators were satisfied with this
line for the western boundary of their Nicolls' grant. Lawrie, it
seems, understood this and concluded that he was free to buy
land beyond the Baker line.† He consequently went ahead and
made a purchase from the Indians of a large section reaching
from the Baker line (which approximated the Minisink Path) to
the Passaic River below Long Hill and then down to a point near
the present-day town of Boundbrook. Meanwhile Baker was
hauled into court by the Proprietors and made to renounce his
purchase and to sustain a fine of ten pounds for violating a law
prohibiting purchases from Indians by private persons.[3]

One can well appreciate the feelings in Elizabethtown when
the Associators found that their move to acquire land within the
purchase of 1664 was blocked by Proprietary-appointed judges
of the Court of Common Right. The dispute over land and quitrents, however, lay dormant for several years following Lawrie's
dismissal in 1686 for endeavoring to grab for himself much of the
best land in the province. During this period the Proprietors
found themselves at the mercy of the great political upheavals that
shook both England and America. In 1686 with James, Duke of
York, crowned King of England, the Proprietors were compelled
to turn their governing powers over to Sir Edmund Andros, once
again back in America with orders to incorporate New York and
New Jersey within his Dominion of New England. Thus Elizabethtown found itself under the jurisdiction of Francis Nichol-
son, Andros' deputy governor for New York and New Jersey. The
change was welcomed by the inhabitants of New Jersey at large
since it offered a way to escape for awhile from the exactions
imposed by the Proprietaries.

Although the rule of James II and Andros was of short duration,
it was followed by another period of uncertainty and of the
absence of effective provincial government in New Jersey. In New

---

* The Shunpike Road in Springfield Township would approximate the
western boundary of the Baker purchase.
† Hatfield thought that the Associators did not give Lawrie to understand
that they claimed no land beyond this boundary. Hatfield, pp. 228-229.

York, upon ouster of Andros in 1688, political power fell into the hands of Jacob Leisler, who held sway for about two years. Many New Yorkers, accused of supporting the dethroned James II and his puppet Andros, were forced to flee to New Jersey where some found refuge in Elizabethtown. Here, too, Andrew Hamilton, deputy governor of New Jersey after Lord Campbell's short term in 1686, and Captain Richard Townley, husband of the widow of Philip Carteret, came forth as champions of the Jacobites who were openly drinking toasts to James II, who had fled to France.

For a time, Leisler's arm was long and his enemies in New Jersey were far from safe. Matthew Plowman, collector of New York, lost over sixty barrels of pork and beef when a body of Leisler's men raided Elizabethtown but failed to catch the owner. Feeling toward the Leisler party of New York was mixed in Elizabethtown but apparently most Associators were sympathetic since his policies favored the common man. However, when he tried to enlist men for his militia in Elizabethtown, he found few, if any, willing to volunteer.[4]

With the advent of William and Mary to the throne in 1689, the Proprietors regained control of New Jersey and again made Andrew Hamilton governor of the province. Since the Proprietors had had quite enough of trying to cope with the Associators by ineffectual orders and threats, they decided to vacate the Nicolls' patents and collect the quitrents by court action. This most assuredly foreshadowed a complete break between the inhabitants and the Proprietors, with a repetition of all the bitterness and struggle for power experienced during the Carteret regime. Barclay's humanitarianism would be shipwrecked on the hard rocks of rival economic interests as the Proprietors came face to face with open rebellion from defiant Associators.

The showdown between the Proprietors and the Associators came in 1693 when a test case arose over rival claims to land within the Elizabethtown purchase of 1664. Among the contenders was Jeffery Jones, one of the first settlers, who owned 180 acres on the Rahway River with a title derived from the Associators. Jones, who had never paid any quitrents, was sued for trespassing on the property of James Fullerton, the Woodbridge schoolmaster, who had patented the Jones farm with the proper proprietary official.

When the case was tried in the Court of Common Right, the jury found for Jones. The judges, however, who represented the proprietary interest, brazenly set aside the verdict and gave a judgment in favor of Fullerton. Abuse of the courts in this manner had been one of the causes for the intense bitterness against the Carterets. Now anger turned against the new Proprietors. Soon the people became so incensed by the proprietary control of the judiciary that, as a result, courts were broken up and judges intimidated.

The Fullerton case, as it turned out, did not end with the action of the judges of the Court of Common Right. The case was appealed to the Privy Council in England where two years later, Lord Chief Justice Holt presiding, the Council reversed the decision of the Court of Common Right. Furthermore, the Nicolls' patent, the Privy Council concluded, was valid. This decision became a land-mark in the long controversy between the Associators and the East Jersey Proprietors. With the highest court of the Realm deciding in their favor, the Elizabethtown Associators henceforth were in no frame of mind to bow to the will of the Proprietors.

In a subsequent case, the Associators won another important victory over the Proprietors. The case involved Peter Noe of Elizabethtown, whose cattle were seized by the baliff for arrears in quitrents. The fundamental issue at stake was whether or not the Proprietors could distrain property to satisfy quitrent claims. Again the jury found in the people's favor with a verdict to the effect that the Proprietors had no legal right to seize goods of delinquents.[5]

Although successful in the courts, fear of the Proprietors was so strong that in 1696 the Elizabethtown Associates came out openly for annexation to New York. Their petition to the King, signed by nearly every man in Elizabethtown, closed with a request for the transfer of government from the Proprietors to the Crown, a step which was eventually realized six years later. "Your petitioners groaning under these and other great Oppressions of the said Usurpers, and in the want of a legal and well-established Government, are humble Suitors to your Majesty," read the letter. For this reason the petitioners asked that Elizabethtown be placed "under the Civil Government of your Majesty's Province of New

York." The Elizabethtown proposal had the hearty support of New York. Governor Thomas Dongan had long advocated such a union as the only means by which New York could protect its trade and commerce.

Fanned by the rising wind of bitterness toward the Proprietors, opposition to the government soon flamed virtually into open rebellion. Tactful and competent Governor Hamilton found it impossible to stem the revolt once it gained heat. During the final stages of the struggle to oust the Proprietors, New Jersey was thrown practically into a state of anarchy.

In defense of their rule, the Proprietors sent the King a long account of the troubles. They pictured the uprising as one led by a minority determined to undermine all authority and "to deprive the Proprietors of their Right to the Soyle and Quit-Rents of the Province derived to them by Grants from the Kings of England, and purchased by them with great sums of money." They even accused the rebels of aiming at making New Jersey independent of any outside authority, whether of Crown or otherwise.[6]

In 1699, after two years of turmoil under Governor Jeremiah Basse, the government was again placed in the hands of Andrew Hamilton. Nevertheless affairs soon went from bad to worse. At Middletown, a mob defied all law by snatching Moses Butterworth (who admitted he had served as a pirate under Captain Kidd) from the hands of the law in open court. In Elizabethtown, the court found it impossible to try Samuel Burwell, held for refusing to support his illegitimate child. When the court adjourned to Newark in the hope of prosecuting the case there, practically every man in Elizabethtown mounted a horse and rode to Newark, club in hand. These were the men of the second and third generation in Elizabethtown, the sons and grandsons of John Ogden, Isaac Whitehead, William Meeker and the other founders.

When the Elizabethtown riders reached Newark, they ordered the sheriff to release the prisoner they had come for. When the sheriff refused to comply with their demands, they shouted that they would release Burwell if they had to break every head in Newark to get him. Helplessly the sheriff and his deputies stood aside as the Elizabethtown men entered the jail, shouting and waving clubs, and made off with the prisoner.

Surviving records do not reveal why Elizabethtown was so aroused by the arrest of Burwell. It is apparent, nonetheless, that the ride was not simply an act of lawlessness. It represented rather the universal resentment of the Proprietors and of their corrupt system of jurisprudence.

At the time of the ride of the Elizabethtown men to Newark, the Proprietors were fully aware that they must give up the government of New Jersey or have it taken from them by the King. Negotiations to that end had been in progress, and in April, 1702, the Proprietors formally turned over the government to the Crown. Henceforth and until 1738, when New Jersey received a royal governor of its own, the Province was ruled by the governor of New York.[7]

After winning the Fullerton case, the Elizabethtown Associators resolved to make use of their good fortune by taking possession of the land purchased fifteen years earlier from the Indians by John Baker. The Associators numbered about 120, since the organization had been enlarged to meet the needs of the sons and grandsons of the founding fathers. To implement their design, the Associators in town meeting chose John Harriman, son of the local pastor, to make the survey. Benjamin Ogden, Benjamin Lyon, John Clarke, Samuel Carter, and Cornelius Hatfield would assist him.

The men appointed by the town meeting lost no time in carrying out the biddings of the Associators. Between December, 1699, and the following March, they surveyed all the land west of the Elizabethtown settlements to the foot of the Watchung Mountains. Upwards of 17,000 acres were surveyed and divided into 171 one-hundred acre plots. Samuel Whitehead, who followed his father as clerk of the town meeting, was granted the first lot in the new survey. The disposal of this land marked the beginnings of the settlement of Westfield, Connecticut Farms (Union), and Springfield.[8]

Naturally the Proprietors were considerably disturbed by the action of the Associators in taking up land for themselves. The Fullerton decision, they contended, was based on technicalities and did not invalidate proprietary right to dispose of all land in East New Jersey or to collect the quitrents. The Associators, they charged, had simply taken advantage of the turmoil in the Province to seize land belonging to the Proprietors. Even the surveys, they maintained, were made by moonlight to avoid detection.

Some of the Clinker Lot Right Men, as the Associators interested in the new survey were called, sold their allotments for five pounds per hundred acres. The price was established by the town meeting, with the understanding that since the land was only worth from two to three pounds per hundred acres, income in excess of this amount should be turned over to a committee chosen by the Associators. The fund derived from sales would be held for defending titles—should the Proprietors attempt to prosecute. Buyers were informed that should they finally lose out, they would in reality suffer no loss since they would be in possession of the land, with its valuable timber, long enough to find the venture profitable.[9]

After the loss of the governing powers in New Jersey, the Board of Proprietors, founded in 1685, became inactive for many years. Meanwhile the Associators or those purchasing from them occupied the land surveyed in 1699-1700. By 1720, with a new generation coming on and the population growing, agitation arose for a new survey within the Nicolls' grant farther to the west. About this time, however, the Board of Proprietors was rejuvenated with the appearance of new men of energy and ability. Foremost among these was James Alexander. A promising young lawyer, Alexander took up residence at Perth Amboy after fleeing Scotland for supporting the Old Pretender during the uprising of 1715.

Realizing once again that they were about to be confronted by a powerful Proprietary organization, the Elizabethtown Associators made preparations for coping with the new threat to their plans for expansion. This time, they knew, they were not likely to get help from England, since the Crown had committed itself to safeguarding the rights of the Proprietors when it assumed the governing powers of New Jersey in 1702. At a town meeting, called on August 2, 1720, the Associators, therefore, revived their committee system to defend themselves against the Proprietors. A new committee was appointed, consisting of Captain Joseph Bonnell, John Blanchard, John Crane, and Joseph Williams. As before, it was instructed to collect subscriptions from the interested parties for defending titles against the Proprietors.

Having become surveyor general and leader in the Board of Proprietors, James Alexander soon found himself right in the center of the contest with the Elizabethtown Associators. For several years, he tried to find a way to settle the controversy by compromise. His overtures, however, came to nothing, as the Elizabethtown men went right on appropriating the lands regardless of the protests of the Proprietors. Meanwhile the Proprietaries were not inactive. They also sent out surveyors, sold land, and gave the buyers their deeds. Surveys in 1722 were made in the area of Turkey (New Providence) whence lines were run up over Long Hill and into the Great Swamp. Farther to the west, the Proprietors made surveys near Mine Hill, Basking Ridge, and Peapack.[10]

By 1735 the contest for the lands beyond the first range of the Watchung Mountains had grown with each passing year. The second generation of Associators had passed away and new names were added to the committee, which consisted of Jeremiah and John Crane, Caleb Jeffery, Samuel Miller, Joseph Halsey, Joseph Williams, and Joseph Bonnell. Joseph Morse was the surveyor for the Associators. As before, lots of one hundred acres were surveyed. In the division of land, third lot rights were given the first drawing out of 280 lots surveyed west of First Range. Second lot rights came in for the second drawing while the first lot rights waited for the final drawing. Out in the Basking Ridge area, Third Right Men received three hundred acres, while the second and first obtained two and one hundred acres respectively. In the Basking Ridge section the committee also put up a large tract for sale for two thousand pounds. This money they planned to set aside to defend the titles against the Proprietors. All sellers were asked, as before, to give the Committee a percentage of their receipts for this fund.[11]

Confronted by the new drive of the Elizabethtown Associates, whose membership had risen to over four hundred, James Alexander called a meeting of the Board of Proprietors at Perth Amboy to devise means for stopping the advance of the Clinker Lot Men. Soon the Board appointed John Vail to study the proceedings of the Elizabethtown Associates and make a report of his findings. Next the Board adopted the system of asking all persons holding Proprietary titles to subscribe to a fund for fighting the claims of the Clinker Lot people. Having decided from Vail's report that it was time to start prosecuting the Elizabethtown "squatters," plaintiffs presently started suits in the county courts.

Meanwhile Joseph Morse and his assistants continued surveying for Elizabethtown. East Jersey proprietors with large holdings in Morris and Somerset counties, the heirs of William Penn and their secretary, James Logan, became very alarmed at the threat to their property. Somewhere in the area west of Long Hill the Elizabethtown surveyors with staff and chains went straight through the green wheat planted by Daniel Cooper; he swore out writs against the trespassers. The case finally came to trial in 1742. After forty hours of testimony, the jury returned a verdict in favor of Cooper and of his claims under the Proprietors. The Proprietors won this case, it appears, because they had succeeded in getting a large number of settlers into Morris County with proprietary titles. The area, indeed, had but recently been made a county for the purpose of defeating the aims of the Elizabethtown men.[12]

Notwithstanding the proprietary victories in the courts, the Board found that, as usual, little was being accomplished in the matter of collecting quitrents. Consequently the Board gradually arrived at the opinion that by an "English Bill in Chancery" all the questions arising from the Nicolls' patents should be settled once and for all. Definite action was taken in 1741 when the Board decided to have the lawyers James Alexander, Joseph Murray of New York, and David Ogden of Newark, draw up a bill in chancery.

James Alexander immediately went to work on the Bill. He spent hours going over all available evidence. He borrowed minute books and ledgers which had belonged to Philip Carteret and took extensive notes for proving his points. Before long, his study of the documents convinced him that the Elizabethtown Associates had no valid title to the land purchased in 1664. When Alexander and Murray finally finished their Bill it was a long involved history of the whole dispute, covering fifteen hundred sheets of manuscript. When the maps were made and the Bill printed, by James Parker of New York, the whole production cost the Board of Proprietors nearly three hundred pounds.[13]

While the Proprietors were preparing this Bill in Chancery, the

Elizabethtown Associators were not idle. Even before the Bill was begun, they had decided that the interest of the town would be served by securing a charter of incorporation. The boundaries of the township as prescribed by a legislative act of 1693 had gone back to the Partition Line between East and West New Jersey, one which extended the boundaries of the town even beyond the thirty-four miles of the Nicolls' patent. Out of this territory the movement arose in 1738 to create Morris County. It was, partially at least, the impending loss of this area that prompted the Associators to seek a charter for Elizabethtown, whereby as much land as possible would be incorporated within the boundaries of the township. Precedent for incorporation was found in Perth Amboy's charter of 1718 and in the more recent incorporation of Burlington and New Brunswick.

In 1738, when New Jersey ceased to share its governor with New York and acquired one of its own in the person of Lewis Morris, Elizabethtown took occasion to present its petition for a charter. Funds for defraying expenses in soliciting the charter were raised by subscription with Matthias Hatfield, Andrew Joline, and John Ogden, forming the committee. Everything went smoothly for Elizabethtown; within a few months after the petition was presented, King George II signed a charter creating the Borough of Elizabethtown. The boundaries of the Borough, Associators were pleased to find, extended to the Passaic River below Long Hill. This area contained most of what is now Union County.[14]

In accordance with the Charter, Governor Morris appointed the mayor and clerk of the market for Elizabethtown. The first mayor was Joseph Bonnell, a resident of Connecticut Farms. Bonnell was the most outstanding leader in Elizabethtown; he had served in the Provincial Assembly and on many town committees for many years. In 1739, when he became mayor, he was speaker of the New Jersey Assembly. Before the end of the year he was again honored when the Governor appointed him as a judge of the Supreme Court. More than anyone, Bonnell was responsible for getting the town incorporated and for securing so much land within its boundaries.

Although Elizabethtown was pleased with its Charter, the Associators had no intention of abandoning their claim to land beyond the boundaries which did not include all of the original purchase. Early in the 1740's, when the Elizabethtown people heard that the Proprietors were raising a large sum of money for a Bill in Chancery, they became alarmed about their claims beyond the First Mountain. After a long discussion, the Associators decided to prepare a history of their claims under the Nicolls' grant and to have it taken to England and presented to Crown authorities. When finished, the document was signed by three hundred and four Associators. Stephen Crane and Matthias Hatfield took the paper to England where it was read by the Privy Council in July, 1744, and referred to a committee. There it apparently died; Crane and Hatfield returned with nothing to show for it all.

When the mission to England failed, the Elizabethtown leaders decided that an answer must be written to the Bill in Chancery. Lawyers were hired and more money was collected from persons with a stake in the western lands. In 1748, Stephen Crane and Robert Ogden (father of Colonel Aaron Ogden) went to Philadelphia to discuss the Nicolls' patent with John Kinsey, one of the foremost lawyers in the country. About this time William Livingston, the future governor of New Jersey, and William Smith, Junior, were hired to write an answer to the Bill in Chancery. Smith, the future judge and historian, was only twenty-three at the time, while Livingston, who had studied law under James Alexander, was twenty-seven. Since expenses already were running high, the Associators borrowed £125 for carrying on its battle against the Proprietors. Thirty-four-year-old Robert Ogden, the treasurer, took a prominent part in all the proceedings. By the time Elizabethtown's brief, entitled *An Answer to a Bill in the Chancery of New Jersey,* was finished and published in 1752, it had cost the Associators nearly two hundred pounds.[15]

Long before the *Answer* was finished, Elizabethtown saw one cause for worry removed when Jonathan Belcher became the governor of New Jersey after the death of Lewis Morris in 1746. Morris had established the Chancery Court, and as governor he became the chancellor. As everyone knew, he was unsympathetic to the Elizabethtown case. But Belcher, who had been governor of Massachusetts, had no ties with the Proprietors and was inclined from the start to favor the Elizabethtown claims. The fact, too, that he was a Presbyterian, as were most of the Associators, no doubt weighed in their favor. Belcher's views apparently explain why the Bill never came before him for adjudication.

The Proprietary-Elizabethtown dispute had become a topic of conversation all over America. Benjamin Franklin favored Elizabethtown, as did Lewis Evans, the celebrated Philadelphia mapmaker, who had made some of the maps for the Bill in Chancery. Evans, indeed, went so far as to say that he believed the Bill in Chancery to be essentially false. During the contest each side accused the other of destroying the Elizabethtown Minute Book containing the records of the founding fathers. The evidence, however, appears to point to someone on the Proprietary side stealing the records about the year 1720. In any event, they have never been seen since that time.

In many areas west of the First Range the contest between the rival factions came to blows. Down in Philadelphia, Proprietary secretary Richard Peters wrote in alarm: "The Elizabethtown gentlemen hath put in two tenants in Mr. Penn's Land, and they are making great havoc in the Best Timber Land." At Turkey, named from the great flocks of wild turkeys found in the area,* the situation got quite out of hand. Rival claimants attacked each other and families were driven from their homes with clubs. Alexander started ejectment proceedings against the Clinker Lot settlers at Turkey in 1744 but he found the courts very slow and that their judgments were disregarded whenever possible.[16] Governor Belcher became very concerned over the rioting and lawlessness in New Jersey, for it had flared up to new heights after he arrived. By then rioting had spread all over the province as Newark, Middletown, and the counties of Somerset and Middlesex followed the lead of Elizabethtown in flouting the Proprietors and in disregarding the law. In Morris County over one hundred armed men came to the aid of Daniel Cooper who momentarily expected the Clinker Lot men to attempt driving him away by force.

Believing that they might be able to make an example of one of the rioters, Somerset officials seized John Bainbridge and took him to Perth Amboy for trial. Soon, over two hundred horsemen

* Summit, N.J. was called Turkey Hill.

descended on the town, armed with clubs and staves. They alighted at the city jail; the sheriff warned them not to break in. In answer the rioters came at the sheriff and his deputies with their clubs. After nearly killing the sheriff, the rioters battered down the door of the jail with sledge hammers and crowbars. After setting Bainbridge free, the rioters, led by a row of fiddlers, paraded through the streets of the town before the eyes of the terrified townspeople.

When Governor Belcher heard of the riot, he angrily threatened to raise a regiment and march against the mobsters. Threats, however, were of little avail and the turmoil continued: public officers were intimidated, courts were prevented from sitting, and jails broken open. In England, Lord Halifax thought that the British government should send an armed force into New Jersey.[17]

With all the uncertainty over land titles, many settlers acquired deeds from both sides. In 1762, a large farm was advertised at Basking Ridge, the title of which was "indisputable both from Elizabethtown and proprietors." Doubtlessly most settlers desired to see an end to the uncertainty and favored any move to terminate the controversy. In 1756, James Alexander, the proprietary leader for forty years, died, his Bill in Chancery still unused. Although Governor Belcher died the next year, sentiment preferred finding a compromise out of court. In 1760 both the Board of Proprietors and the Elizabethtown Associators signified a desire to reach a compromise. Robert Hunter Morris indicated in a letter to Cortlandt Skinner that both parties might settle the controversy by dividing the disputed area between them. On July 20, 1762, John Stevens, a proprietor with much at stake, wrote "that there is a probability of settling in an amicable manner the long dispute between the proprietors & the Elizabethtown people" since "an agreement with the People of Elizabethtown is now on the Carpet." Time passed, however, with little progress made in bringing the controversy to a close. Finally the issue was shoved aside during the turmoil of the American Revolution.[18]

After the War for Independence, the state adopted a policy of recognizing land titles whenever people had long been settled with deeds from either the Proprietors or from the Associators. Morris County, which had resisted the advance of the Clinker Lot men, generally had proprietary titles. Most of the patents up to Long Hill, however, were derived from the Nicolls' grant, since this area was settled and held by the Associators.

The long struggle between the Proprietors and the Elizabethtown Associators, which began in the days of the founding fathers and continued generation after generation until the outbreak of the American Revolution, was a significant episode in American history. The pioneers of Elizabethtown were men highly imbued with a sense of their rights as Englishmen. Therefore, although economic interest lay at the root of the struggle between the rival parties, the feeling that the Nicolls' grant was valid and that the Proprietors continuously resorted to illegal measures to achieve their ends, caused the dispute to become involved in the highly significant question of rights so dear to the hearts of the English yeomen. With the coming of the American Revolution, the sentiment for resisting oppression, which had characterized the long contest with the Proprietors, was carried over and became the rallying point which was extended and finally ended in independence.

VI

The Great Awakening

During the first sixty years of eighteenth century Elizabethtown, the story of the times centers around religious life and related events quite as much as it centers around the Proprietary-Clinker Lot struggle. Religion in colonial days exerted a powerful influence over the lives of the people; Elizabethtown was no exception. Even the Elizabethtown-Proprietary controversy had its religious overtones, with the Associators nearly all Presbyterian (Independents before the change to Presbyterianism) and the Proprietors after 1700 mostly of the Episcopalian faith. As might be expected, the Presbyterian ministers were stout defenders of town rights, while the Episcopalian clergy tended to favor the Proprietary cause. Later, during the War for Independence, the same lines remained. Presbyterian ministers thundered against the tyranny of the British, while the Episcopalian clergymen generally felt obliged to stand by the mother country.

Many ministers of the colonial period found it necessary to supplement their pastoral income with earnings from other sources. No better example of the minister-entrepreneur can be found than the life of the Reverend John Harriman. Harriman was already thirty-nine when he became the town's pastor in 1687, after the pulpit had stood vacant for five years. He came from Connecticut, where he had helped Robert Vauquellin, Carteret's surveyor of former times, in running a boundary line between New York and Connecticut. In his boyhood, he had studied under Jeremiah Peck, Elizabethtown's first minister. After graduating from Harvard, Harriman alternately preached and kept school. Having married Hannah Bryan when he was twenty-five, he came to Elizabethtown with a wife and six children. Three more children were born in Elizabethtown. No wonder that the

69

Reverend John Harriman gave thought to earning more than the sixty pounds which he received for his pastoral services.

Upon making application to the Proprietors after moving to Elizabethtown, Harriman was granted one hundred acres of good farm land. Calling upon his congregation for volunteers, he soon had his farm cleared with an outlay of "beer, Cake and rum." Thereafter, with the labor of his older sons and one or two slaves, the farm became for him an important source of income.

Having become a man of capital, the Reverend John Harriman branched out into other lines of endeavor. With Benjamin Ogden, he leased John Ogden's old "corn mill," since fallen into the hands of a New York merchant. The owner received a yearly rent of twenty-five pounds. Nathaniel Whitehead was hired to operate the mill. Besides managing his farm and mill, Harriman dabbled in real estate, kept a store, owned a cider mill, and for many years conducted a boarding school. He even found time to serve in the Provincial Assembly.

All of the Reverend Harriman's transactions were meticulously tabulated in ledgers. Thus we find that he received five shillings a week for boarding students, and three shillings for teaching the art of navigation. A barn cost him seven pounds; a slave, forty-eight pounds. His parishioners paid their tithes in produce or services, the value of which were entered in an account book. John Woodruff in February, 1696, was credited for making a coffin for the minister's son, Leonard. In September the pastor lost another son, for whom Woodruff made another coffin. Other credits were entered for the shoemaker, the tailor, and the like. Occasionally someone paid in wampum.[1]

Toward the end of John Harriman's busy life, Episcopalianism began to make headway in Elizabethtown. Prior to 1700, the few Episcopalians (who were generally governing officials) went to church on their visits to New York or sometimes attended the meetings of the Independents in Elizabethtown. In 1702, George Keith, having given up Quakerism for the Church, visited Elizabethtown on a proselytizing tour of America for the Society for the Propagation of the Gospel in Foreign Parts. There he sowed seeds which generated a desire in the community for the introduction of Episcopalianism. A few years later their hope was fulfilled when the Society for the Propagation of the Gospel sent the Reverend John Brooke to found a church in Elizabethtown.

At first, Reverend John Brooke, a graduate of Emmanuel College, Cambridge, held his services in Colonel Richard Townley's brick house, the one built for Philip Carteret in 1680. Within a few months, when his house grew too small for the expanding congregation, services were held in a barn until the summer's harvest forced the worshippers to seek other quarters. From the start, the Reverend Harriman was deeply annoyed by Reverend Brooke and his undisguised campaign to win over as many Independents to Episcopalianism as possible. In fact, he died of a heart attack in his fifty-eighth year, while he was standing in the pulpit "railing against the Church."

Following the death of their minister, the Elizabethtown Independents offered to share their meetinghouse with the Episcopalians. Apparently the Reverend Samuel Melyen, Mr. Harriman's assistant and successor, found no objection. The kind offer was accepted; thereupon the Anglican service followed that of the Independents, which ran from eight in the morning until ten. In the afternoon, both congregations held another service.

When the Independents opened their church to the Episcopalians, they asked only that Mr. Brooke refrain from reading from the Book of Common Prayer. The promise was given but apparently the Reverend Mr. Brooke, who was young and zealous, had no intention of honoring the commitment, for he at once proceeded to learn his prayers "by heart" and recite them during the services. What the Independents thought is not known, but in any event they continued to allow the Anglicans to use their church until they had one of their own. The hospitality of the Independents to a rival church, bent on expanding at the expense of its host, demonstrates the degree of tolerance among Elizabethtonians. Unfortunately the liberality of the Independents was not reciprocated by the Anglicans, who continuously exhibited a narrow, unbending attitude toward all dissenters.

Although in some ways the Independents were surprisingly broadminded, the time had not arrived when they would tolerate card playing, stage plays, or other devices of Satan. At a Quarter Sessions in 1712, George Jewell and several other Elizabethtonians were indicted for card playing in their homes. When they paid their fines, however, the indictments were quashed. No doubt, had their fines remained unpaid, the guilty would have served time in the town's stocks in front of the Court House.

Only a few weeks after they began sharing the meetinghouse with the Independents, the Episcopalians started building a brick church of their own. Colonel Richard Townley, his wife Elizabeth, and his son Effingham were the principal benefactors of the church in Elizabethtown. The Townleys not only appropriated the ground for the church but gave a considerable sum for its construction.* Due, however, to the slowness of the money coming in, St. John's, as the church was named, was not finished for ten years. Altogether the church cost over four hundred pounds, most of the money coming from the Society for the Propagation of the Gospel and from private donors in England and America. Much of the funds raised in America was solicited by the Reverend John Brooke, who rode horseback through New York and Pennsylvania in search of subscribers. Young and strong, he could endure hard riding but his clothes, much to his distress, wore out faster than he could replace them.

The Reverend John Brooke was at Elizabethtown less than two years when his career ended in tragedy. The eccentric Lord Cornbury, governor of New York and New Jersey, became angry when Brooke's friend, the Reverend Thorowgood Moore of Burlington, criticized his morals and indecent behavior. As a result, Moore was seized, brought to New York, and thrown in jail. Hearing of the plight of his friend, Brooke made a dash to New York and succeeded in helping Moore to break jail. After that, neither dared stay any longer in America; both took passage for England to lay their troubles before the King. During the voyage, the ship was lost and all on board perished.

Mr. Brooke's successor, the Reverend Edward Vaughan, enjoyed a long and distinguished career. Installed as rector of St. John's within two years after Mr. Brooke's demise, Vaughan served the community until his death thirty-eight years later. Like the Reverend John Harriman, he was not a poor man, although he acquired his wealth in a more direct manner. Four years after arriving at Elizabethtown, he married Mrs. Mary Emott, a widow considerably older than he was. Colonel Richard Townley's stepdaughter, she had a dowry of two thousand pounds.

* The land was deeded to St. John's in 1711.

The Reverend Jonathan Dickinson.

During Vaughan's ministry, his congregation steadily grew; he was well-liked and respected. Converts primarily were made from among the Quakers and Presbyterians, who suffered from internal differences from time to time. Since most of the members were quite poor, only a fraction of the minister's support was raised by the parish. Apparently not a few were attracted to St. John's by the knowledge that most of the expense of maintaining the church fell on other shoulders. Vaughan recognized the attraction of a charity-supported church when he wrote that should he ask the people to support him: "it would very much tend to the dis-service of the Church, in causing our proselytes to start from us rather than bear the weight of such burthens." [2]

In the year Mr. Vaughan came to Elizabethtown the Independents found a new minister—in the person of the Reverend Jonathan Dickinson. Having graduated from Yale in the first class, 1706, Dickinson came to Elizabethtown two years later; he was then twenty-one. Within a year, he married a sister of Samuel Melyen, who had filled the pulpit for a short time after the death of John Harriman. From the start, it became apparent that Mr. Dickinson was to be no ordinary minister.

At the time Jonathan Dickinson became the pastor of the old church in Elizabethtown, the Independent or Congregational churches in New Jersey were rapidly succumbing to the Presbyterian movement in America. Dickinson favored the Presbyterian system and thus it was not long before he had persuaded his congregation to affiliate with the Philadelphia Presbyterian Synod. Henceforth the church would be known as the First Presbyterian Church of Elizabethtown.

Upon becoming a member of the Synod, Dickinson at once became an important figure in Presbyterian circles. For a number of years he served as clerk for the Presbytery at Philadelphia. Finally, in 1733, when the Presbytery of East New Jersey was formed, he became its acknowledged leader. He was instrumental in extending the jurisdiction of the East New Jersey Presbytery to include the Long Island Presbyterian churches.

At home in Elizabethtown, Dickinson was as enterprising and constructive as he was in inter-church affairs. Under his guidance, the old meetinghouse, built by the founding fathers, was pulled down and a new church erected. The new edifice was a frame building, like the old one, with shingled roof and sides. Unlike its predecessor, however, it had a belfry and steeple in the Georgian style of the times. As before, pews were sold, the price ranging according to the location in the church. When an owner failed to pay his annual dues, the trustees had the power "to enter into said pew, and rent the same to highest bidder by public outcry." Pews sold for as much as forty-four pounds.[3]

During his pastorate, the Reverend Jonathan Dickinson became one of the outstanding religious writers in America. Much of his writing was directed against the Deists, whose teachings were finding converts in America. Other publications arose from controversies with the Anglicans. Later, when the Great Awakening reached the shores of America, Dickinson joined the movement and used his pen to further the cause. As the years passed and one book followed another, Dickinson's reputation as a religious thinker spread to the British Isles. Dr. John Erskine, a noted Edinburgh clergyman, later declared that "the British Isles have produced no such writers on Divinity in the Eighteenth Century as Dickinson and Edwards." [4] A century after his death, the works of Dickinson were still being published and read. Except for Jonathan Edwards, no other eighteenth century religious leader exerted such a lasting influence on American Protestantism.

In 1739, when the Reverend Jonathan Dickinson was about fifty, he became very much concerned about the low state of religion in the world. Ministers seemed lifeless, the people devoid of Godliness. But the Reverend had barely spoken before a great transformation appeared. People seemed to awake from their lethargy as though struck by an electric bolt. It was not an isolated phenomenon. Rather, it was a general awakening all over the Christian world. Starting in Germany, the revival quickly spread to other countries. In England, a great evangelist appeared in the person of the young and dynamic George Whitefield, who came to America on a preaching tour in 1739.

George Whitefield reached Elizabethtown in November. He was cordially welcomed by Jonathan Dickinson, who threw open the doors of his church to the famous evangelist. Taking the people to task for their apathy in religious matters, Whitefield wrote that "God was pleased to open my mouth against both ministers and people among the Dissenters, who hold the truth in unrighteousness contenting themselves with a bare, speculative knowledge of the doctrines of grace, but never experiencing the power of them in their hearts." A year later when he returned to Elizabethtown, Whitefield estimated that two thousand people came to hear him. Flanked by twelve ministers, Whitefield delivered another of his stirring evangelical sermons so dear to the heart of his host, Jonathan Dickinson.

Unlike the second, George Whitefield's first visit to Elizabethtown was disappointing to the Reverend Jonathan Dickinson. At Newark the people responded to Whitefield with a great outburst of religious emotionalism. But at Elizabethtown they remained calm and collected. While others were flying to Christ, bemoaned Dickinson, his congregation "could not be awakened out of their Sleep." Nonetheless, pastor Dickinson kept trying to move them. "To that End, there were frequent Lectures appointed for the young people in particular, but without any visible success," wrote the unhappy pastor.

Not long after Whitefield's second visit to Elizabethtown Mr. Dickinson had his hopes fulfilled when the revival suddenly burst upon his congregation without warning. It began while he was preaching "a plain, practical Sermon, without Pathos or Pungency, or any special Liveliness or Vigor." Then, during a moment's pause, Dickinson noticed "a sudden and deep Impression which visibly appear'd upon the Congregation in general." "There was no Crying out, or Falling down (as elsewhere has happen'd) but an inward Distress and Concern of the Audience discover'd itself, by their Tears, and by an audible Sobbing and Sighing in almost all Parts of the Assembly." "From that Time," wrote Dickinson with satisfaction, "we heard no more of our young People's meeting together for Frolicks and extravagant Diversions,—but instead thereof, private Meetings for religious Exercises were by them set up in several Parts of the Town." [5]

Soon after the revival struck Elizabethtown, Dickinson began writing in support of evangelism. Not all religious bodies, however, succumbed to the infection. The Quakers and Anglicans, especially, were cool to the movement. In Elizabethtown, for example, the Reverend Vaughan gave Whitefield a cold shoulder and refused to open St. John's for revival purposes. In most of the other Protestant denominations, evangelism caused a serious division to arise. Division was especially severe among the Presbyterians, who became divided into Old and New Lights. Men like Jonathan Dickinson, who denounced fanaticism, tried to keep the church together, to no avail. Finally the New Light, which espoused evangelism, torn by discord, formed a new synod at New York. The first meeting took place at Elizabethtown with Jonathan Dickinson acting as moderator.

With Yale College under the control of Old Lights and seemingly discriminating against youths with New Light persuasions, Jonathan Dickinson and his friends decided that it was time to found an institution for higher learning in New Jersey. In Pennsylvania, the New Lights had founded a Log College at Neshaminy, led by Gilbert and William Tennent, the success of which was inspiring to Dickinson. After a preliminary meeting, Dickinson's committee, in 1746, applied to John Hamilton, president of the Council and acting governor by the death of Lewis Morris, for a charter. The request was granted; the College of New Jersey was born and Jonathan Dickinson was appointed its president by the Board of Trustees.

The Reverend Jonathan Dickinson was well-fitted to be president of the new college. Besides being a scholar, author, and minister, he had for nearly forty years conducted a boarding school for classical studies.

It was the month of May and the eight or ten boys who reported for college were exuberant over the prospect of attending classes in a town well stocked with pretty girls, if a little short on educational facilities. The college which was in the parsonage on Jelf's Hill on the west side of the river, near the Stone Bridge, was, in fact, not much more than the old classical school under a new name. As required by the charter, the college was open to boys of all denominations. Caleb Smith, who had assisted Dickinson in the classical school, was retained as usher or instructor.

Unfortunately, Dickinson's presidency of the College of New Jersey was cut short by his death within a few months after the college opened. When word that he had died reached Mr. Vaughan, who himself was very sick and would die within a few days, he exclaimed, "Oh that I had hold of the skirts of Brother Jonathan." After Dickinson's death, the college was moved to Newark where for nine years the Reverend Aaron Burr, pastor of the Presbyterian church, served as president. Following the death of Burr, the College of New Jersey was moved to Princeton and renamed after its new home.[6]

During the latter part of Dickinson's life, he became most interested in promoting missionary work among the Indians. In this period, Presbyterians supported several missionaries who gained fame for their work with the Indians. One of these was the Reverend Azariah Horton, who ministered to the Indians on Long Island.* Another was David Brainerd, a young mystic supported by the Scottish Society for the Propagation of Christian Knowledge and the New York Presbytery. Coming to New Jersey in 1744, Brainerd found help and encouragement from Mr. Dickinson before beginning his work among the Indians.

Life among the natives was hard; before long Brainerd contracted tuberculosis. Leaving the Indians, he stayed a winter with Pastor Dickinson, from whom he received encouragement and spiritual nourishment. Not long after Brainerd (whose diary, published in 1746, had earned him recognition as a missionary and a philosopher) followed Dickinson to the grave at the age of twenty-nine. His death occurred while he was visiting the great divine, Jonathan Edwards, at Northampton. His brother, John, who was also well-known in Elizabethtown, continued the work among the Indians. While on his way to the Indian mission at Cranberry, New Jersey, in 1749, he was kindly entertained by Samuel Woodruff in his new house on East Jersey Street.

Ministers in colonial days were often doctors; none, perhaps, deserves more credit in this field than Jonathan Dickinson. Diphteria, called septic sore throat, carried off a great many people each year. So lethal was the disease that Dickinson, who had studied and practiced medicine most of his life, set himself to work on the diagnosis and treatment of the infection. The popular remedy was a gargle with a preparation of honey, vinegar, and alum. This treatment did no more than furnish some relief from the soreness.

As a result of his study, Dickinson published in 1740 a treatise entitled *Observations on that Terrible Disease vulgarly called Throat Distemper*. The study, published in Boston, demonstrated Dickinson's unusual skill as a diagnostician. At a time

* He was afterward the minister at Bottlehill (Madison, N.J.).

when the stock cure for the average doctor consisted of ineffectual remedies and a debilitating treatment of bleeding, blistering, and purging, Dickinson was trying to discover effective ways to combat the disease. Considering the degree of medical ignorance in Dickinson's time, it is not surprising that Dr. William Douglass of Boston advised people to stay away from most doctors if they wished to live long.[7]

While Jonathan Dickinson was absorbed in the great religious revival, there occurred in Elizabethtown a blot on its history, one that is difficult to explain because its people were generally not given to excesses. Be that as it may, two or three Negroes were burned at the stake before the Court House in Elizabethtown in the year 1741. Hysteria over rumors of a slave revolt had first appeared in New York where, before the panic ended, one hundred and fifty Negroes were imprisoned and fourteen were burned at the stake. Twenty white men were charged with having a part in the plot; four were hanged. In desperation, some Negroes fled to Elizabethtown. Soon several of them were apprehended and brought to trial, found guilty of conspiracy to murder the people, and sent to the flames. Sheriff William Chetwood was in charge of the burning. Records show that several townsmen received pay for furnishing the wood for the execution.[8]

Psychologists may see a connection between the religious frenzy rampant at the time and the burning of the Negroes. The revival, it is true, aroused a great excitement, which was not a very favorable atmosphere for a calm consideration of wild rumors and charges against runaway slaves. When it is remembered, however, that punishment for crimes was still very severe, the torturing of the Negroes seems less extraordinary. In 1745, for instance, Sheriff Chetwood was paid for burning Harry Hartwell in the hand, presumably for stealing. In such an environment the burning of slaves accused of plotting murder, aroused few qualms. Everyone, of course, approved of the laws prohibiting slaves from owning firearms or from hunting, except with their masters.

By Dickinson's time slavery had become very common in Elizabethtown, with many people of property owning several Negroes. Some Indians, mostly women, were also slaves. In 1701, the Reverend John Harriman bought an Indian girl for nineteen pounds. Another minister, the Reverend Simeon Horton of Connecticut Farms, advertised in 1744 for his Indian "wench" named Sarah, who had run away. In Elizabethtown, Cornelius Hatfield, one of the town's leading citizens, was a slave dealer.[9]

Governor Jonathan Belcher, who moved to Elizabethtown in 1751 after living three years in Burlington, was a man who firmly believed in the teachings of Jonathan Dickinson. Above all, Governor Belcher was both deeply religious and interested in the advancement of learning.

Elizabethtonians were proud to have among them a man of Governor Belcher's character and devotion. Perhaps, however, the fondness for the Governor arose more from the knowledge that he favored the legality of the Nicolls' grant, so close to the hearts of most Elizabethtonians. In any event, Elizabethtown leaders had been active in securing the appointment of Belcher as governor.

When Belcher first came to New Jersey to take up the reins of government, he was warmly received in Elizabethtown. Mayor John Ross, flanked by Samuel Woodruff, Robert Ogden, Jonathan Hampton, and other leaders, gave a welcoming speech in which he lamented the disorders in the province. This condition, he felt, would improve rapidly with Mr. Belcher the governor. "We cannot but lament the Uneasiness that the present tumultuous Circumstances of your Government must create in your Excellency's Mind, and yet we cannot but comfort ourselves with Hopes, that Providence has designed your Excellency as the happy Instrument of quieting our Confusions, and of stilling the Tumults of the People," the Mayor concluded.[10]

Jonathan Belcher was sixty-six and failing in health when he became Governor of New Jersey. Having inherited a large fortune as a young man, he had lived lavishly and entertained in great style. Now, however, his fortune had dwindled and he had found it necessary to live on a modest scale. A Harvard graduate with a keen interest in knowledge, Belcher had cultivated the friendship of men of learning in America and the British Isles. From the first he had evinced a deep interest in the College of New Jersey. Unfortunately, while attending the commencement exercises in 1750, he suffered a severe stroke which left his right side partially paralyzed. So acute was the affliction that for eighteen months after the attack he could not hold a pen.

Harkening to the doctors who told him he was likely to enjoy better health near salt water, Belcher decided to leave Burlington and try the air at Elizabethtown. However, since he was nearly seventy and ailing, qualms arose over the thought of moving. He liked his surrroundings at Burlington, only taking exception to the Quaker laxness in the observance of the Sabbath. But at Burlington he had been much afflicted with "the fever and the ague" and the move seemed imperative. At least he had one consolation. His second wife, Mary Louise Teale, whom he had married after coming to Burlington, was younger and strong enough to assume much of the work of moving to Elizabethtown.

Arrangements were soon made with Mayor Samuel Woodruff for Belcher's wife and step-daughter, Elizabeth, to come to Elizabethtown to see about a house. Upon arriving, Mary and Elizabeth stayed with the Woodruffs in their large new house, part of which was used as a store.* In his day, Samuel Woodruff was one of the principal men of Elizabethtown holding such offices as magistrate, councilman, and mayor of the Borough.

A short distance from the Woodruffs was the Ogden house, part brick and part frame, standing on the lot granted to John Ogden, Jr., in 1665. This is the house that Benjamin Ogden willed to his sons in 1722. The records do not show who owned the house in 1751 or if Governor Belcher rented or purchased the property. In any event, it pleased Mrs. Belcher and Elizabeth, especially after Woodruff agreed to have the house enlarged and otherwise made more attractive for the Governor.[11]

Since Governor Belcher had much furniture and other belongings, three sloops were hired to transport his property to Elizabethtown. Late in the summer, accompanied by one or two servants, Elizabeth left Burlington to get the house settled before the Governor and his lady arrived. With her went the family cows, driven behind the coach by a boy.

By the time the Belchers arrived in the autumn, Elizabeth had the house all settled and ready for living. Samuel Woodruff had purchased sixty cords of oak, walnut, and hickory for the five large fireplaces. He also, at the Governor's request, had purchased twelve barrels of cider at Matthias Hatfield's cidermill. From

* Today this house is of historic importance, having subsequently been the home of Elias Boudinot and later of Jonathan Dayton.

New York he had bought a stock of good wines and tasty beer. Woodruff, indeed, had overlooked nothing which the Governor might want. Apples, pears, vegetables, flour, and all manner of supplies for the pantry were in the house and ready for use.

Riding in their coach drawn by four black horses, Governor and Mrs. Belcher arrived at Elizabethtown on a bright October day. From the start, they were delighted with their new home. Its gardens and orchards covering much of the six acres from Jersey Street to the King's Highway were especially pleasing to the Governor, who prided himself on his botanical knowledge. The Governor was pleased, too, with the new wing in Flemish bond which had nearly doubled the size of the house.

As the Governor entered the center hall, painted apple green, he found his gun case precisely where he wanted it, with its array of muskets, pistols, and swords. To the right, in the new section, was the parlor where Elizabeth had hung the large looking glass and arranged the mahogany table with the silver inkstand. In this room, too, with the mahogany table and walnut chairs, she had placed the tall grandfather's clock, the terrestrial globe, pictures of the King and Queen, and the Governor's coat of arms, carved in wood and resplendent in its paint and gilt. The room itself, pleased the Governor with its fireplace flanked by deep alcoves. The walls, above the usual wainscoting, were plastered and painted a deep blue. Beneath the two large windows on each side of the room were squab seats which Elizabeth had fitted with pretty velvet cushions.

In the dining room to the left of the hallway, Elizabeth had placed the Governor's large painted carpet, which went well with the dining room set of mahogany chairs and table. Apparently she thought that the Governor would use this room a good deal since she had the two elbow chairs by the fireplace at the end of the room near the doors which led to the kitchen in the old frame section.

On the second floor were two large bedrooms and a small one just at the head of the stairs. The west bedroom, where the ailing Governor had many council meetings, was a dark blue. The shutters for the windows, when open, gave color to the room with their orange paint made from brick dust and buttermilk. The alcoves, which flanked the fireplace as on the first floor, were complete with shelving and double doors, also lined in orange. In the mode of the day, the closet ceilings were fashioned with meticulous care in the form of scallop shells, the alternate bars of which were painted a soft grey and blue. The closet to the right of the fireplace was made into a cellaret, with glasses waiting on the shelves and the cabinet well-stocked with wines to please the Governor's palate.

The bedroom to the east was unique in that the right alcove served as a bathroom warmed by a small fireplace off the big chimney. The other alcove was a study with a large desk and shelves for several hundred books. Here, it is said, the Reverend Jonathan Edwards worked on some of his sermons or essays while visiting his friend, the Governor.

On the day Governor Belcher and his wife arrived, Elizabethtown held a large reception in his honor. On the platform sat Mayor Samuel Woodruff with his Aldermen and Common Council. The Reverend Elihu Spencer, who had succeeded Dickinson, offered the prayers and gave a sermon. Mayor Woodruff then gave the welcoming address. Four years had gone by since Belcher had come to New Jersey and the people of Elizabethtown were well-satisfied with the Governor. With the Bill in Chancery still in the hands of its authors, no wonder the Mayor praised the Governor for "protecting our Liberties and Privileges" by a "mild, wise, and just Administration." [12]

When Jonathan Belcher came to Elizabethtown in 1751, it had slowly evolved from a crude pioneer settlement into an attractive village of about seven or eight hundred inhabitants. Here and there was a house of stone or brick, but most of the dwellings, as in former times, were of frame construction covered with shingles. As from the beginning, the houses which numbered about one hundred and fifty, were on plots of four to six acres. Many houses had acquired additions bespeaking the economic circumstances of the occupants. Each premise was surrounded by a wooden fence to keep out the wandering fowl and pigs as well as the cattle as they were driven along the streets to and from the town range. Back of the houses were the gardens and orchards, as well as the numerous outbuildings. Many of the families owned either a two or four wheel riding chair drawn by one or two horses. Indeed, the age of traffic accidents already had arrived.

Just before Belcher arrived, two women were killed in Elizabeth-town by falling out of riding chairs, which often were driven too fast over the rough, uneven roads.[13]

The center of the town remained that section lying near the Old Stone Bridge by the Court House and the First Presbyterian Church. Since the Court House and both of the churches had acquired bells, the silence was broken repeatedly by their ringing. Bells were rung for church, for weddings and funerals, for fires, for the opening of court, and for the opening and closing of the market. To the east of the Stone Bridge was the landing place where merchants had built wharves to tie up the sloops and ferries which carried the town's shipping. Here and there along the King's Highway and Old Broad Street west of the bridge were tiny shops and stores. Often a shop was attached to the house or occupied space in one of the outbuildings. Shade trees lined the streets and in front of the Court House the road widened suf-ficiently to form a parade ground for the militia. Here, too, were the stocks and the whipping post for disciplining culprits.

By Belcher's time, taverns in Elizabethtown had become larger and more commodious. After the death of Colonel Richard Town-ley, the White House, as Philip Carteret's mansion came to be called, was purchased by Arent Schuyler and given to his son, Peter, a noted colonial soldier and public official. In the 1720's and 1730's the mansion was owned by Benjamin Hill, who used it for a tavern called the Sign of the Ship. From that time until it was demolished in the nineteenth century, the White House was usually a tavern or a boarding house under one name or another. Early in the 1760's, the White House was run by Mrs. Johnson and called the Sign of the Nag's Head. Later she changed the name to the Duke of Rutland.

Other taverns dating back to Governor Belcher's time were the Sign of the Unicorn and the first Sign of the Nag's Head next to the Old Mill. The Sign of the Unicorn on the north corner of Broad and East Jersey streets was built in the 1750's by Dr. John Clark who operated it until his death. In 1770 his widow married William Graham and for the next twenty years this fa-mous tavern was known as Graham's Tavern as well as the Sign of the Unicorn.

The Nag's Head tavern between the Old Mill and the Court

House was run by William Chetwood as early as the 1730's. After he died and his widow had married James Johnson and moved to the White House, the Nag's Head was purchased by Barnaby Shute in 1761 and renamed the Marquis of Granby. Long and low like the Sign of the Unicorn, the Marquis of Granby, or part of it, conceivably could have been the house of John Ogden, the founder of Elizabethtown in 1665. The later history of both the Graham's Tavern and the Marquis of Granby will be resumed in chapters seven and eleven.

Usually one or two taverns did most of the business and were better kept than their competitors. Of all public places, the taverns were the most frequented since they served a greater variety of purposes. Here the stage coaches stopped with the mail and brought travelers from afar. People congregated in the taverns for merriment, to talk and gossip, and hear the newspapers read. Any mail left around was read by anyone. Taverns were the scene of constant business transactions, auctions, and horse trading. Politicians gathered there to decide on slates for the elections and to plan their course of action. There was always a bustle about an inn as people came and went and stages arrived and departed.

In the main room on the first floor of the tavern would be found a great fireplace kept well-supplied with wood in winter by a Negro boy. Most of the alcoholic beverages were in barrels or pipes which lined the wall back of the bar. Meals and drinks were served by plump bar-maids, often indentured servants brought from Holland or Germany. The second floor was usually made into a large hall for dances, political gatherings, or any community affair demanding a large room. In the back part of the tavern lived the proprietor and his family, while upstairs were rooms for servants and slaves.

The newspaper ordinarily found in Elizabethtown taverns was the *New York Gazette* established by William Bradford in 1725. In Belcher's time it was published by James Parker, the printer of both the *Bill in Chancery* and the *Answer*. Since New Jersey had no newspaper of its own before the Revolution, the *New York Gazette* contained advertisements from New Jersey as well as accounts of crimes, some political coverage, and items of local interest, such as death notices.

The paper used for the *New York Gazette* was long made in a papermill in Elizabethtown. About 1726 Bradford purchased either a mill or a mill site and constructed a papermill on the Elizabeth River. It was situated about half a mile above Trotter's Mill on the northern outskirts of Elizabethtown.[14] Bradford's papermill in Elizabethtown was the third papermill built in America.*

It is not at all surprising that Bradford erected a papermill to go with his printing business since he had been a partner of William Rittenhouse and two others in building the first papermill in America on the Wissahicken Creek near Germantown, Pennsylvania, in 1690. After moving to New York, Bradford sold his interest in the Pennsylvania mill. Having learned the art of paper-making from Rittenhouse, he soon had his mill in operation at Elizabethtown. Vats and presses were installed and the mechanism was harnessed to the water wheel. Vatmen, pressers, and sizers were procured and linen rags collected for making the paper. One workman, a paper-maker by trade, was an indentured servant from England named James Roberts. He ran away from the mill in 1729.[15] When finished after sizing with a preparation of glue and alum the paper was a soft greyish white product well-suited to absorb the ink on the old printing presses. It is paper, moreover, that has stood the test of time; indeed much of what we know of our colonial past has been preserved on the paper made at Elizabethtown.

When Jonathan Belcher came to Elizabethtown, there were several mills in the town. The old "corn mill" built by John Ogden at the Stone Bridge was still in use, though it had passed through several hands since his time. After his son Benjamin Ogden and the Reverend John Harriman operated it, the mill was purchased by William Williamson, who in turn sold it to Barnaby Shute. Williamson also had a fulling mill near the bridge for processing wool before the busy housewives made it into cloth. Another fulling mill was found near Trotter's sawmill, three quarters of a mile above the Stone Bridge. In 1764 this fulling mill was owned by John Hardy. Elizabethtown had several cider mills with Hatfield's near the Race Course being the most patronized. Often cider mills were built on hillsides so that the apples could be

* The second papermill was erected on Chester Creek, Delaware, in 1741.

unloaded from above and pass down through the grinder before going into the press. For power, hillside cider mills used horses walking a treadmill or beating a path around a turn-post.

With few exceptions the occupations pursued by the men of Elizabethtown had not changed since the days of the founding fathers. But since the town had grown and the demand for goods had increased, the number of craftsmen had multiplied accordingly. Even the most influential men had their trade. John Ross, the mayor in 1748, was a shoemaker. As so often happened he had trouble with his help. On one occasion, his apprentice, Abraham Hendricks, not only ran away but took his master's tools with him. Since cobblers traveled from town to town and from house to house, staying with a family until all were fitted with shoes, no doubt young Hendricks found life on the road more pleasant than in John Ross's shop.

Some of the craftsmen of Belcher's time were Thomas and John Clauson, bricklayers; Joseph Hindes, James Howard, and David Oliver, weavers; Jonathan Dayton, tailor; Geishom Higgins, Joseph Little, and Baker Hendricks, blacksmiths; Abraham Hetfield and John Ross, cordwainers; David Marsh, millwright; Jonathan Morrell, nailmaker; Ebenezer Spining, cooper; Aaron Miller, clockmaker; Jonathan Hampton, coachmaker, and Benjamin and Matthias Halsted, silversmiths. Another silversmith was James Bruff who, like Aaron Miller, became involved with the law for making molds and dies for counterfeiting coins.

Elizabethtown merchants conducted a modest business, one not to be compared with that of the lords of trade of New York. However, barrels of meat, flour, and other commodities were often loaded on schooners at Elizabethtown for the West Indies. Ships were also loaded with barrel and pipe staves for cooper shops in all parts of the world. That most of the staves were shipped out rather than made into barrels at Elizabethtown is further indication that the export trade of Elizabethtown was not very large when compared with many other towns and cities in America.

Besides the barrel staves, Elizabethtown received lumber from the fine stand of timber, especially hickory and oak, of the backcountry. Iron from Morris County also found its way to Elizabethtown. With the lumber and iron, a few schooners and sloops were built in Elizabethtown from time to time. Most of the lumber and iron, however, found a market elsewhere. Except on a minor scale, therefore, the Elizabeth River did not afford the size or depth for much commerce or shipbuilding.

For the farmers and for the convenience of the townspeople, Elizabethtown had a produce market opposite the old mill at the Stone Bridge. While the market was open during a few hours in the morning, the clerk was a busy man, letting out stalls and seeing that all the rules of the market were observed. In the autumn, the Borough conducted a yearly fair, similar to the medieval fairs from which it owed its origin. The fair, which like the market will be described more fully in chapter ten, was held at the Race Course on the way to Halsted's Point.

Soon after arriving at Elizabethtown, Governor Belcher sought the services of a physician. Most likely he called Dr. Ichabod Burnet, a graduate of Edinburgh and a physician of long experience. His methods were simple but he performed greater cures, it was said, than others by their "pompous prescriptions." Furthermore his fees were modest. Burnet died in 1774 at the age of ninety.

Another physician, Dr. William Barnet, a student of Dr. Staats in New York, was just starting his career when Governor Belcher came to Elizabethtown. After Belcher's death, Dr. Barnet gained renown for his smallpox inoculations during the epidemic of 1764, when he was called to Boston to combat the disease. He was put in charge of a hospital at Shirley Point near Boston where his services soon proved effective in curtailing the spread of the disease. Years later after his colleague, Dr. Burnet, had died, Barnet became a distinguished soldier and surgeon in the American Revolution. As was the custom, both doctors were apothecaries with a drug store in their homes. They were supplied by New York merchants dealing in drugs and apothecary supplies. Both doctors became leaders in the formation of the Medical Society of New Jersey, founded in 1766. Through their society, doctors were able to secure legislation requiring physicians to be licensed to practice in the province. After the Revolution, Dr. Barnet became president of the New Jersey Medical Society. While president, he read an essay to the Society in Latin on the "Proper Use of the Lancet in Pleuritic Cases."

In 1748 while at Burlington, Governor Belcher granted Princeton College a new charter which gave the struggling institution more freedom of action, especially over matters of finance. Keenly interested in education, Belcher wrote to many friends throughout America and England soliciting funds for the College. In one letter he told the Reverend Elisha Williams, formerly Rector at Yale, that the New Jersey Assembly had done little to help the College. He hoped, however, that New England would come to the aid of the College and that New Hampshire would proceed with its intention of setting up a lottery for Princeton. Before he died, Belcher bequeathed his library of over four hundred volumes to Princeton. Almost all of the books, unfortunately, were lost in the fire which consumed Nassau Hall a half century later. Although probably no one had done more for Princeton than Governor Belcher, he refused to allow the trustees to name the new building after him. Instead, at his suggestion, it was named Nassau Hall after William I, Prince of Orange and Count of Nassau, the defender of Calvinism against the fury of the Spanish.

While living at Elizabethtown, Governor Belcher granted a charter of incorporation to the First Presbyterian Church. In the charter, Stephen Crane, Jonathan Dayton, and several others were named trustees with the right of "perpetual succession": they could appoint trustees when vacancies arose. As in the case of Princeton, incorporation made it easier for the church to raise funds, especially for buildings.

A kind man, Governor Belcher was concerned for the welfare of the poor and needy. In colonial days every community took care not to become the haven for the poor of other towns. Magistrates could examine travelers and compel any persons to leave town who seemed likely to become public charges. Laws consequently hindered the poor from improving their condition. Some towns tried to remove obstacles by issuing a guarantee that if any of their people became public charges in another town, they would take them back.

In caring for the poor, Elizabethtown followed the usual pattern of appointing an Overseer of the Poor in town meeting. When a person appealed for help, the Overseer would auction off the pauper to the lowest bidder for board and lodging. There can be no doubt that this system put the least strain on the taxpayer.

But the plight of the unfortunate poor at the mercy of a miserly keeper must have been pitiful.

It was to help the conditions of the poor that Governor Belcher secured an act from the legislature which allowed Elizabethtown to erect a "Poorhouse, Workhouse, and House of Correction for the care of orphans, paupers, and vagabonds." The records, however, do not disclose any attempt on the part of the Borough to implement the measure. Apparently the town ignored the legislation and continued to auction its poor to the lowest bidder.[16]

Many of Jonathan Belcher's friends were made through his membership in the Masonic Lodge, which he joined in England when a young man. One of Belcher's Masonic friends was Benjamin Franklin, who offered to come to Elizabethtown and give the Governor some electrical treatments for his paralysis. Being somewhat afraid of Franklin's apparatus for administering electrical shocks, Belcher wrote to Dr. Cadwallader Colden of New York for advice. Still apprehensive, he wrote again to Colden asking him to seek the advice of Dr. McGaw. Whether or not Franklin came to Elizabethtown to treat the Governor is not known. However, Belcher continued to correspond with Franklin, who was engaged in founding the College of Philadelphia. Franklin's ideas on practical education coincided with those of Belcher, who thought that Princeton could profit by taking note of what the Philadelphia philosopher was doing.

In 1754, Governor Belcher and his wife had the pleasure of entertaining several luminaries who came to Elizabethtown during the year. Two were John Winthrop, Professor of Astronomy and Mathematics at Harvard, and his brother Samuel, a judge of the Supreme Court of Massachusetts. Belcher had been a good friend of their father and he found great satisfaction in entertaining them and discussing earthquakes with Professor Winthrop, one of the leading authorities on the subject. After the visit, Belcher gave his guests letters of introduction to friends in Philadelphia, where they expected to spend some time. Captain Jonathan Hampton, for one, was not at all impressed by many of the Governor's distinguished visitors. They were, he snorted, "a numerous Train of Bostonians, whining and Praying and Canting Continually about our streets." [17]

Another caller at the Belcher home was George Whitefield whom the Governor had known before coming to New Jersey. "I am now at Governor Belcher's," wrote the evangelist. "His outward man decays, but his inward man seemed to be renewed day by day. I think he ripens for heaven apace." Jonathan Edwards, who also visited the Governor on occasions, agreed with Whitefield. "He labors under many of the infirmities of age, but savors much of a spirit of religion, and seems very desirous of doing all the good he can, while he lives." Acts of benevolence, as the great divine perceived, were foremost in the Governor's mind.[18]

During the last two or three years of his life, Belcher persuaded the Assembly to meet in Elizabethtown out of regard for his failing health. Jacob Spicer, a delegate from Cape May, dined with the Governor at his mansion and found him quite helpless, but mentally alert.[19] In spite of poor health, Governor Belcher was largely responsible for New Jersey's commendable support of the French and Indian War, notwithstanding the fact that it had no stake in the lands beyond its borders.

When war was declared against France in 1756, following the outbreak of hostilities the previous year, Governor Belcher called a mass meeting in front of the Court House. Flanked by Mayor Woodruff and his Aldermen and Common Council, the Governor read the declaration of war while the militia stood at arms. His call for volunteers, which followed, met with a good response. Elias Dayton, age nineteen and son of tailor Jonathan Dayton, was commissioned a lieutenant and put at the head of a company raised among his townsmen.

Lieutenant Dayton and his men served with General Wolfe during the famous campaign that led to the capture of Quebec in 1759. Later, as a Captain, Dayton and his "Jersey Blues" helped quell Pontiac's uprising. Leaving Elizabethtown Point for the west, Dayton and his men sailed for Albany early in 1764. After marching to Oswego and sailing over Lake Ontario and Lake Erie, they finally reached Detroit to find the Indians suing for peace. This ended campaigning for Captain Dayton and his men until the Revolution carried them into a conflict of far greater proportions.[20]

Although a port of small consequence, Elizabethtown supplied privateers for the French and Indian War. In 1757, the privateer

Sturdy Beggar was built by John Dally at Elizabethtown and sent to cruise in the Caribbean. As everywhere, Elizabethtown craftsmen found it difficult to prevent their help from running away to join the armed forces. John Dennis, hatter, lost his apprentice when he ran away to join a privateer—perhaps the *Sturdy Beggar*. Apparently not all that happened at Elizabethtown was of a patriotic nature. No less a person than Mayor Samuel Woodruff, part owner of the *Charming Betsy*, was accused of trading with the enemy through the Dutch island of St. Eustatius. Woodruff swore, as did his clerks, that the ship was loaded at his wharf for the British island of St. Christopher. If Woodruff were guilty of trading with the enemy he had plenty of company among the great names in America.[21]

Altogether New Jersey furnished about one thousand men for the French and Indian War. In addition it raised army supplies, built forts on the northwestern borders of the province, and constructed barracks at Trenton, Burlington, and Elizabethtown. The barracks at Elizabethtown, built on Cherry Street west of the river, held about three hundred men. When finished, it was occupied by British soldiers until the Revolution. During the Revolution both British and Americans used it at one time or another until it was burned by Loyalists. For the French and Indian War, New Jersey raised an average of forty thousand pounds a year, an expense which bore heavily on the taxpayers of the little colony.

Jonathan Belcher died in 1757, leaving a wife, two sons, and a daughter. The Reverend Aaron Burr (who would himself die ten days later from smallpox) preached the funeral sermon. After the funeral, Mrs. Belcher stayed for awhile with Robert Ogden's family, "being disconsolate, having lost the kindest and dearest of husbands."

In his will, Belcher bequeathed fifty pounds to his wife, Mary, for a ring to wear in his memory. She also received an annuity of sixty pounds as long as she remained single. The remainder went to his sons, Andrew and Jonathan Belcher. Samuel Woodruff and Robert Ogden, the Governor's closest friends in Elizabethtown, acted as executors in the absence of Andrew Belcher, who was chief justice of Nova Scotia.

When Jonathan Belcher died, the Clinker Lot controversy was

on the wane. The Great Awakening as a religious movement had also run its course and the division in the churches was healing. A different kind of awakening, however, was appearing during the lives of Dickinson and Belcher. Jacob Spicer illustrated the new way of thinking when in reference to Cotton Mather's writings he declared that the author must have been "either a Stupid Bigot, or a Hypocritical Puritan, or else he would never have published so much about Demonism, & Witchcraft, things as even rendered by the author monstrously ridiculous & absurd." [22] The age of the "Enlightenment" was dawning in America. Another generation receptive to the new outlook on life was emerging. In Elizabethtown, as in New Jersey at large, nothing did more to broaden men's minds in preparation for the Revolutionary movement than the founding of Princeton College. This was Dickinson's and Belcher's supreme contribution to a new epoch signaled by the Declaration of Independence.

VII

The Revolutionary Groundswell

In Elizabethtown on October 28, 1764, an ox was roasted in front of Barnaby Shute's tavern, the Marquis of Granby, between the Court House and the river. The celebration marked the one hundredth anniversary of the purchase of Elizabethtown from the Indians. The spirit of festivity, however, had barely subsided before ominous reports came from over the ocean. Parliament, it was learned, was preparing to levy a stamp tax on America, a move without precedent in the life of the colonies. When word came that the act was passed and would go into effect on the first of November, 1765, a wave of indignation swept the colonies. Taxation without the consent of the colonies was declared to be both unconstitutional and a formidable threat to American liberties.

Since Robert Ogden was speaker of the Provincial Assembly and the spokesman for the people, the full weight of the crisis for New Jersey fell upon his shoulders. For a quarter of a century he had been one of the leading citizens of Elizabethtown, having taken a prominent part in the Clinker Lot controversy and other affairs of the town. As an able lawyer and a friend of Governor Belcher, he had received many favors by appointment to public offices. As early as 1749 he was appointed clerk of the Court of Common Pleas for Essex County. After that, one appointment followed another. In 1750 Belcher made him Recorder for the Borough of Elizabethtown. Two years later he was made Register of the Court of Chancery. Soon he was a member of the Governor's Council. Just before his death, Belcher appointed Ogden the Barracks Master for the King's troops in Elizabethtown. With his reputation as a public official well-established, he continued to be the recipient of other appointments. In 1761 he became Judge of the Essex County Court, and two years later Surrogate of the Orphans Court of New Jersey. After serving ten years in the Provincial Assembly from Elizabethtown, he became the speaker of the House in 1763.

Born in 1716, Robert Ogden was a great grandson of John Ogden, the founder. He inherited his father's double stone house and lot on the King's Highway about a half mile to the east of the Court House. His father also gave him his tanyard across the street from the house and extending to the river. Here was the bark house, bark mill, the nauseating tanning vats, and all the equipment for making leather.

Upon reaching the age of twenty, Robert Ogden married Phoebe, daughter of Matthias Hatfield, one of the principal defenders of the Clinker Lots. Robert and Phoebe had twenty-two children but only eight lived to grow up. Not long after his marriage Robert Ogden began the practice of law and soon was well on his way as a leading citizen of Elizabethtown. Always active in the Presbyterian Church, Ogden as the ruling elder attended the New York Synod for several years. Long a sponsor of Princeton College, to which he sent his three sons, Ogden once headed a time consuming lottery for the College.

Upon hearing that Parliament intended to tax America, Ogden wrote to Attorney General Cortlandt Skinner voicing his alarm. "The affair is Serious and Greatly Concerns all the Colonies to unite & Exert themselves to the utmost to Keep off the Threatening blow of Imposing Taxes, Duties, etc., so destructive to the Libertys the Colonies hitherto enjoyed," he told Skinner.[1] By these words he voiced the general sentiment in America. After the Stamp Act was passed, however, even the most zealous patriots were astonished by the intensity of the resentment that swept the country.

Regardless of the unpopularity of the Stamp Act, New Jersey's Governor William Franklin chose to defend the interests of the Crown and took counsel on how to enforce the hated measure. From England Benjamin Franklin, who was close to Grenville, the author of the Stamp Act, advised his son to enforce the law which he thought would be accepted after a season of ineffectual protesting. Never did Benjamin Franklin so misjudge the temper of his countrymen. Finding that the stamps would be unsafe in New Jersey, Governor Franklin coaxed Captain James Hawker into keeping the stamps on board one of his warships in New York Bay until the crisis ended.

Since it would be illegal to do business without stamps after the first of November, 1765, at the instance of Massachusetts a meeting of representatives from all the colonies was called at New York. Upon hearing of the Massachusetts action, Richard Stockton of Princeton wrote to Robert Ogden advising him to ask the Governor to call the Assembly into extra session. If New Jersey did not send a delegation, said Stockton, it would look like "a speckled bird" among her fellow colonies. As would be expected, Governor Franklin declined to call the Assembly. His refusal, however, did not block New Jersey's participation at the New York meeting. With the backing of the whole province, Speaker Ogden took the bold step of personally convening the Assembly, an action which constituted a direct challenge to British authority in New Jersey. When the Assembly met at Perth Amboy, it chose Robert Ogden, Hendrick Fisher, and Joseph Borden to represent New Jersey at the Stamp Act Congress in October.

At the Stamp Act Congress Robert Ogden heartily endorsed the resolutions condemning the stamp tax as unconstitutional and destructive of the liberties of America. But he joined with Timothy Ruggles, president of the Congress, in opposing the sending of the resolutions directly from the Congress to Parliament and the King. In the end he refused to sign the resolutions, which he thought should be presented to the British authorities by the legislatures of each province. The other New Jersey delegates signed the Stamp Act Resolutions.

Upon returning to Elizabethtown, Robert Ogden found he had few supporters anywhere in New Jersey. Everywhere he was denounced and held up to ridicule and scorn. In many towns his burning effigies lit the streets by night as crowds shouted approval of the proceedings of the Stamp Act Congress. With his prestige vanished like smoke, Ogden resigned from the Assembly and stayed close to home to weather the storm. But unlike Timothy Ruggles, of Massachusetts, who became a Loyalist, Robert Ogden continued to denounce the British colonial policies and by degrees regained the favor of his countrymen.

After the adjournment of the Stamp Act Congress, a mass

meeting was held at Elizabethtown, where resolutions were adopted approving the action taken at New York. By this time the most radical element in New Jersey, following the example of New York, had assumed the name Sons of Liberty. After the first of November when the Stamp Act became law, no business requiring the use of stamps could be conducted. Since this situation soon became intolerable, the Sons of Liberty began to pressure the lawyers and public officers to issue the necessary papers without the use of stamps. For awhile the lawyers refused to bow to public opinion. Finally, however, they capitulated and at a meeting at New Brunswick in February they resolved to disregard the law and issue legal papers without stamps.

In Elizabethtown, where the Sons of Liberty were strong, gallows were erected near the Court House to frighten anyone advocating the use of stamps. The Reverend Thomas B. Chandler, rector of St. John's since the death of Vaughan, tried to reason with his parishioners and townspeople and to caution them against extreme measures. But few would listen. "Such an opinion of oppression prevails throughout the Colonies as I believe was scarcely ever seen on any occasion in any country on Earth," Chandler declared. In his letters to England he advised leniency from that quarter or America, he warned, would be driven into open rebellion.[2]

It was a glad day in early spring when the welcome news reached Elizabethtown that Parliament had repealed the hated Stamp Act. On the commons in front of the Court House a great celebration was held for the joyous occasion. Speeches on liberty were made and expressions of gratitude were offered to King George the Third. When night fell, bonfires lit the skies as the people continued their merrymaking. At home the Reverend Thomas Chandler was pleased with the thought that perhaps his letters to superiors in London had contributed something to the happy ending of the bitter dispute between the mother country and her colonies.

The Reverend Thomas Bradbury Chandler had come to Elizabethtown from his native Connecticut eighteen years before the advent of the Stamp Act crisis. After serving four years as Catechist and missionary at St. John's the young man made a trip to London where he took the holy orders of the Episcopalian

The Reverend Thomas Bradbury Chandler. Courtesy St. John's Episcopal Church, Elizabeth, N.J.

Church. He returned to St. John's as its rector at the age of twenty-five. Having been raised a Congregationalist, his conversion to Episcopalianism was accompanied by all the enthusiasm of a proselyte. His zeal aroused discontent among his parishioners, who generally were more tolerant than their pastor. Criticism first arose when Chandler, following the example of Vaughan, refused the use of St. John's to George Whitefield on one of his visits to Elizabethtown. Criticism over his attitude toward Whitefield, however, was mild compared to the dissension which arose when he chose to preach on disloyalty to the King during the Stamp Act upheaval. Some parishioners left the Church, a harbinger of what would follow when the Revolution turned into open revolt against the mother country.

Although pleased with the demise of the Stamp Act, the Reverend Chandler was troubled by the failure of Parliament to provide the Anglican church in America with a bishop. This neglect, he felt, placed the church under a great handicap. The prospect of obtaining a bishop, he realized, was not encouraging since the British government was anxious to avoid a controversy over religion which might become as explosive as the Stamp Act. Dissenters everywhere feared the Anglican church, with its claim to special privileges as the King's church. Even in Virginia, where the majority were Episcopalians, most parishioners preferred not to see the exercise of more power over their local churches through the establishment of an American bishopric. But notwithstanding the widespread opposition, Thomas Chandler was one of those who believed it was time to launch a crusade for an American bishop.

In 1766 (the year he received a doctor's degree from Oxford) Chandler joined other Anglican ministers in openly advocating a bishopric for the colonies. At Elizabethtown, Chandler was the host to nearly two score Episcopalian clergymen from Connecticut, New York, New Jersey, and Pennsylvania. Together they mapped out plans for a campaign for securing an American bishopric. Soon essays by Chandler and others began appearing in newspapers advancing the needs of the Anglican church.

Opponents did not allow the editorials to remain unanswered. Foremost among those who attacked the arguments of the churchmen were Dr. Francis Alison of Philadelphia and Dr. Charles

Chauncy of Boston. For a time the excitement generated by the debate over an American episcopate was intense, especially in New England. Not all dissenting ministers, however, were unalterably opposed to an episcopate. At a meeting at Elizabethtown in 1768, a group of dissenting clergymen went on record as not opposing it, provided the bishop's powers were strictly confined to matters within the Anglican church.

Sympathetic as were the British authorities to the desires of the American Anglican clergymen, they still did not wish to incur colonial resentment by meeting their demands. In Elizabethtown, itself, Chandler received little encouragement from his parishioners who, like those in other places in America, were content with a minimum of ecclesiastical supervision. Within a few years the movement for an American bishopric was drowned out in the rising tide of the Revolution as one crisis succeeded another.

While the Reverend Thomas Chandler was immersed in the campaign for an American episcopate, the British government made its second attempt to tax the colonies. This time the tax, which took the form of duties on imports, proved no more acceptable than the Stamp Act. After some months, during which the colonies resorted to non-importation of British goods, Parliament repealed the Townshend duties except for the tax on tea. As was done elsewhere in America, the merchants and shopkeepers of Essex County met at Elizabethtown and resolved to maintain non-importation until the tax on tea was also removed. The boycott, however, did not survive much longer as one place after another resumed trading with the British. Only tea remained conspicuously absent in the cargoes arriving from the mother country.

New Jersey, as well as the other colonies, nourished another grievance against the mother country that was generally irritating. Recently Parliament had passed an act prohibiting the use of paper money as legal tender in America. Fuel was added to the flames of discontent when the Privy Council disallowed a New Jersey paper money bill calculated to circumvent the Parliamentary prohibition. Governor Franklin declared that the Assembly was indignant over the fate of the measure and would seek revenge by withholding funds for supplying the King's barracks in New Jersey.

Although the citizens of Elizabethtown were of one mind on

the paper money question, contrary to opinion in some other parts of the province, they had no objection to having a barracks in their midst. The officers and soldiers were good spenders, a factor which more than compensated for the occasional disturbances that might arise. At the inns, the market place, the churches, and at the dances and balls, the townspeople and the soldiery mingled freely and amicably. In 1770 a company of the 26th Regiment which was especially well-liked by the inhabitants left for another post. In its place came men of the 29th who had recently been involved in the Boston Massacre. What the people thought is not known but no incident occurred in Elizabethtown while the company was there.

In 1774, when Captain Richard England's company belonging to the 47th Regiment left Elizabethtown, the townspeople bade them a fond farewell despite the mounting tension between the Redcoats and the people of Boston. In a note to Captain England, Mayor Stephen Crane and the town fathers expressed their deep appreciation for the harmony that had existed between the soldiers and citizens. Captain England returned the compliment by expressing how much his company had enjoyed the hospitality of the town. With sorrowful hearts many a young maiden watched the column of Redcoats march away to join General Thomas Gage, who was confronted by open rebellion in Massachusetts.

Once, however, a company of British soldiers left Elizabethtown with a marked absence of good humor on either side. That occurred in 1767 when some officers of the 28th Regiment decided to leave town without paying their bills. In the nick of time, Elizabethtown creditors had them brought into court and made them pay. "As the inhabitants had used them so very ungenteelly as to make them pay their debts," a gang of officers ranged through the streets at midnight doing what damage they could. Windows of the Presbyterian Meeting House were broken. Then the mob turned on the Court House and jail, breaking the windows and threatening the gaoler. When the latter pointed a gun at the rioters, they tried to pull it out of his hands. The gun went off and a soldier was wounded in the leg. By this time the Court House bell was ringing, since the gaoler had taken the precaution of releasing the prisoners so that they could help him. Soon, from all over the town, men and boys with clubs in hand were flocking to the Court House. When the gaoler opened the door to let in the townsmen, some of the officers crowded in; a fight ensued. The affair ended when the officers, finding they were outmatched, beat a hasty retreat. In their flight they met a file of soldiers who with fixed bayonets escorted them back to the barracks. The next day the company left for Amboy. They were preceded by magistrates from Elizabethtown who appealed to the Chief Justice for satisfaction. Hearing of the trouble, Sir John St. Clair, in command of the troops in New Jersey, brought the incident to a close by having the officers apologize and pay a fine of twenty-five pounds.[3]

After the passage of the "Coercive Acts" by Parliament, following the Boston Tea Party, the Revolutionary movement in America moved into high gear. Most explosive of all was the order from England for closing the port of Boston until Massachusetts paid for the tea destroyed by its citizens. The closure of the port on June 1, 1774, caused a wave of resentment to sweep the colonies. Committees were organized, military organizations were formed, and a Continental Congress was called to consider the crisis.

In Newark, Essex County leaders met to consider Virginia's call for a Continental Congress. From Elizabethtown came Mayor Stephen Crane, William Livingston, William Peartree Smith, John De Hart, John Chetwood, and Elias Boudinot. Since they knew better than to expect the cooperation of Governor Franklin and since the Assembly was not in session, the Essex County leaders decided to call a provincial convention at New Brunswick. Mayor Stephen Crane, who presided at Newark, was left in charge of the arrangements.

Mayor Crane was the son of the Stephen Crane who had taken a prominent part in the Clinker Lot controversy twenty-five years earlier. The father was still living in Elizabethtown. It was Stephen Crane, Jr., who was elected to the Assembly to take the place of Robert Ogden when the latter lost favor during the Stamp Act episode. In 1771 he was chosen speaker of the Provincial Assembly. The next year he became mayor of Elizabethtown.

According to plans, the Provincial Convention, with Stephen Crane presiding, met at New Brunswick on July 21. The Convention chose William Peartree Smith to head a committee of correspondence for the province. Five men, three of whom came from Elizabethtown, were chosen delegates to the Continental Congress. The three from Elizabethtown were Stephen Crane, William Livingston, and John De Hart.[4]

With the establishment of a provincial committee of correspondence, New Jersey was prepared to keep in close touch with Whigs in other colonies. Chairman William Peartree Smith was a good choice for heading the committee, being well-known beyond the borders of the colony as well as locally. In 1742 he graduated from Yale with William Livingston, his life-long friend. Although trained in law, Smith never practiced it, having been left a fortune by his father, Port Royal Smith, one time governor of Jamaica. Not long after graduating from Yale, Peartree married Mary Bryant and about 1758 moved to Elizabethtown and purchased the Belcher Mansion from a member of the Ogden family. From that time on, he was active in civic affairs. He was a devout Presbyterian, a patron of Princeton, and, for a time, mayor of Elizabethtown. When the American Philosophical Society was founded at Philadelphia by Franklin and others, Smith and Livingston became charter members.

With the Smiths in the Belcher Mansion, the place took on a much different appearance than it had in the quiet days when Governor Belcher was there. Catherine and Belcher Peartree Smith were small children when the family moved into the house. Soon there was a third child, William Pitt Smith, destined to become a professor at Columbia. With plenty of servants and almost anything money could buy, the Smiths lived in great style at their home on East Jersey Street.

Naturally William Peartree Smith was very pleased when his old friend William Livingston decided to move to Elizabethtown with his wife and family. On the outskirts of the town, Livingston had bought a large tract of land on which in 1772 he built a commodious mansion. Here, for a while, the teen-aged Alexander Hamilton came to live with the Livingstons during his attendance at Francis Barber's classical school.

William Livingston was fifty years of age and one of America's leading lawyers when he moved to Elizabethtown in 1773. Having been the principal author of the *Answer* for the Clinker Lot people, he had many friends in Elizabethtown. Like Thomas Jefferson, whom he resembled in appearance, he was plain in dress and manners and a student of history and philosophy. About a year after the family moved into their new home, which Livingston called Liberty Hall, an elegant wedding was held in the house when the eldest daughter, Sarah, married the gifted New York lawyer, John Jay. Thereafter the Jays were frequent visitors at Liberty Hall. John Jay and Livingston had much in common. They both were ardent Whigs and enjoyed the sport of hunting and fishing and hiking in the woods.

After the meeting of the Continental Congress in September, 1774, Elizabethtown Whigs found much to do for the patriotic cause. A sloop loaded with provisions purchased with money given for the relief of Boston was despatched to the suffering city. Following the recommendation of Congress, Elizabethtown freeholders met at the Court House where, with Mayor Crane presiding, they chose a large and imposing Committee of Observation. Jonathan Hampton was selected chairman for the committee. Among its members were Matthias Williamson, Elias Dayton, Isaac Woodruff, Dr. William Barnet, Dr. George Ross, Cornelius Hatfield, John Blanchard, Abraham Clark, Robert Ogden, Jr., Richard Townley, Jr., and Jonathan Dayton. Most of these men would serve in many another important capacity before the close of the Revolution.[5]

The Elizabethtown Committee of Observation found much to do after it was organized. James Rivington's *New York Gazette* was banned for not supporting the American cause. Merchants on Staten Island not cooperating with the Continental Congress were put on a black list. In view of the boycott of British merchandise, steps were taken to increase the supply of woolen cloth. Spinning and weaving were given every encouragement and young ewes could not be killed. Even members of the committee failed to escape its surveillance. Goods from Bristol for Matthias Williamson, a staunch Whig and member of the committee, were seized and put up for public auction.

It was not long before the failure of men on Staten Island to abide by the resolutions of Congress further roiled the tempers of the Elizabethtown Whigs. Dr. George Ross, clerk for the Committee of Observation, noted that his fellow committeemen

St. John's Parsonage. Top, 1764; Bottom, 1817.

would resort to violence if the culprits on Staten Island did not mend their ways. Matters came to a head when Elizabethtown Sons of Liberty seized a boat belonging to James Jackson of Staten Island and with a team of horses dragged it to the liberty pole and gallows in front of the Court House. Some of the citizens of Elizabethtown, including Elias Boudinot and John Blanchard, criticized the demonstration which to them smacked too much of mob violence. Not wishing to alienate the conservatives, the Committee of Observation ordered the liberty pole and gallows to be taken down.[6]

For his part in the affair, Committee of Observation Chairman Jonathan Hampton was accused of instigating excesses and of being intoxicated when the boat was dragged to the Court House. Witnesses declared that the charge was not true. Hampton, nonetheless, was in favor of using a strong hand against Tories and did not share the fears of Boudinot that the demonstrations would get out of control. Recently he had tried to prevent the march of the Royal Regiment of Ireland through New Jersey to join the British forces at Boston. But his efforts to prevent the regiment from procuring wagons and the use of the ferry proved futile.

Jonathan Hampton was an Episcopalian who did not at all relish the Tory-slanted sermons he was hearing from the Reverend Thomas Chandler. He was the grandson of Andrew Hampton, a Scotch Quaker who came to Elizabethtown and built a brick house in 1696 which became the parsonage for St. John's after 1749. Part of the building is still standing. In 1762, Jonathan Hampton, having been foremost in securing the permission of St. John's Grand Lodge in Boston to found a chapter, became master of Temple Masonic Lodge in Elizabethtown. By profession he was a surveyor. In the capacity of deputy surveyor for James Alexander, he was active in the proprietary effort to frustrate the Clinker Lot men. He had also been the agent for Thomas and Richard Penn in looking after the lands in New Jersey inherited from William Penn, their father. Naturally, like most colonial surveyors, he was a land speculator. In Elizabethtown, Hampton owned a prosperous coach and harness-making business.

Jonathan Hampton had long been a holder of public offices. During the French and Indian War, he was commissary for the New Jersey troops. After the war, he served at times as high sheriff for Essex County, as justice of the peace, assemblyman, and vestryman for St. John's. By 1774, he was one of the most influential Whigs in Elizabethtown. Besides his chairmanship of the Committee of Observation, he was chairman of the Essex County Committee of Correspondence. With his second wife, Ann Frances, Hampton lived in a large brick house on a three-acre plot on Broad Street in the center of town. Unfortunately the life of this Revolutionary worthy ended when, at the age of sixty-five, he died while rejoicing over the surrender of Burgoyne in 1777.

In March, 1775, Jonathan Hampton and the Committee of Observation apprehended two New York merchants found smuggling two tons of merchandise into Elizabethtown from the ship *Beulah,* recently arrived from London. The ship was owned by Isaac Woodruff of Elizabethtown, who had no knowledge of the smuggling. However, Ichabod B. Barnet, who had a store and warehouse at Elizabethtown, was found to be on the receiving end of the goods. After admitting everything and promising never again to violate the Non-Importation agreement, the culprits were pardoned. All the goods were confiscated. Canvas found in the shipment finally was sent to the Continental Army for tenting.[7]

On June 24, 1775, Elizabethtown was full of excitement. George Washington, newly created Commander-in-Chief of the Continental Army, had stopped at William Livingston's on his way to Cambridge. Since the stop-off was but for a few hours, everyone was out to see the General ride through Elizabethtown, escorted as he was by the local Light Horse and by militia. Six months later, Martha Washington came through town on her way to join her husband at Cambridge. She rode in "a chariot and four, with black postillions in scarlet and white linens." Like her husband, she was escorted by the local Light Horse, which was always pleased with an opportunity for parading.

During the siege of Boston, the Elizabethtown Committee was most active collecting and forwarding ammunition to the American army. In June, powder collected at New Brunswick and Woodbridge was despatched from Elizabethtown to the army in Massachusetts. After Washington arrived at Cambridge, the powder supply became very critical. In July and August, the situation was eased when over fifty casks of powder from Philadelphia were sent to the army via Dobb's Ferry. More than anyone else, Jonathan Hampton was responsible for getting the supplies through to the army. Spurred by the Committee, a powdermill was soon erected below the dam near the Stone Bridge in Elizabethtown. As an incentive, the Committee offered twenty pounds for every hundredweight of saltpeter made in Elizabethtown during the first three months of operation. Thereafter the price would be much less.[8]

After the outbreak of hostilities in Massachusetts, America became the scene of military preparations from Maine to Georgia. Since Elizabethtown had several men with officer experience in the French and Indian War, it became a center for military recruiting and training. In October, 1775, sixteen companies of militia belonging to Elizabethtown and neighboring communities were reviewed on the parade ground in front of the Court House. Most eye-catching was the company of plummed Light Horse commanded by Colonel Matthias Williamson.

Colonel Williamson was a well-to-do harness and saddle maker who lived in a large mansion across from the Court House at the intersection of Broad and the King's Highway. His mother, after the death of her second husband, William Chetwood, had become the well-known tavern keeper in Elizabethtown. In the 1740's when his father was still alive, young Williamson had served as a lieutenant with a company of cadets in the King George's War. In 1757, he became high sheriff of Essex County, after which he held other public offices. With the advent of the Revolution, Williamson became one of the most active Whigs in Elizabethtown, serving on various committees. Like Jonathan Hampton, he was an Episcopalian with no high regard for the Reverend Chandler's prayers for the King of England. Williamson was very proud of his company of Light Horse, officered by such noted townsmen as Dr. William Barnet and Obediah Meeker.

Already some of Elizabethtown's young men had gone to join the embattled farmers facing the British army in Boston. One of these was Matthias Ogden, son of Robert Ogden who had outlived his mistake at the Stamp Act Congress and was serving on the town's Revolutionary committees. Matthias Ogden was but twenty-one when he left to fight the British. He had grown up with Aaron Burr, who, left an orphan, had been raised by Matthias' sister, who had married Burr's uncle, Timothy Edwards, son of the Reverend Jonathan Edwards.

Bosom pals, Matthias Ogden and Aaron Burr had attended Tapping Reeve's Classical School in Elizabethtown. Next they went to Princeton where they read Voltaire and Chesterfield and graduated with distinction. Although occasionally slowed down by attacks of asthma, Matthias was a swashbuckling youth of enormous strength who loved a good joke. One time, for the fun of it, he wrote a letter to Kitty Alexander, daughter of Lord Stirling, and signed another lad's name. More than anything, Matthias and Aaron loved to sail and fish in the bays and narrows near Elizabethtown. Often they would watch an eagle chase a fish hawk until the latter dropped its catch and left it to the larger bird. One day, while crabbing alone, Matthias ran his knife deep into one of his legs. After bandaging it up as best he could, he rowed to Dayton's wharf where he happened to find Dr. Bennett. Supplied with a needle by Mrs. Dayton, the doctor sewed up the wound as Matthias "grinned and bore it" with the help of some wine provided by Mrs. Dayton.[9]

Having gained his father's permission, Matthias left the tanvats and after kissing his sweetheart, Hannah Dayton, set off for the fighting front. With him went the diminutive and sporty Aaron Burr who had come to Elizabethtown so that they could leave together. The two were not long at Cambridge before the call went forth for volunteers for a hazardous march through the wilds of Maine against the British in Canada. Both Matthias and Aaron volunteered. Husky Matthias Ogden became a captain in a regiment of Grenadiers under Lieutenant Colonel Christopher Greene. After untold hardships, they finally joined the main force with General Richard Montgomery under the walls of Quebec. While storming the fort during the fatal night of December 31, Ogden was wounded in the shoulder. Among others severely wounded at Quebec was Ogden's friend, William Crane, son of Mayor Stephen Crane.

When the not-to-be-forgotten trials of the Canadian campaign were over and the defeated Americans were back in New York, Ogden found time to marry Hannah, daughter of Colonel Elias Dayton. Finding Elizabethtown fairly swarming with pretty girls,

Matthias sent a warning to Aaron Burr, who however would remain unwed for a long time to come. Another friend, William Paterson (who would become famous as the author of the New Jersey Plan at the Constitutional Convention in 1787), was fully aware of the pitfalls of Elizabethtown. "There is certainly something amorous in its very air," he told Burr. Consequently, he always drove through town "as quickly as possible, lest the soft infection" should steal upon him. Ogden, however, was confident he had picked one of the fairest in Elizabethtown and only laughed at the timidity of his friends. Not long after their marriage, Hannah joined the exodus from Elizabethtown seeking the safety of the backcountry. Matthias was gone, too, having left again for the northern frontier to help General Philip Schuyler hold off the British, Tories, and Indians.

Although the war was still far from the doors of Elizabethtown, there had been excitement enough to keep everyone keyed up. Late in the month of January, 1776, word reached Lord Stirling, in command of the patriot forces in New Jersey, that a British supply ship named the *Blue Mountain Valley* had been driven into Princess Bay near Sandy Hook by a storm. Without hesitation, the intrepid Lord Stirling decided to attempt the capture of the ship. After hearing of Stirling's intentions, word came to Elizabethtown that a British naval craft was leaving New York to help the *Blue Mountain Valley* get into port. Realizing that Stirling, at Amboy, might be overpowered, Jonathan Hampton and the Elizabethtown Committee called for volunteers to go to his aid. All were promised a share in the booty if the ship were taken. As soon as the word was out, the youth of Elizabethtown (many of whom were already members of one regiment or another) volunteered for the daring raid. Within a few hours all were ready and the volunteers set off to join Stirling.

The Elizabethtown volunteers were commanded by Colonel Elias Dayton, the veteran of the French and Indian War who after serving as muster master had just been put in command of the Third New Jersey Continental Regiment. Next in command was Lieutenant Colonel Edward Thomas, Elizabethtown storekeeper. Schoolmaster Francis Barber was in third place as major. Most of the one hundred and ten men from Elizabethtown who took part in the expedition were young lads, such as Aaron Ogden and William and Brockholst Livingston, sons of the future governor. One of the older men was Dr. William Barnet, who was ready to patch up the wounds should the raid prove bloody.

Reaching Amboy during the night in three sail boats, the Elizabethtown men found Stirling with about forty soldiers ready to leave. Together they sailed for the open seas with the icy wind in their faces. Not until shortly after daybreak did they sight their prey. Silently they drew alongside the *Blue Mountain Valley,* fearing each moment to be greeted by a blast of gunfire. None came, however, and before the enemy was aware of it, the raiders were clambering up the side of the ship and over the rails. Fifty-year-old Lord Stirling with sword in hand was the second man over the gunwales, with Aaron Ogden hard on his heels. Finding himself surprised and out-numbered, Captain John H. Dempster surrendered without firing a shot. Loaded with coal, flour, meat, powder, and other supplies, the *Blue Mountain Valley* was brought to Elizabethtown Point where Stirling turned it over to the Committee of Safety to await the orders of Congress. Since the cargo was eventually sold at public vendue, the participants in the raid must have received their share of the proceeds.[10]

Francis Barber's participation in the capture of the *Blue Mountain Valley* just about marked the end of schooling in Elizabethtown during the Revolution. The tall, modest, blue-eyed Francis Barber, who had conducted the Classical School for several years, had closed his desk to become a major in Dayton's Third New Jersey Regiment. Ahead of him lay a distinguished military career but he never again would return to the classroom. When the long war was drawing to a close, the heroic Barber was killed by a falling tree. While keeping school, Francis Barber had married Mary Ogden, a sister of Matthias and Aaron. Poor Mary, however, died at the age of twenty-one. Following her death, Barber continued to live with his father-in-law, Robert Ogden, until he left for the war.

A graduate of Princeton, Francis Barber taught for a short time at Newbridge, Hackensack, before taking over the school at Elizabethtown. He succeeded Joseph Periam, a talented mathematician, who served as master of the Classical School for about two years. Before Periam, the school had been under the charge of Tapping Reeve, the future founder of the famous Litchfield Law

School. Sponsored by the Presbyterian Church, the school apparently had been in operation for some years before Reeve took it over. As early as 1760, it appears to have been under a schoolmaster named John Jones.

New life was injected into the Classical School in 1768 when Tapping Reeve moved into a new schoolhouse provided by funds contributed by public-minded persons. The wooden building, surmounted by a cupola with a bell, stood to the west of the old burying ground on Broad Street. Here Tapping Reeve had many promising students, prominent among whom were Matthias and Aaron Ogden, Aaron Burr, and Francis Barber. After Barber took over the school, one of his best students was the fourteen-year-old Alexander Hamilton, from the West Indies. At the time of the outbreak of the Revolution, Aaron Ogden was one of the instructors in Barber's school.

Several other schools were conducted in Elizabethtown during the prewar period. Robert Cather opened a boarding school for boys in 1762, with emphasis on English oratory and moral virtues. Another schoolmaster, James Conn, started a school which stressed the practical studies. Accounting was taught according to the Italian method. Instruction was also given in mathematics, navigation, and drawing. In his spare time, Conn could be hired for making shop bills, bills of exchange, or "any kind of Writing for the Rolling Press." One could also hire him for drawing maps and charts "either Plain, Mercator, Spherical, or Conical." [11] Another school was opened in 1775 by William and Sarah Long; it was for young ladies. They took over the large house on the Old Point Road made available by the death of its owner, Colonel Jacob Ricketts. Apparently none of these purely private schools lasted for long. A small school founded before the Revolution on the northern outskirts of the town, however, experienced a long life. This was the North End School, built on land provided by Edward Thomas. The bell which hung in the cupola was given by Captain David Lyon and was made by David Ross, the well-known Elizabethtown craftsman. [12]

During the exciting times of the Revolution, the bells on the Court House, schools, and churches were frequently rung to call town meetings and warn the people of approaching danger. Doubtlessly the earliest bells were made by Aaron Miller, an Elizabethtown clockmaker and craftsman of rare ability. In London, in 1765, Franklin mentioned an improved type of compass developed by Aaron Miller "an Ingenious Man in the Province of New Jersey." As early as 1747, Miller was advertising his wares: all kinds of clocks, compasses, surveyor's instruments and chains, church bells, and other things demanding fine workmanship.[13]

In the 1760's, Miller was making bells for public buildings both near and far. David Ross was at that time his helper. Besides bell-making, Ross was kept busy with threshing, hauling hay, cutting wood, trimming the orchard, and butchering. But bell-making was his principal line of work. In 1767 he helped cast a bell for Amboy. Bells for Hopewell, Millstone, Burlington, Woodbridge, Staten Island, and other places were in turn made by Aaron Miller and his helper, David Ross. Often the bells were defective and had to be recast. Preparatory to casting, Ross was employed pouring copper pigs, making charcoal, and cleaning and lining the furnace. His wages were generally eight shillings, eight pence a day. After he went into business for himself, he made a dinner bell for Sir William Johnson of Mohawk Valley fame.[14]

During the Revolutionary period, the Presbyterian Church was still the largest and most stately building in Elizabethtown. About a decade before the Revolution, it was enlarged to accommodate the growing congregation. For miles around people could hear its bell and get their bearings from its lofty spire. The clock placed in the tower in 1759 and the weather vane on top of the spire were of constant use to the villagers in their daily round of living.

The sexton for the church was a busy man, especially on the Sabbath. One of his main duties was to wind the clock. He also kept the fence repaired around the church and burying ground. Inside the church he kept the benches clean and the floors swept. For the evening lectures the church was well-lighted with candles. During the service the sexton was busy snuffing and lighting candles as the occasion demanded. If on Sundays he found difficulty in keeping the boys quiet, he was at liberty to call on any magistrate present to lend a hand.[15]

In 1762 the Presbyterian Church received for its rector the man who was destined to be its most famous pastor. This was the Reverend James Caldwell. Born in Virginia in 1734, Caldwell graduated from Princeton and then spent several years preaching in the South. When he came to Elizabethtown he was twenty-five, burning with enthusiasm, a tower of strength for any church. Mr. Chandler found him zealous to a fault, holding services two or three times on Sundays and extending the time devoted to the Thursday night lecture. He was a prodigious house-caller, praying and exhorting wherever he went. Not even the Negroes were forgotten by Pastor Caldwell, who urged them to come to church and join in the devotion. Soon the Reverend Chandler found some of his parishioners leaving his church and going over to the Presbyterian. Chandler thought he could understand this, since members of both churches seemed little concerned with matters of doctrine and took the view that it did not much matter where they went to church. Although seemingly always on the go, Caldwell was devoted to his family and gave much attention to bringing up his children. He loved to work in his garden next to the red saltbox parsonage. Occasionally he found time to sit with a caller on the long porch shaded by several large elms and a sycamore tree.

By 1774, with the Reverend Thomas Chandler making no effort to conceal his Tory feelings, the old toleration of the dissenters for the Anglican church was severely tried. A new church which, when finished, would be slightly larger than the Presbyterian edifice, was being built for St. John's. With the Anglican church growing more unpopular all the time, people wondered how the new building could be paid for and who would be left to worship in it.

By 1775 the Whigs were so wrought up by Chandler's denunciations of the Revolutionary movement that Episcopalians had to guard St. John's by night to prevent vandalism. The plight of the church was not eased when Dr. Chandler left for England —not to return until after the war. With no minister and with the stigma of having been the King's church, the remnants of the congregation waited for a brighter day when the war would end. Meanwhile St. John's, used by both the British and Americans for quartering and storage and even for a stable, became a shambles.

During the years leading up to the Revolution, social life in the colonies became marked by more extravagant living and more

leisure for indulging in pastimes. The manner of holding funerals
became so extravagant that a movement developed for curtailing
expenses. In 1764, fifty families of Elizabethtown agreed to reduce
expenditures for funerals by doing away with the giving out of
scarfs, veils, gloves, and other articles of mourning. In the future
they would use only the black band around the arm. They also
agreed to curtail the use of liquor at funerals.

Everyone looked forward to the yearly Fair held at Elizabethtown in October where there was much to buy and plenty of
merriment. The Fair was probably held near the race track owned
by Isaac Hatfield on the road leading to Halsted's Point, about a
mile from the Court House. Horse racing was one of the chief
attractions at the Fair. In 1759, the horse winning three heats
"carrying ten stone" won a prize of fifteen pounds. From time to
time New Jersey passed laws against betting on races. To avoid
trouble with the law, Elizabethtown Freemasons in 1765 ran
a horse race on the first day of the Fair on Staten Island opposite Halsted's Point. For years, Captain Samuel Smith, Elizabethtown tavern keeper, entered horses for the races at his inn.[16]

To the fairs and public gatherings came people from all classes
of society. Slaves, servants, apprentices, and laborers, of whom
Elizabethtown by the time of the Revolution had a goodly number, mixed freely with persons of quality and refinement. Most of
Elizabethtown's menfolk, however, belonged to the artisan class.
Like their fathers and grandfathers, they owned their little shops
where they worked with perhaps the help of one or two assistants.
Some craftsmen were men of means and were considered the
equal in every respect to the merchants, lawyers, land speculators,
and others who did not work with their hands. Social distinctions,
however, were becoming more pronounced with the passing of
time as the gulf widened between the moneyed class and the
less fortunate. Elizabethtown, following the example of larger
towns and cities, was coming to have its "carriage class" with
coats of arms embellishing the doors of the coaches and carriages.
For the ladies of the affluent families, Richard Morris, staymaker
from London, had a shop where ladies "who are uneasy in their
shapes" were fitted "without any incumbrances." [17]

The Belcher Mansion, which had been owned and occupied by

William Peartree Smith since Governor Belcher's death, represented the type of living of the affluent class in Elizabethtown. Beautiful furniture graced each room. In the parlor a spinet afforded Peartree's wife and daughter hours of enjoyment, as well as music for many social occasions. For conversation pieces, there was a mahogany case of wax work and another of ornamental shells. Peartree also had a "glass in case with fifty perspective views," doubtlessly an early stereoscope. Busts of William Pitt and other celebrities occupied niches above the doors and fireplaces. Peartree's large bookcase with sixty panes of glass held forty ponderous law books. Another case contained fifty maps. In the dining room, the coin silver spoons and ivory-handled knives and forks, the dozens of pewter plates, the fine chinaware, all bespoke the grace of living at the Belcher Mansion. On the floors were painted "cloths" and bearskin rugs. Here and there were ornate brass candlesticks holding their tall tapering candles.

Back of the mansion were the stables and carriage house. A large coach suspended on leather straps and drawn by four horses was the family vehicle. A one-horse riding chair was used by Peartree to get around the town and countryside. The children had their ponies and chariot, and, as soon as they were old enough, their riding horses and saddles. Coachman and stableboys for the livery and servants and slaves for the mansion provided the necessary help for the Smith estate.[18]

Between the years 1750 and 1775, a number of houses of mansion proportions were built in Elizabethtown. One of these was the Old Chateau, built for Thomas Pollock by Elihu Pierson. Erected on land acquired from Cavalier Jouet, the mansion was called the Chateau in honor of Madam Tousard, wife of the French consul at New Orleans who was once a guest at the house.* Another house constructed during this period was the brick mansion on East Jersey Street, built for Dr. William Barnet by Captain William Brittin, a noted local architect and builder. About the same time Samuel Woodruff had a mansion built on East Jersey Street; he used it for a store as well as a home.† Other large houses of the third quarter of the eighteenth century were

---

* Now occupied by the Elizabeth Manor Nursing Home.
† Now Boxwood Hall or the Boudinot Mansion.

erected for Matthias Williamson, Moses Ogden, Barnaby Shute, John De Hart, Joseph Jelf, and William Livingston.*

During the Revolutionary period with people coming and going more than before, taverns did a thriving business. The principal taverns continued to be Graham's Sign of the Unicorn and the tavern next to the Old Mill. Toward the end of the war, the Williamson house on the corner of Water and Broad streets also became a tavern.

William Graham ran the Sign of the Unicorn from 1770, when he married the widow of Dr. Clark, until his death nine years later. After that, Widow Graham ran the tavern until her son-in-law, Morris Hatfield, took it over for about two years in 1788 and called it the Sign of the Two Lions. In 1791 Widow Graham married her third husband, Robert Forest of Hanover, New Jersey, who ran the tavern until it was rented by Joseph Lyon in 1793.

Graham's tavern was a busy place during the years of its existence. Officers of both the American and British armies often stayed there and used it for headquarters. One of the faithful patrons of the Sign of the Unicorn was Dr. William Barnet, who lived a few doors farther down East Jersey Street. Going by, Dr. Barnet seldom failed to stop for a bowl of grog or toddy or for some snuff. Although a good customer, the Doctor was not so good at settling his account; by 1777 it had risen to seventy-eight pounds.[19]

After Barnaby Shute purchased the Nag's Head next to the Old Mill, in 1761, and renamed it the Marquis of Granby, this tavern rivaled the Sign of the Unicorn in popularity. Officers and soldiers congregated at this tavern during the Revolution. During the 1760's the Marquis of Granby was successively operated by John Joline, John Graham, Barnaby Shute, and Broughton Reynolds. Between 1771 and 1776 it was owned by Samuel Smith and called the Sign of the King's Arms. With the outbreak of the Revolution, Smith renamed his tavern the Red Lion Inn. In 1780, and for about a year, it was run by Dr. William Winans. Then

---

* The houses were located as follows: Williamson's on the corner of Broad Street and the King's Highway (Elizabeth Avenue), Ogden's on the King's Highway near the end of town, Shute's next to the Court House on Broad Street, De Hart's on Pearl Street near the Barracks, Jelf's on Jelf's Hill near Pearl Street, Livingston's on the western outskirts near Trotter's Mill.

Jacamiah Smith operated it until 1785 when Samuel Smith, the owner, took it over again. Other proprietors followed. After the turn of the century it was known as the Indian Queen.

Probably the first proprietor of the tavern in the Williamson house on the corner of Water and Broad streets was Joseph Crane, who occupied the house in 1781. This house was built by Matthias Williamson before the Revolution. During the war, especially while General Williamson was away, the house was severely damaged by the soldiery of both armies. The property was well situated for a tavern and the house was large and commodious. The building had three stories, dominated by two huge chimneys at either end. A porch ran along the front of the building on Water Street. Back of the tavern were the stables which fronted on Broad Street.

Samuel Sayre succeeded Crane as the proprietor of the new tavern on the busy corner in 1782. Sayre was a good tavern keeper; he put up a sign almost as catching as a modern-day singing commercial for people traveling up Broad Street and over Golden Hill. "Before you do this hill go up, Stop and drink a cheering cup." For those coming the other way, the sign read: "You're down the hill, all dangers past, Stop and drink a cheerful glass." Over the taproom door, Sayre had these words for his customers: "Samuel Sayre, he does live here, and sells a pot of good strong beer; His liquors good, his measure just, but Sam's so poor he cannot trust." After the Revolution this busy tavern became known as the Wales Tavern, having been taken over by a man of that name.

In the taverns American etiquette came under the scrutiny of foreigners, especially of the French officers and travelers. All Americans, the foreigners noted, ate with their knives, using the fork only to hold meat while cutting it. Napkins were unknown. Handkerchiefs were used for wiping the face and hands but not for blowing the nose. More than anything, foreigners marveled at the dexterity with which an American blew his nose by holding it with his fingers.[20]

Since more speed was required with the advance in the tempo of living during the Revolution, the schedule for stages was accelerated accordingly. John Mercereau advertised in 1774 his "Flying Machine" with its leather curtains, as carrying passengers from New York to Philadelphia in two days. Stages were not only faster but larger and more comfortable. Accidents, as usual, sometimes occurred when horses ran away or brakes failed. Generally the drivers were experts who guided with great dexterity their four or six spirited horses, clothed in harness trimmed with shining brass. When a stage pulled up at a tavern, off jumped the driver's helper to assist the ladies and tend to the luggage. Usually everyone in the tavern hurried out to see who were arriving and hear the news.

European visitors found the American stages very interesting. They were surprised to find ladies traveling alone, usually too absorbed in listening to the conversation to be bothered by the heavy tobacco smoke. Most of all, foreigners were amazed by the inquisitiveness of Americans as well as the way in which even a common laborer conversed freely with the most polished gentleman. Foreigners were captivated by the drivers. Usually he waited until the travelers had pried everything of interest out of each other before taking over and monopolizing the talk. Then he appeared as a perambulating philosopher, historian, newspeddler, and dispenser of all kinds of information. Often to the bewilderment of the foreigner he was a militia captain or even a colonel. Nobody disputed the driver. He sat like a magistrate and settled every point that arose. Along the road he knew the occupants of every house and all about their business. When it came to politics, he seemed versed in every aspect of the most involved situations. The American stagecoach driver, for versatility, has seldom seen an equal.

In March 1776, the siege of Boston finally ended and the British sailed away for Halifax to await reenforcements from England. Meanwhile Lord Stirling, who had been made a brigadier general in the Continental Army, was ordered to New York to direct the erection of defenses against the impending return of the British. With Stirling and the New Jersey Brigade went the men and boys of Elizabethtown to help defend their country. Early in the summer, the British sailed into New York Bay with thirty thousand troops on more than four hundred transports guarded by a powerful fleet. The war was about to descend upon New York and New Jersey. Soon Elizabethtown would be transformed from a quiet little village into a town swept by war and devastation.

VIII

War Comes to Elizabethtown

"Went to church: never was in church before," wrote Timothy Tuttle, a private in Lord Stirling's First New Jersey Battalion on January 1, 1776.* Timothy Tuttle came from Hanover and, like many another recruit from the back-country, he was getting his first thrills from joining the army and living in a "big town." Next day Tuttle saw "the mulatto" whipped and drummed out of the battalion for stealing. Directly afterward, orders came that no soldier would be allowed out of barracks after sunset. The following day four soldiers were whipped for misbehavior. The next culprits were put in the "dark hole" but escaped by breaking open the door. On January 29, Tuttle stood guard on the *Blue Mountain Valley*. That Stirling and his officers were working hard to make soldiers out of the raw New Jersey yeomanry can be read in the notes scribbled by Timothy Tuttle.[1]

By May, all of New Jersey's three battalions had left Elizabethtown and were in New York erecting defenses against the return of the enemy. The New Jersey Continentals, however, were at New York only a short time before they were ordered to join Major General Philip Schuyler, who was holding the lines on the New York frontier against the British, Loyalists, and Indians. Colonel Dayton (who closely resembled Washington in appearance) was assigned the task of guarding the Mohawk Valley. In Dayton's Battalion were Major Francis Barber, Second Lieutenant Jeremiah Ballard, Paymaster Jonathan Dayton (son of the Colonel), Chaplain Reverend James Caldwell, and Dr. William Barnet, Surgeon, all from Elizabethtown. With Colonel William

---

* By "church" Tuttle meant St. John's since he was a member of the Reverend Jacob Greene's Presbyterian congregation at Hanover.

Winds' Third Battalion were also many Elizabethtown men. Matthias Ogden was Lieutenant Colonel; William De Hart, Major; and Aaron Ogden, Paymaster. Other Elizabethtown volunteers in the Third Battalion were Captain Joseph Meeker and Ensign George Ross.

Most of the Elizabethtown soldiers were members of the Presbyterian church. During the war over forty commissioned officers and many more non-commissioned officers and privates were Elizabethtown Presbyterians. No wonder the members of the church, although sorry to see the Reverend Caldwell leave the pulpit, were happy with the thought that their beloved pastor would be with their boys in all the danger of the war.

The first section of the British Army, commanded by Major General William Howe, arrived during the last days of June, 1776. Throughout the succeeding six weeks, troops continued to arrive like a "swarm of locusts escaped from the bottomless pit." On July 12, Admiral Lord Richard Howe, the general's brother, appeared with ten ships of the line and twenty frigates. In all, nearly thirty-two thousand troops arrived on more than four hundred transports. Witnessing an armed might never before seen in America, Elizabethtown and all the country within miles of Staten Island, where the enemy landed, were seized with paroxysms of fear and excitement.

By the time the invading host had arrived, Governor William Franklin had been arrested and imprisoned in Hartford, Connecticut; Congress had declared America to be free and independent; and New Jersey was in the process of writing a constitution for the state. Sensing the gravity of the hour, Abraham Clark, signer of the Declaration of Independence and a native of Elizabethtown, declared, "We are now embarked on a most Tempestuous Sea." [2]

With the first appearance of the enemy in New York Bay, an exodus from areas exposed to invasion began. On July 4, a traveler found the roads out of Elizabethtown and Newark crowded with wagons and carts piled high with household goods, headed for the back-country.[3] As soon as the refugees had left, many of their homes were taken over by the militia for billeting.

After Lord Stirling and his Continentals left for New York, the Elizabethtown area came under the command of William Livingston, brigadier general of the New Jersey militia. Confronted by no end of work, Livingston was fortunate in having for an aide-de-camp the hard-working and conscientious Elias Boudinot, who would soon become Washington's Commissary General of Prisoners. In June, Livingston came under the command of Brigadier General Hugh Mercer, appointed by Washington to head the militia of New Jersey, Pennsylvania, and Maryland (collectively known as the Flying Camp), gathered to defend the shores of New Jersey. Local authority, however, continued to be exercised. On one occasion the Elizabethtown Committee sent its Light Horse on a daring raid into Staten Island after livestock, wagons, and horses.[4]

With New York the immediate target of the enemy, Washington called upon New Jersey to send all the militia it could spare to assist in defending the far-flung lines surrounding the city. In answer Thomas Morrell, an Elizabethtown merchant who many years later became the first Methodist minister in the Borough, called for volunteers to meet on the parade ground in front of the Court House. Within a matter of hours, Captain Morrell filled his company. The volunteers then chose Samuel Lyon and Jonathan Pierson for lieutenants. During the battle of Long Island (August 27, 1776), Morrell's company stood its ground although it was literally cut to pieces by the enemy. One of the men, nineteen-year-old Morris Hatfield, after firing nine rounds at the enemy, was about to be run through by a charging Grenadier. Just in time, Hatfield shot his adversary who fell dead at his feet. Minutes later, Hatfield, with a hole in his cheek from a musket ball, was taken prisoner. Heroes, however, do not always resist temptation. A year later after his exchange, Hatfield (who in after years became the proprietor of the Sign of the Two Lions)* was thrown in jail for passing counterfeit bills.[5]

The Flying Camp, which at its peak numbered about five thousand, was slow in forming. By August, Mercer had only two thousand militia, most of which were posted at Elizabethtown, Newark, Woodbridge, Amboy, and nearby points. A soldier from Pennsylvania noted the widespread destruction caused by the men wherever they were stationed. Orchards and fences were destroyed for firewood, houses were damaged and pilfered; every-

* Formerly Graham's Tavern or the Sign of the Unicorn.

thing showed the ravages of war. When Catherine Livingston returned for a visit to Liberty Hall in 1777, she found it a shambles. An artillery company stationed there by General Philemon Dickinson of the New Jersey militia had stripped even the locks and hinges from the building. St. John's Church, long used as a barracks, was gutted by the wanton soldiers.[6]

In August, William Livingston became governor of New Jersey. Thereafter he saw little of his once beautiful home, which lay too close to the enemy to permit his staying there for any length of time. At the election which chose him governor, the legislature found it difficult to choose between Livingston and Richard Stockton. The die was cast when John Stevens made known that Stockton had refused to allow his team of horses to be used by the army. Upon becoming governor, Livingston was glad to turn his command over to Matthias Williamson, the organizer of the Elizabethtown Light Horse, since he had little liking for generalship.

Just before the Battle of Long Island, the British on Staten Island gave Elizabethtown a taste of war by bombarding the American works at Elizabethtown Point. The cannonading was part of Howe's stratagem to divert attention while he launched his drive against the Americans on Long Island.[7]

Following the British victory at Long Island, fear gripped Elizabethtown as each day increased the danger of invasion. Fifteen-year-old Hannah Ogden, sister of Matthias and Aaron, told of the excitement. Writing to her brother-in-law, Major Francis Barber with the New Jersey Continentals, she told of a false alarm that the enemy was crossing the ferry at Elizabethtown Point.

"We were almost distracted," wrote Hannah, "for we hadn't sent away anything at all not even our Clothes and could not bear to leave everything behind us to be burnt as we expected it would be as soon as they came up; we catched every one what cloathes we could not do without and huddled them into empty barrels, Hogsheads and anything that came first at hand, & kept horses by the door ready to set off as soon as we saw them coming, which we expected every minute. The whole town was in an uproar: Women and Children running out, some on horseback, some on Carts & many on foot." The British did not appear this time, but Hannah had had enough; off she went to her Uncle's at Connecticut Farms, leaving her stout-hearted mother who declared she would not budge until she actually saw the Redcoats coming.

Hannah's father, Robert Ogden, had been serving as commissary for the militia but had found the work too exhausting. Consequently he had turned the job over to his son, Robert, who, unlike Matthias and Aaron, could not go to war because of a childhood injury. Robert, wrote Hannah, was "almost worry'd out of his Life with supplying the soldiers who are very saucy." [8]

The first move of the British against New Jersey was the seizure of Paulus Hook following their capture of New York City. With the enemy on New Jersey soil, the exodus from the eastern counties increased daily. Elias Boudinot sent his family to his farm in Basking Ridge, Robert Ogden took his family to Sparta, and Governor Livingston's wife and daughters went to stay with his sister, Lady Stirling, at Basking Ridge. Later the Governor's family moved to Parsippany. Others were gathered at Springfield, Chatham, Morristown, and other back-country communities. Many families had recently been bereaved of loved-ones since a siege of sickness had ravaged the country. Before the Daytons left Elizabethtown for Springfield, Colonel Dayton's father died in his chair with his grandchildren playing around him. [9]

After capturing Fort Washington and driving the Americans out of Fort Lee, the British triumphantly entered Elizabethtown on November 29. At Elizabethtown the British found a great quantity of military stores including twenty tons of musket balls abandoned by the Americans. New Jersey, it seemed, would soon be subdued. In anticipation of the event, General Howe had appointed Cortlandt Skinner, the former attorney general, lieutenant governor of the province. After entering Elizabethtown, the inhabitants were asked to accept General Howe's amnesty by taking an oath of allegiance to the King. Some men came forward and accepted the offer, but most of the men still in town held back. The strong appeal for patriotism made by Mrs. Hannah Arnett, while the men were meeting at her husband's house on East Jersey Street to consider Howe's terms, is said to have persuaded many not to go over to the British. It was too bad there was not a Hannah Arnett up in Morris County where General Matthias Williamson exhausted himself in trying to round up enough militia to enable Washington to make a stand behind the Raritan at New Brunswick. Few, however, would join Williamson and Washington was compelled to flee across the Delaware.

One of the Loyalists who helped the British during their march through New Jersey was Cavalier Jouet. Born in Jamaica in 1757, Cavalier inherited a large fortune and a fifty-five acre farm in Elizabethtown from his Huguenot grandfather. During his youth Cavalier was tutored by the Reverend Thomas Chandler whose teachings may have conditioned him for loyalism. By the time of the Revolution, Cavalier had married his second wife, Mary Hampton, daughter of the staunch Whig, Jonathan Hampton.

When Cavalier Jouet found himself the target of the Sons of Liberty after coming out openly for the King, he received no sympathy from his father-in-law. Apparently Cavalier was not much concerned with what his friends and relatives thought. On one occasion he signed his name to a Whig paper and immediately scratched it out to show his contempt for the Sons of Liberty. With the invasion of the state imminent, the Committee of Safety sent Cavalier into the interior after making him post a bond for one thousand dollars as a guarantee of good behavior. This, however, did not prevent him from fleeing from Basking Ridge to the British lines when Howe invaded New Jersey. The rebellion, Jouet thought, was collapsing and he wanted to help bring it to a speedy end. During the days while Washington was retreating to the Delaware, Jouet collected information for the British, pointed out the loyal from the disloyal, and acted as a guide for parties of British dragoons that scoured the country for leaders of the rebellion.[10]

Unlike Jouet, the conservative Boudinots chose to go along with the Whigs though they had no stomach for the more extreme element in the country. Of the two brothers, Elias and Elisha, Elias was the elder and the more gifted. Of Huguenot extraction, Elias was born in Philadelphia in 1740 and baptised by George Whitefield, the English evangelist. At Princeton he had studied law with Richard Stockton, who married Boudinot's sister. Elias reciprocated by marrying Stockton's sister. In 1762 Boudinot purchased the large mansion (Boxwood Hall) on East

Jersey Street from the heirs of Samuel Woodruff. Here he lived and had his law office for his growing practice.

Conservative by nature, Elias Boudinot's presence on the Revolutionary committees and congresses was a restraining influence upon more radical temperaments. In June, 1776, when the question of independence came to a head, Boudinot opposed the measure. It was too risky, he maintained. Furthermore, he was opposed to a republican form of government which he considered impractical. England, he said, had tried republicanism in the seventeenth century and it had failed. Reconciliation, therefore, was the proper course to pursue, in his opinion.[11]

When the die was finally cast and independence declared, Elias Boudinot chose to remain with the Whigs rather than espouse loyalism. It was a difficult decision. However, once it was made, he did not flinch or look back. With his family safe at Basking Ridge, he continued his public services. His most important work during the war began in 1777 with his appointment as Commissary General of Prisoners. Through his efforts, treatment of American prisoners in the hands of the enemy became acceptable to the standards of war. Hundreds of Americans, however, would never forget the barbaric treatment they had experienced as prisoners of war during the early months of the Revolution.

With the reversal in the fortunes of war occasioned by Washington's spectacular victories at Trenton and Princeton, the remaining British garrisons in New Jersey were forced upon the defensive. The New Jersey militia, which had faltered during Washington's retreat, rallied and reaped vengeance upon an enemy guilty of pillage and murder. On January 8, 1777, Brigadier General William Maxwell and his New Jersey Continentals drove the enemy out of Elizabethtown with the help of Matthias Williamson's militia. They took fifty Waldeckers and forty Highlanders, as well as a schooner loaded with precious war supplies. Freeing their town was a happy event for all the Elizabethtown officers and men who took part in the operation.[12]

Early in January, from his headquarters at Morristown, Washington took measures to defend himself against the large number of persons of doubtful loyalty in New Jersey. By proclamation, all who had taken General Howe's protection were commanded to turn over their papers and take an oath of allegiance to the

United States of America. Those not wishing to comply must move within the enemy's lines. When General Maxwell reported that there were numbers of men in Elizabethtown who refused to comply with the proclamation, Washington commanded him to rigidly enforce the orders. "These fellows at Elizabethtown, as well as others who wish to remain with us (till the expiration of the 30 days) for no other purpose than to convey intelligence to the Enemy, and poison our People's minds, must and shall be compelled to withdraw immediately within the Enemy's lines," wrote Washington.[13]

With the presence of the Livingston girls and many other young ladies in the Morristown area, a marked improvement in the morale of Washinton's young officers was discernable. One of the General's aides was the spirited Alexander Hamilton, who knew the Livingston girls from his schooldays in Elizabethtown. Writing to Catherine, Hamilton swore that if she would play the role of Goddess, he would write the appropriate verses. He wanted to walk with her "in the flowery walks, and roseate bowers of Cupid." She would not be disappointed, he assured her, for he was renowned for his gallantry.[14]

Late in May, 1777, Washington gathered his army on the heights above Middlebrook overlooking the British at New Brunswick. To the camp being erected on the heights by General Nathanael Greene, Colonel Ogden marched his regiment from Elizabethtown, which it had guarded since its recovery in January. The defense of Elizabethtown and the surrounding country was left to the militia under Brigadier General Nathaniel Heard, the successor to Matthias Williamson, who had resigned for reasons of poor health.[15]

Finding that Washington could not be drawn into a major battle, Sir William Howe returned to Staten Island and late in July sailed for Philadelphia. To help defend New Jersey against raids from Staten Island, Washington sent Colonels Dayton and Ogden with their regiments to Newark and Elizabethtown while he marched the army toward Philadelphia. Together, Dayton and Ogden had but four hundred men, badly clothed and nearly all barefoot. A little less ragged were the militia, units of which came and went as dictated by their six weeks of service. The only well-groomed corps guarding the area was the Elizabethtown Light Horse, now commanded by Dr. William Barnet.

Colonel Matthias Ogden had scarcely time to get his troops posted at Elizabethtown before word came that Major General John Sullivan, bringing up the rear of Washington's army, was marching from Hanover with his division for the purpose of launching a surprise attack upon Staten Island. This was exhilarating news for the officers of the New Jersey line. Nothing, too, would do more for the morale of the people of Essex and Monmouth counties than a smashing defeat of the British and the hated Loyalists on Staten Island.

Arriving at Elizabethtown on the evening of August 21, Sullivan launched his attack early the next morning. With the brigades of William Smallwood and Prudhomme Deborre, Sullivan crossed the Arthur Kill at Halsted's Point. Simultaneously Dayton and Ogden crossed at the Old Blazing Star Ferry farther to the south. The attack, however, failed miserably. Dayton and Ogden managed to capture about one hundred prisoners, but their success was more than offset by Sullivan's loss of several hundred men before he could get back to the safety of the New Jersey shore. Colonel Frederick Frelinghuysen, who led part of the militia, blamed Sullivan. "Nothing but the most unpardonable neglect will be found the cause of our loss," he told Governor Livingston.[16]

Within two weeks after Sullivan left Elizabethtown accompanied by the New Jersey Brigade, the British invaded the state on a foraging expedition with a force of fifteen hundred. Led by General Clinton whom Howe had left in command of New York, the British landed at Elizabethtown Point and at Fort Lee to the north. Collecting livestock wherever found, the enemy marched through Elizabethtown without opposition and headed for Newark. North of Newark they met the troops who had landed at Fort Lee. After that the force returned to Staten Island by way of Bayonne. Altogether the march netted the enemy four hundred cattle, two hundred milk cows, and four hundred sheep. Foraging by both armies virtually kept the area stripped of livestock during the war. During the expedition, the British were fired upon by small parties of militia whose numbers were never large enough to risk making any kind of a stand.

After Clinton's mid-summer raid on the livestock of Essex and Bergen counties, General Philemon Dickinson, commander of the New Jersey militia, by orders of the Council of Safety, rounded up all the remaining livestock in the exposed areas and sent them inland. Hoping to retaliate, Dickinson launched an attack on Staten Island with fourteen hundred troops. The raid, however, failed to accomplish more than the capture of a few prisoners among Cortlandt Skinner's Royal Greens. The remainder of the year, Elizabethtown enjoyed a season of comparative quiet due to the large number of militia called upon to protect the area.

While Elizabethtown and the surrounding country braced itself against enemy raids, its sons did yeomen service with Washington in the bloody battles of Brandywine and Germantown. At Brandywine, Francis Barber, as lieutenant colonel of artillery, took an active part in saving two brass cannon captured from the Hessians at Trenton.*

When the enemy finally abandoned Philadelphia in June, 1778, Washington followed and fought the Battle of Monmouth. During the battle, Major Aaron Ogden, whose unit was not engaged, volunteered and served as an aide-de-camp for Lord Stirling. It was through information he gained from reconnoitering that Washington secured the advantage over Clinton on this memorable day. While the battle raged, the temperature rose to one hundred degrees. Smoke lay in dense clouds over the field. Many of the heavily clad British and Hessians died from exhaustion and heart failure. In the battle Francis Barber received a wound that laid him up long enough so that he could get married again.

After the Battle of Monmouth, the New Jersey Brigade was once again stationed at Elizabethtown and nearby posts. During this time Francis Barber's marriage to the charming Nancy Ogden, a cousin of his deceased wife, was not the only accomplishment on the part of Cupid in Elizabethtown. In October, wedding bells rang for Catherine Smith and Elisha Boudinot, who were married in the Belcher House amid great festivities. Catherine had wanted a fancy wedding dress and to please her William Peartree Smith had tried to smuggle one in from New

---

* These cannon are now at the Lafayette Headquarters near Chadd's Ford. The nozzles are worn from dragging the cannon during the rout following the battle.

York. But it was "Seized and Sold according to Law, and the poor Bride put under the Mortification of being married in her Old Cloathes." However, Lord Stirling, who was one of the guests, admitted that it was a very grand wedding.[17]

Believing Elizabethtown was a fairly safe place once more with the New Jersey Brigade in its midst, many citizens returned home during the winter of 1778-1779. Colonel Elias Dayton became comfortably settled with his family at his home on East Jersey Street near Broad. With much business to attend at Elizabethtown, he turned down a nomination as delegate to Congress. Besides attending his duties, he was needed at home, he admitted, to protect his property against his own soldiers and even some officers who were known to walk off with anything not nailed down.[18]

Occasionally during the winter, Elizabethtown people were pleased to hear a sermon by their busy minister, the Reverend James Caldwell, who had become a deputy quartermaster for the Continental Army. There is a story that one day Congressman Abraham Clark appeared before Caldwell's office at Springfield and, looking up, saw the letters DQMG over the door. "What do those letters mean?" asked the visitor. "What do you think?" rejoined the minister. "I cannot conceive," replied Clark, "unless they mean Devilish Queer Minister of the Gospel."

Besides Quartermaster Caldwell and the army officers, another important official in Elizabethtown that winter was Elias Boudinot, the Commissary General for Prisoners. By this time Boudinot was quite satisfied with the British treatment of American prisoners. On visiting New York and Long Island in March 1778, he found the prisoners living under quite satisfactory conditions. Officers were usually allowed to board with a family and were often permitted to go home on parole. Belcher Peartree Smith, a prisoner on Long Island in 1780, found good company among his fellow prisoners as well as among the inhabitants, who often loaned him their books.[19]

With the main part of the Continental Army camped at Middlebrook in the winter of 1778-1779, many officers stopped at Elizabethtown on their way to winter quarters. Arriving on December 3, Washington stayed for nearly a week. He probably stayed at Graham's Tavern or the Red Lion Inn, the most commodious and popular inns at Elizabethtown during the Revolution. With Lord Stirling, General Maxwell, Colonels Dayton and Ogden, and other officers, Washington discussed military problems. From Elizabethtown, he sent many despatches pertaining to the march which was then in progress of the Convention troops from Massachusetts to Virginia.*

It was a cold night late in February, 1779, when Henry Woodruff came pounding at the door of the house where General Maxwell and his aide-de-camp, Major Aaron Ogden, were sleeping. Excitedly he related that a picket had heard the sound of many oars on the narrows beyond the Point. At once Major Ogden volunteered to reconnoiter the road leading to Crane's Ferry where the sounds were heard. On approaching the Ferry House standing by the salt marsh, Aaron saw a light. Pulling his horse to a walk, he moved cautiously ahead. Suddenly from out of the dark men appeared as if from nowhere. Instead of dismounting as ordered, Ogden wheeled and put spurs to his horse but not in time to escape the thrust of a bayonet which pierced his side. Notwithstanding his wound, Major Ogden made it back to town to confirm the alarm.

Although the Americans did not know the enemy's strength, they were soon to find that it was no small raiding party. Lieutenant Colonel Thomas Sterling with one thousand men had landed in the salt meadows about a mile to the east of Crane's Ferry. Guided by Cornelius Hatfield and several other Elizabethtown Loyalists, the main body reached Woodruff's Farm by wading through the marsh.

When the first report of the enemy's landing reached Elizabethtown, the Reverend Andrew Hunter, chaplain for Maxwell's Brigade, hurried to Liberty Hall to sound the warning. Reaching the mansion he found that the Governor was with friends a few miles away and was presumably out of danger. On his return, Hunter was captured by the British who had directed their march to Liberty Hall in the hope of capturing Governor Livingston.

Upon arriving at Liberty Hall, Colonel Sterling found the Governor's wife and daughters, Susan and Catherine. When Sterling, who was as polite as a deacon, asked for the Governor's papers,

* The Convention troops were General Burgoyne's army captured at Saratoga a year earlier.

Susan had the presence of mind to steer him away from a box of state papers to a drawer full of worthless correspondence intercepted at sea. Believing he had the Governor's papers, Sterling politely bade the girls and their mother goodby and left for Elizabethtown.[20]

By the time the British arrived at Elizabethtown, Maxwell had withdrawn his troops to the southward to await reinforcements. With pickets guarding the roads, Sterling sent out foraging parties to round up all the livestock in town. Meanwhile others ransacked the village looking for military stores. On leaving, they set fire and burned to the ground the barracks, a blacksmith shop, and the Academy. Somehow the women of Elizabethtown (all the men and boys were gone with Maxwell) heroically rescued twenty-six barrels of flour from the flaming Academy before the fire drove them from the building.[21]

When word reached Middlebrook that the enemy had attacked Elizabethtown, Washington sent St. Clair and Smallwood with the Pennsylvania and Maryland divisions to help Maxwell. Before the reinforcements reached Scotch Plains, however, the enemy was gone. As the British retired, Dayton and Matthias Ogden pressed so closely with their regiments that all the cattle was retaken. Upon reaching the meadows, the British found the tide had risen. Before reaching their boats, in many places the enemy were compelled to wade waist deep through the icy waters.[22]

Not long after the raid on Liberty Hall, Livingston wrote Sir Henry Clinton a sarcastic letter. In it Livingston assured the General he was certain that he had nothing to do with the price of two thousand pounds put upon the Governor's head by Cortlandt Skinner. In closing, Livingston warned the General that two could play the game of assassination as well as one and that Clinton's life could be taken at any time. Although noted for his wit and sarcasm, Livingston decidedly came off second best in his exchange with Sir Henry Clinton. "I should not blacken myself with so foul a crime," Sir Henry assured Livingston, "to obtain so trifling an end." Then in reply to Livingston's boast that Clinton could be assassinated, he wrote: "Sensible of the power you boast (of being able to dispose of my life, by means of intimates of yours, ready to murder at your command), I can only congratulate you on your amiable connections, and acknowledge myself your most humble servant." [23]

While the New Jersey Continentals guarded Elizabethtown, their neglect by the state became almost unbearable. The officers could not buy one shirt with four months' pay. In contrast, most other states had relieved the suffering of their soldiers with bounties or advances in pay. A British officer on a pass within the American lines found the swarthy and homely General Maxwell dressed in a threadbare blue coat and shabby hat like an "invalid Corporal."

In April the officers of the New Jersey line finally served notice on the legislature that unless relief was immediately forthcoming, they would be compelled to leave the service. Colonels Dayton, Ogden, Barber, and sixty other officers signed the protest. Other letters and petitions followed. On May 6, Major Aaron Ogden and twenty others informed the legislature that they were penning their last remonstrance. Unless they were given assurance that help was forthcoming, they would resign in three days. Their demand again went unanswered. Probably all would have resigned had not Washington intervened with a strong rebuke for the officers. The General's reprimand, however, did not go unanswered. They loved their country, they declared, "but when that country is so lost to virtue and justice as to forget to support its servants, then it becomes their duty to retire from the service." [24]

When summer came again, the New Jersey Brigade left their posts in the Elizabethtown-Newark area and marched off to join the force being led by General Sullivan against the Six Nations in western New York. As before, the militia and state troops were left to defend the eastern area. With the Continentals gone, the enemy did not wait long to strike. The first raid from Staten Island came in June, 1779, when Cornelius Hatfield, the most hated of the Elizabethtown Loyalists, crossed at Halsted's Point to commit acts of vandalism. Other raids followed in rapid succession, with the New Jersey militia indulging in some of their own on Staten Island.

In August, the exasperated Elizabethtown Committee demanded the expulsion of all suspected persons in the area. Governor Livingston, however, would not consent since he believed the action would increase the number of enemies by forcing neutrals to take sides. One of the persons suspected of supplying the enemy with information was the wife of the Reverend Thomas Chandler. More alarming, however, than the ubiquitous raids was the discovery of a plot among the Negro slaves in Elizabethtown to rise and murder their masters. All Negroes believed to be involved in the plot were locked up, while the others were kept under close surveillance.[25]

Although Elizabethtown was having its troubles with Loyalists, it again answered Washington's call for aid by sending a company of militiamen to the Hudson Highlands. When Wayne captured Stony Point in July, 1779, he found in the fort a brass cannon with a long history. The cannon was cast at Strasburg, Germany, in 1758, for the French government. Louis XV sent it to Canada, where it was captured by Wolfe the following year. The cannon was still at Quebec when General Richard Montgomery stormed the town in December, 1775. Seemingly, grape shot from this cannon killed Montgomery and wounded Matthias Ogden and William Crane of Elizabethtown. After the capture of the cannon by Wayne, Washington gave it to the Elizabethtown volunteers who had acted as a reserve during the storming of Stony Point. After the Revolution the cannon belonged to the Elizabethtown Artillery Company. For many years it was a familiar object in all the Fourth of July celebrations in the town. Today it rests on a foundation in front of the Union County Court House.

When Sullivan returned from ravaging the towns of the Six Nations, Colonel Dayton was sent to Elizabethtown while the rest of the New Jersey Brigade camped near Morristown. Not long after, General William Irvine brought his brigade to Crane's Mill * to help cover the exposed areas. As usual both the officers and privates were ragged and destitute. General Anthony Wayne, at his camp on Second River, thought Congress saw no need of hats for the heads or shoes for the feet. "If they find we can bare it tolerably well in the two extremes," he wrote, "perhaps they may try it in the center."

In December, 1779, Washington brought his main army to Jockey Hollow near Morristown for winter quarters. Right after

* Now Cranford, N.J.

the army arrived, a series of great snow storms accompanied by bitter cold swept the country. Soon the army was on the verge of starvation, the storehouses empty and the roads closed by huge drifts. For some days Washington allowed the soldiers to roam the countryside begging for food, while General Greene worked frantically to open the roads. Colonel Matthias Ogden, by Washington's orders, was charged with collecting provisions in Essex County. Finally the crisis passed as the snow let up and provisions began to arrive with the help of the farmers and magistrates.[26]

But the cold remained intense. Not for forty years had there been such a winter. With the waters between the mainland and Staten Island frozen solid, raiding parties from either side took advantage of the bridge of ice. On one raid, men from Staten Island captured a sleighing party near Rahway. Leaving the astonished and bewildered girls behind, the raiders drove the three sleighs to Staten Island with the boy friends as prisoners. The next day the sleighs were driven to New York on the ice.[27]

As soon as the supply problem had eased and the storms had abated, Washington and his generals decided that a major attack on Staten Island was worth a try. The heavy-drinking and gout-afflicted Lord Stirling was selected to command the attacking army of twenty-five hundred men. The first move was taken when Colonel Moses Hazen advanced with one thousand troops from Morristown to Connecticut Farms on January 12, 1780. Meanwhile Greene made preparations for sending down the supplies and ammunition. As ordered by Greene, Colonel Joseph Lewis gathered planking to build the platforms for getting the cannon off the sleighs and onto the ice at Arthur Kill. From Greene also went out a call for the justices of the peace to impress three hundred sleds and have them on hand at sunrise, January 14, at the farm of Peter Kemble or on the Morristown Green.[28]

Acting on orders from Stirling or Major Aaron Ogden, his aide-de-camp, General Irvine and Colonel Hazen readied themselves for the attack. Colonel Hazen's corps would compose the left column and cross at De Hart's Point with Dayton's regiment. The regiments of Stewart and Hall, coming from Morristown in sleds, would advance, join Irvine, and cross at Halsted's Point. The troops and the militia were warned against taking any private property except livestock, horses, wagons, and other items of military value. All were promised a share in the legitimate spoils of war. The militia, however, to Washington's indignation, paid no attention to the orders and returned with everything they could find worth the taking.[29]

After the American forces had crossed to Staten Island, it was discovered that the enemy, numbering about twelve hundred, had been warned and were collected in their fortified positions. Since it might prove very costly to storm their redoubts, Stirling decided to return before the enemy received reinforcements from New York. A channel, it was reported, had been opened through the ice from New York and the British were preparing to despatch reinforcements to Staten Island.

The ice over the Arthur Kill proved to be a bridge for the enemy also. Tipped off by spies in Elizabethtown, the Loyalists launched a counter-raid ten days after Stirling's abortive attempt on Staten Island. Entering by Halsted's Point, one hundred and twenty Loyalists and twelve dragoons under Lieutenant Colonel Abraham Buskirk pounced upon and captured nearly the entire Continental garrison of sixty men at Elizabethtown. Included among the captives was the commanding officer, Major John Eccleston. Guided by the revengeful Cornelius Hatfield, the raiders also carried off Belcher Peartree Smith and one of General Williamson's sons. With his own hands, it is said, Hatfield set fire to the Presbyterian Church, of which his father was a deacon. The Court House, used for military purposes on occasion, was also burned with the town records. Returning by way of De Hart's Point, the Loyalists burned the house at the Point before shoving off for Staten Island.

On the night of the Elizabethtown raid, a simultaneous one on Newark resulted in the destruction of the Academy and in considerable pillaging. Joseph Hedden, a commissioner for the confiscation of Loyalist estates, was snatched from his bed and carried half-clad to New York to die from frost bite and beatings.

After the raids on Elizabethtown and Newark, Washington provided the towns with more protection by sending into the area Major General Arthur St. Clair with two thousand Continentals. The sight of so many soldiers was a genuine relief to the hard-pressed citizens of Elizabethtown. Many people returned to their homes and church services were resumed: Deacon Hatfield opened his large red storehouse for worshipping. However, in spite of all, small parties continued to raid from Staten Island, as revengeful Tories sought to retaliate for the loss of their property. In May, 1780, the Loyalists tried again to capture Governor Livingston when a band led by Ensign James Moody made a daring raid into the state. Moody, however, was captured and his men either killed or made prisoners.

Bored by inactivity in New York and believing that the American cause was becoming unpopular in New Jersey, Lieutenant General Wilhelm von Knyphausen, in command of the King's army in the absence of Clinton, decided to test Washington's strength. He had been told that the Connecticut line was ready to mutiny and that the Pennsylvania troops were in a like frame of mind. Furthermore, Washington was weakened, having detached sections of his army for service in the South. Discouraged by the fall of Charleston, the New Jersey militia, he was informed, was not likely to give Washington much support. A powerful and quick thrust toward the American main base at Morristown, therefore, might result in the seizure of most of Washington's supplies and, possibly, in a devastating defeat of the American army. That Knyphausen's information was not entirely without validity can be gathered from a letter to General Gates. "The people are tired, the lower Class whether Whig or Tory regret the English Times, and curse the present Rulers," read the letter.[30] A better informed writer, however, wrote that since the loss of Charleston the Patriotic cause had received new life. "The change is indeed wonderful. Private concerns seem now to be forgotten, and nothing is talked of but the public cause," he wrote.[31] As events proved, Knyphausen would have been better advised had he listened to reports like the latter.

With fully six thousand troops—including Jaegers, Grenadiers, artillery, and dragoons—Knyphausen began crossing from Staten Island to Elizabethtown Point early in the evening of June 6, 1780. The ferrying, done with flatboats, was not completed until three in the morning. Knyphausen, prepared for an extended march into New Jersey, brought along his carriage. The first division under General Thomas Sterling came upon a small picket of Dayton's corps at the Crossroads (Union Square, Elizabeth). The

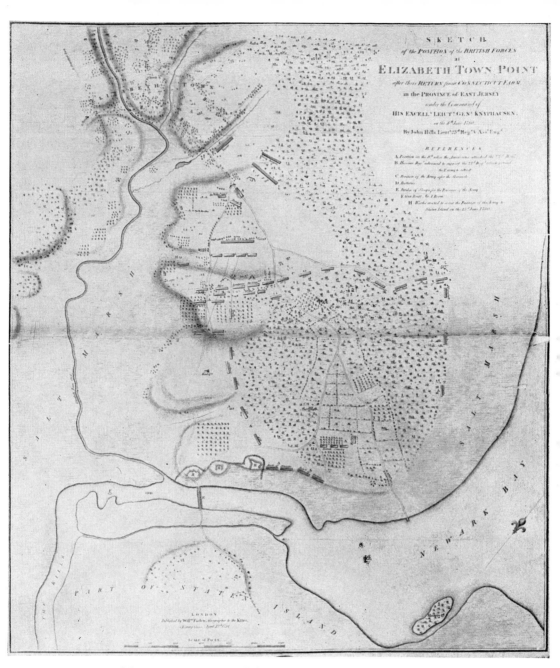

Map, 1780. Courtesy of the New Jersey Historical Society.

Americans fired and ran, but not before a musket ball struck and mortally wounded the British general.

Firing from time to time, Dayton's regiment, which had been stationed in Elizabethtown, retreated along the Galloping Hill Road toward Connecticut Farms. In a skirmish near the present-day intersection of Colonial Road and the Galloping Hill Road, a son of Major William Crane's was bayoneted to death by the enemy. Another Elizabethtown lad killed before the day was done was Ensign Moses Ogden, a brother-in-law of Lieutenant Colonel Barber.

At Connecticut Farms (Union, New Jersey) Dayton was joined by General Maxwell with most of the New Jersey Brigade. Although the Americans were strategically posted in the defile near the Presbyterian Meetinghouse, the British launched a frontal attack because they believed that the resistance would be slight. They found, however, quite the reverse: it was three hours before they pushed the New Jersey men out of Connecticut Farms. At one time the Americans drove the Hessian Jaegers, equipped with their short barreled and deadly rifles, back at the point of the bayonet. Besides Colonel Dayton, most of the other Elizabethtown officers were there, including Colonel Ogden, Major Ogden, and Lieutenant Colonel Francis Barber. Finally, with the enemy reinforced and preparing to outflank them, the New Jersey Brigade retired along the road to Springfield.

With the Jaegers again taking the lead, the British column moved forward like a great dragon after its prey. Following the Jaegers came Colonel Von Wurmb with Buskirk's Loyalists and a train of artillery. Then came a long column of blue-coated Chasseurs wearing tall black hats. In back of these was Colonel Birch with three hundred Dragoons in their short green coats and shining helmets, topped with queues of streaming horsehair. After the Dragoons came the Cold Stream Guards under General Edward Matthews. These were followed by other regiments, led by General William Tryon and General James Robertson (acting as a volunteer). Behind these were the columns of Hessians led by Generals Hackenberg and Lossberg. In the rear was another corps of horsemen. What an army compared with the few hundred New Jersey Continentals and the sprinkling of militia who dared to contest every inch of ground on the road to Springfield!

After the Americans had left Connecticut Farms, most of the houses and the church were burned to the ground by the invaders. In one house, some distance from the fighting at the defile, Mrs. Caldwell, wife of the fighting parson, was waiting out the battle with some neighbors. Standing by a window and peeking out, Abigail Lennington, a girl in her teens, saw a short squatty soldier in a red coat come around the side of the house. When nearly opposite the window, the man fired. Glass came flying into the room and Mrs. Caldwell who was sitting on the side of the bed, gasped and fell back unconscious. The next instance several soldiers came rushing into the house apparently expecting to find some of the men who had been firing at them all morning from the houses and barns. They were followed by General Tryon who expressed his sorrow for the accident. Mrs. Caldwell who had died almost instantly was carried to a neighboring house while the one in which she was killed was burned like the others.

From the moment Mrs. Caldwell was killed all kinds of rumors arose as to how it happened. Soon it was the talk that the enemy had orders to kill her on sight. One woman, it was said, was mistaken for Mrs. Caldwell and came near being shot earlier in the day. Although the truth became quite apparent after testimony was given by the ones in the house when Mrs. Caldwell was killed, Americans preferred to believe that she had been murdered in cold blood. That the enemy had been fired upon from nearly every house along the way and that they had had to rush many houses in order to drive out the rebels, was never considered. Nor have historians been any better than the people of the Revolutionary generation in arriving at the truth. Long after, in 1847, Captain William C. De Hart, an aide-de-camp for General Winfield Scott and a hero of the Mexican War, attempted to write an unbiased account of the incident. For his pains, Captain De Hart, who had come back to Elizabethtown to die from a disease contracted in Mexico, was verbally crucified by irate townspeople, especially the Reverend Nicholas Murray, the author of a rather romantic history of Elizabethtown.[32]

Probably no "atrocity" during the Revolution excited Americans more than the killing of Mrs. Caldwell, save the murder of Jane McCrea by Long Jim, the Cayuga Indian with General Burgoyne. As the stories of Mrs. Caldwell's death spread like wild fire, a wave of indignation swept over New Jersey that brought the militia swarming in from all sides to battle the invaders. "I never saw soldiers pant for revenge more than ours do—not a deserter from us since we came to the ground," wrote an observer. To the British, however, the kind of warfare waged by the Americans wore a different look. "A soldier is received with smiles one moment," wrote a British officer, "and the following instant butchered (for in a military view it merits no other name) by a set of people, who by their clothing and appointments cannot be distinguished from the quiet inhabitants of the Country." [33]

By the time the New Jersey Brigade drew back from Connecticut Farms, large numbers of militia from the surrounding country were arriving at Springfield. From Morris County came Colonel Sylvanus Seely, whose profanity disturbed Asbel Green, a young militiaman and son of the minister at Hanover. Placing his men in a woods near the Rahway River, Seely swore he would kill any man firing without orders. By this time the New Jersey Brigade was over the bridge at the Rahway after making the Jaegers fight for almost every inch of ground from Connecticut Farms.

Posting his men near the bridge, Colonel Dayton soon brought a four-pounder into play as the Jaegers sought cover and waited for reinforcements. Minutes later the British opened upon the New Jersey men with several cannon under the command of Colonel Von Wurmb. Asbel Green heard the cannon balls zooming overhead and saw several men hit by them as they ricocheted and fell from the trees. Casualties, he thought, would have been greater had the enemy aimed lower.

As the day was growing late and Washington was known to be approaching from Morristown with the main army, Knyphausen disengaged his forces and fell back to Connecticut Farms. He had hoped to surprise the Americans and catch them off balance but he failed. His failure was due to the valor of the New Jersey Continentals, who almost single-handedly had held back an enemy many times their strength. Philip Schuyler at Morristown said that the day could have ended on a much different note. "Had the enemy," he wrote, "pursued what we generally believed to be their object, our heavy cannon and stores would inevitably have fallen into their hands, as our military force was incompetent to their protection, and the means for conveying them to places more distant for want of horses and carriages, not of our power." [34]

Late in the afternoon, the British returned to Connecticut Farms. Since he planned to continue the fighting the next day, Knyphausen ordered redoubts to be thrown up and camp prepared. About six o'clock Americans attacked the British in force at several points but, after they were fired upon with cannon, all withdrew. Colonel Seely with his militia made camp at Thompson's Mill about a mile to the west of the British, while the New Jersey Brigade camped on the road to Springfield. Neither army had tents and all prepared to sleep in the open or under makeshift cover.

That morning at the time the British began their march, Old Sow, the signal gun on the Heights above Springfield, had warned Washington at Morristown that the enemy was coming. General Greene, the Quartermaster General, at once issued orders for loading the wagons for a full scale battle. When all was ready, Washington started toward Springfield about noon while the fighting was still in progress at Connecticut Farms. By the time Washington reached the Heights above Springfield, Knyphausen was on his way back to Connecticut Farms. Not wishing to advance any further, Washington pitched camp in battle formation on the slopes of the mountain. Greene commanded the right wing, Lafayette the left wing. Steuben commanded the second line with the brigades of Hand and Stark. Stirling was sent ahead with a strong corps to join the New Jersey Brigade near the enemy lines. Washington's final words for Stirling were to keep his men in the woods as much as possible to avoid attack by the enemy dragoons.

About ten o'clock, Knyphausen came to the conclusion that it was too dangerous to remain longer at Connecticut Farms. A deserter from the American lines reported Washington's position and Stirling's advance. Orders were immediately given to break camp and return to Elizabethtown Point. The British, however, did not leave unnoticed, and soon Stirling moved to intercept the retreating enemy. Not long after, the night became pitch dark and a violent thunderstorm arose. For awhile the British could advance only by the flashes of lightning that lit up the road for an instant. Meanwhile Stirling's force missed the road and failed to intercept their enemy.

There is a legend that upon passing Liberty Hall some Hessians entered the house to get out of the storm. Just then a flash of lightning lit up the hall stairs; on it stood Catherine Livingston, terrified but determined, if possible, to save the house. Believing that the girl, who was as pale as a sheet, was the ghost of Mrs. Caldwell, the Hessians ran from the house amid the thunder and lightning and pouring rain. A less dramatic account reports that Mrs. Livingston and the young ladies were saved when a Tory neighbor persuaded the enemy to leave the house.

For a running fight that lasted all day, casualties on either side on June 7th were comparatively light. Nonetheless, the Jaegers, who bore the brunt of the battle for the enemy, suffered over sixty casualties out of a corps of four hundred. In all, the British sustained nearly double the losses of the Americans whose casualties were confined almost entirely to the New Jersey Brigade.[35]

After the night of storm, day broke clear and bright over the heads of the opposing armies. Finding that the British were encamped in an area surrounding Elizabethtown Point, Stirling ordered Brigadier General Edward Hand to attack the enemy with fifteen hundred Continentals and a body of militia. Hand crossed the old Stone Bridge at Elizabethtown and advanced against the British outpost manned by the Twenty-Second Regiment. Although the British fought from behind breastworks, Hand's attack was so strong that they would have been completely overpowered had not two regiments of Hessians arrived in time.

Although Hand's attack was repulsed, the British pulled back nearer to the Point. That night the Jaegers and the Dragoons, who had been ferried over to Staten Island on the night of the retreat, returned to join the army on the mainland. The next day the Jaegers advanced and took up position near the Belcher House. After this there followed days of skirmishing especially around the Stone Bridge where the ashes of the Court House and the Church were plainly visible. The American forces which kept to the area west of the Bridge, except during an attack, were now commanded by Baron von Steuben. His superior, Lord Stirling, had set up headquarters at Connecticut Farms. The main army with Washington and Greene remained at Springfield.

As the days passed it became apparent that Knyphausen would not launch another invasion of New Jersey without reinforcements. These, however, he would soon have: his stay in Elizabethtown was more than a gesture of defiance. While waiting for reinforcements, the Hessian General had fears that Washington, whose army was swollen by great numbers of militia, might attempt a major attack. His fears were not reduced when the New Jersey Brigade and a body of militia launched a savage attack on the Jaegers at the Stone Bridge and the Wooden Bridge at Crane's Mill. Bullets, according to a Hessian, were flying in all directions. One Elizabethtown boy who saw much of the fighting during these days was Ichabod Cleveland, a drummer boy. He lived on the corner of West Jersey and Cherry streets. Much to his relief, Knyphausen was soon reinforced when Clinton, who had returned from the South, landed his Grenadiers, the Queen's Rangers, and other units on Staten Island and sent them over a newly-constructed pontoon bridge at Elizabethtown Point to join their beleagured comrades.[36]

During the fighting at Elizabethtown most of the houses on the east side of the river were systematically looted by the British. Regarding the pillaging of his home, Dr. William Barnet wrote: "They emptied my feather beds in the streets, broke in windows, smashed my mirrors and left our pantry and storeroom department bare. I could forgive them all that, but the rascals stole from my kitchen wall the finest string of red peppers in all Elizabethtown." The Belcher House suffered most from the looting. William Peartree Smith afterward claimed losses amounting to £899.

One house, according to legend, escaped without having anything stolen or damaged. This was either the house owned by Robert Ogden or that of Moses Ogden on the King's Highway. The British, it seems, on entering the house, found over the mantle a picture of General James Wolfe at Quebec. Believing the house belonged to Loyalists they immediately left with profuse apologies to the occupants.

After holding a council of war, General Clinton directed Knyphausen to march with his now formidable army against the American forces at Connecticut Farms and Springfield. At the same time Clinton prepared to move up the Hudson with a body of troops. If Knyphausen should find that Washington had moved far enough toward West Point with the main part of his army, he was to press on and secure control of the Morristown area. If, however, Washington should return to confront Knyphausen, Clinton promised to sail back and come to his assistance.[37]

In obedience to Clinton's orders, Knyphausen marched out of his camp at Elizabethtown on June 23, 1780, and again took the Galloping Hill Road to Connecticut Farms. On the way he met with some resistance from small parties of Continentals and militia. By sunrise, however, the British had reached Connecticut Farms. Here, as on the previous occasion, they met stubborn resistance from Colonel Dayton's corps and a swarm of militia. This time, with the Jaegers again in the lead, the British were held up for about an hour before Dayton signaled a retreat on reports that he would soon be outflanked. As Knyphausen continued with the main force down the Springfield road, General Matthews turned to the right with the Queen's Rangers, Skinner's Battalion, and a body of Hessians to circle Springfield by way of the Vauxhall Road.

With the Cold Stream Guards in the main column was a dashing young officer, Lieutenant Colonel Cosmo Gordon. During the march to Connecticut Farms, Gordon and Lt. Colonel Ludwig Johann Adolph Von Wurmb paid a visit to Liberty Hall near which his troops had skirmished with a party of Americans. Riding up to the house guarded by Livingston's wife and daughters, the two officers drew rein opposite Susan, standing near some roses. In his broken English, Lt. Colonel Von Wurmb enquired if he might pick a rose. Susan consented. She then asked Colonel Gordon, whom she knew, if he would like one too. He would be delighted, he answered, as he took the red rose from the smiling Susan. Charmed by his pretty hostess, Gordon declared that in exchange for the rose he would place a guard at Liberty Hall for its protection. As he pinned the rose to his hat, Susan vowed it would protect him from the bullets of her countrymen. (Unfortunately, the charm did not work for before the day was done Gordon received a severe wound.) As he rode away from Liberty Hall, however, Gordon's thoughts must have gone back to the days of his youth when Susan's uncle, Lord

Stirling, had visited Gordon Castle, the colonel's family home in Scotland. Never would he have thought then that he would some-day be fighting his guest on American battlefields.[38]

When Knyphausen marched from his base at Elizabethtown against the American forces at Connecticut Farms and Springfield, Washington with the major part of the army was at Rockaway Bridge, eight miles north of Morristown. Here he was waiting to see if Clinton would make a thrust at West Point or would con-trive to bring his combined forces against General Greene in com-mand at Springfield. In any event, Washington was in a position to move in either direction as the occasion demanded.

Nathanael Greene was left with about twenty-five hundred Continentals, including the New Jersey line with such veteran officers as Elias Dayton, Matthias Ogden, Francis Barber, Israel Shreve, William De Hart, and Aaron Ogden. In addition he had General John Stark with his brigade and Colonel Israel Angel's crack Rhode Island regiment. There was also "Light Horse Harry" Lee with his green-coated Dragoons, the pride of the American army. Before the day was done, upwards of five thousand militia under General Philemon Dickinson turned out to help battle the enemy. A good share of the militia remained far from the center of fighting, posted as they were on outlying roads to protect the main army against flanking movements. Units such as these were with General Nathaniel Heard, watching the roads west of Con-necticut Farms. As before, practically the entire Morris County militia was on hand under the colorful Colonel Sylvanus Seely. With Seely was Captain Jacob Arnold with his veteran Morris-town Light Horse who, as despatch riders, performed a most important service.*

After the British left Elizabethtown, "Old Sow" atop the Short Hills began booming out its call to the militia. All through the morning "the militia were running" over the dirt roads leading to Springfield. At eight o'clock, General Greene, who for the first time was commanding an army of his own, was calmly eating breakfast at Bryant's Tavern back of Springfield as he received messages and issued orders for his fighting formation.

* Accounts differ as to the American strength but the evidence indicates a force of about 7,500.

At the main bridge over the Rahway from which the planks had been removed, Greene placed Colonel Israel Angel's corps with artillery under Lieutenant Colonel Thomas Forrest. They were joined by Colonel Dayton's regiment after it had slowly retired from Connecticut Farms. To the west along the little river were General Dickinson's militia watching the flank. To aid Dickinson, who had his hands full with the poorly disciplined militia swarming into town, Greene sent several Continental officers, including Major Aaron Ogden.

General Greene was a brilliant tactician as well as a strategist. At Springfield he fully displayed his genius with a formation that defied the British and Hessians. Near the Presbyterian Meetinghouse at the Second Bridge, less than half a mile back of his first line, Greene placed Colonel Shreve's New Jersey regiment with an accompaniment of militia and artillery. Back of these on a rise by the old mill was a third line consisting of Stark's brigade and some of the New Jersey Continentals with General Maxwell. A mile to the left in the Vauxhall area were Colonel Matthias Ogden and Lee's cavalry to check any forces attempting to outflank the lines in that direction. Greene's adjutant general for the day was Lieutenant Colonel Francis Barber, who was cited for his assistance in drawing up the battle formations.

When Knyphausen arrived at the Rahway Bridge his troops met an intense fire from the men under Angel, Dayton, and Forrest. So concentrated was the fire that it was forty minutes before the British could force a crossing by wading waist-deep through the river. Doubtlessly it was during this phase of the battle that Quartermaster Caldwell, according to tradition, brought out a stack of Watt's hymnals from the church and distributed them to the soldiers for wadding. As he passed along the line he is reputed to have shouted above the roar of battle "Give 'em Watts, boys, give 'em Watts!" How much would the enemy have relished an opportunity to get their hands on preacher Caldwell, "the Retailer of Sedition on Sundays, and Ammunition, Shoes, and Boots, the Week Days!"

By the time the Americans gave up defending the crossing at the first bridge, Angel's men had sustained heavy losses, when one considers the numbers involved. According to Captain Stephen Olney, only five out of the forty men serving the single cannon escaped without being killed or wounded.*

The stand at the Second Bridge was short, since Greene had received word that Lee and Ogden had been forced to retire from the Vauxhall area. This meant that General Matthews would soon be driving upon Springfield from the rear. For a slightly longer time Greene held to his third line on the rise near the mill, but knowing that he was no match for the enemy in full-scale battle he brought his forces back to the top of the Short Hills. Here he intended to give a good account of himself should the enemy attempt to push over the mountain and march for Chatham.

To check the enemy while he drew back to the hills, Greene sent Lieutenant Colonel Ebenezer Huntington and Colonel Henry Jackson with a strong detachment and a cannon to stop the advance on his left. He also sent a strong force under Lieutenant Colonel William S. Smith into an orchard in front of the mill. Here for half an hour or longer the advanced units of the enemy were pinned down by a murderous fire from the Americans. Until Smith was forced to retire by a flanking movement, the Redcoats in the orchard lay prone on their stomachs not daring to lift a head.[39]

Most of the British army on this hot and humid day never advanced beyond the old mill or Bryant's Tavern. The Cold Stream Guards, however, and some of the Jaegers, pushed up to a point near the pass † just below the signal cannon where the sides of the ridge are very steep. Here it became apparent that it would be suicide to try to climb the slopes in the face of the American fire. Having gained the lower elevation below the ridge, the Guards lay stretched on the ground, exhausted from their exertion and cringing from the bullets fired by some of the more intrepid Americans who had climbed part way down to meet them. Colonel Gordon stood with his hat off wiping his forehead, seemingly oblivious to the enemy's fire. The rose given him by Susan Livingston was still on his hat though he knew it was a target for the Americans. After resting a bit, the Guards beat a

---

* Francis Barber reported thirteen killed, forty-seven wounded, and nine missing among the Continentals. His report admittedly was inconclusive.
† Hobart's Gap.

retreat and were soon back in Springfield where Knyphausen was forming his men for the march back to Elizabethtown.[40]

Before the enemy left Springfield, the meetinghouse and most of the houses in town were given over to flames. The officers tried to restrain the men but the soldiery, who had been fired upon from most of the buildings, could not be restrained. Long years afterward, an old lady told how one house was saved when the British found several women locked in a closet. Believing they were Loyalists, a guard was stationed by the house which, standing in the line of battle, had been repeatedly struck by cannon and musket fire.*

It was late afternoon when Knyphausen, with the heroic Jaegers and the cavalry as rear guards, started back for Elizabethtown. Greene sent Stark's brigade after them but they could not be overtaken. Militia, however, responded more swiftly and harassed the enemy as they withdrew. By eight o'clock the baggage and cavalry were over the pontoon bridge at Elizabethtown Point; by one in the morning all were on Staten Island and the bridge dismantled.

Casualties during the day as on the previous invasion were comparatively light, the greater part occurring at the Rahway Bridge. In all, the two-week campaign cost the British about five hundred men, killed, wounded, and missing. Although not in itself a serious loss, it was a high price to pay for nothing gained. Altogether, American losses were less than half those sustained by the British.

The fighting on June 23 at no time reached the proportions of a full-scale battle. Greene held back the enemy at strategic points until the pressure became threatening. Then he withdrew to his next line of defense. Confronted by an army much stronger than his own, no competent general would have done otherwise.

As for Knyphausen, he could not at any time be charged with audacious generalship. Had he been able to carry out his intentions of reaching Morristown during the first invasion, he might have crippled the American army severely. On his second incursion, a defeat of Greene's army at Springfield would have

* From the location of the house described by the woman, it would appear to be the present-day Cannon-Ball House. MSS, Edward J. Grassmann Collection, Elizabeth, N.J.

had a like effect. If, however, Knyphausen had pushed an un-defeated Greene to the Passaic River at Chatham, he would doubtlessly have found himself trapped. Washington would have advanced from Rockaway Bridge to Springfield, encircling the British. The result would have been the annihilation of a British army larger than Burgoyne's at Saratoga. In this way the war might have ended in New Jersey rather than at Yorktown.

After the battle on June 23, Greene left New Jersey's defense in the hands of General Dickinson and the militia and moved his continentals northward to join Washington. Soon after, finding that Clinton was not likely to launch a major drive on West Point, Washington detached Colonel Dayton for duty at Elizabethtown. With Dayton came his wife and family. Not long after, Mrs. Dayton and the wives of Dr. Barnet, Elisha Boudinot, Governor Livingston, and others undertook to raise money for the New Jersey Continentals, once again ragged and barefoot. Help for the Brigade, however, also came from an unexpected source when Lafayette, returning from France, provided the men with cloth-ing and other necessaries. To his close friend, Matthias Ogden and to each of the officers of his regiment, he gave a fine sword. In their new blue uniforms with hard leather helmets topped with a crest of horsehair, the New Jersey troops for once looked fully as good as they were.[41]

Although the people of Elizabethtown were once again thank-ful for protection, the soldiers' services were offset by their de-mands upon the community and by the stealing that went on. In the fall, Stephen Moylan's Light Horse, on the way to join Wash-ington, went about town impressing cattle and horses without warrants. This time, however, the aroused citizens caused the magistrates to use the militia to force the cavalry to give up the stolen animals.

Notwithstanding the presence of troops, living in the Elizabeth-town area remained hazardous. One night in November, 1780, Colonel Matthias Ogden and Captain Jonathan Dayton, sleeping at Herd's Tavern in Connecticut Farms, were surprised and car-ried off to Staten Island by a raiding party led by the arch villains to all Elizabethtown patriots, Cornelius and Smith Hatfield.

As captives, Ogden and Dayton were sent to New York where they were allowed the freedom of the city. The gay young Matthias Ogden became a favorite among the British officers and a constant guest at their mess. One day a newly-arrived officer from England offered a toast to the "damnation of all rebels." To the astonishment of the diners, Ogden threw his wine in the officer's face while he shouted an appropriate oath. For a minute there was silence. Then each officer, including the offender, turned and offered Ogden an apology. Thereafter Matthias Ogden suffered no more insults while a prisoner among the British.[42]

Not long before his brother's capture, Major Aaron Ogden had an unforgettable experience. He was selected by Washington to go within the British lines at Paulus Hook with an offer to exchange Major John André for the traitor, Benedict Arnold. On reaching the fort, Ogden was politely received by the commanding officer who in turn forwarded his message to General Clinton in New York. The answer was prompt and decisive. The British never gave up a deserter. "Your horse is waiting for you, Major Ogden," said the commanding officer as he brought the interview to a close.

It was the summer of 1781 when events led to Cornwallis's surrender at Yorktown and the end of the war. In August, Washington heard that Admiral Comte Francois de Grasse was sailing to the Chesapeake with a fleet which would provide naval superiority in American waters. Given the help of General de Rochambeau and his strong expeditionary army encamped near Peekskill, this was the time to trap Cornwallis. Washington acted promptly.

Within a few days after the intelligence arrived, the American and French armies began marching. Making it appear that New York was the object of the move, the New Jersey Brigade in the lead came and pitched camp at Springfield, New Jersey. Matthias Ogden, having been exchanged, was once again at the head of his regiment. Most of Washington's army camped near Chatham where bake-ovens were built to deceive the enemy into thinking that the troops were preparing for a long siege of New York. Since only the top officers knew their destination, much perplexity existed throughout the army. Colonel Alexander Scammel wrote: "The refinement of the Commander-in-Chief's manuevers & movements eludes the sagacity of the army, and I presume of the enemy. Some say Virginia is the place of Destination, others that we are going to begin our approaches to New York by way of Staten Island." But what deceived Clinton more than bake-ovens was an intercepted letter written by Chastellux to Luzerne in which he boasted of convincing Washington that a siege of New York was the best course to pursue.

Breaking camp and marching swiftly toward Trenton late in August, Washington left New Jersey to the protection of its militia. General Dickinson directed Colonel Seely with the Morris County militia to take post at Connecticut Farms and to send advanced parties into Elizabethtown, Woodbridge, and Amboy. That the enemy had a healthy respect for the New Jersey militia is attested by the fact that they made no move to attack the state while Washington was gone.

Close on the heels of the American army came the well-disciplined and flashily-dressed French expeditionary force. So well-trained were the French soldiers that cornfields and apple orchards along the line of march remained untouched. To the inhabitants, the French army was a thrilling sight. "The people—flocked from all sides to see them, the regimental bands played in the evening whenever the troops camped." Never would the country girls forget dancing with the courtly French officers whose smiles more than compensated for their lack of English.[43]

At Yorktown, the New Jersey "light troops" with Elias Dayton, Matthias Ogden, and Francis Barber were in the thick of the storming of the British works. Serving as an aide-de-camp for Lafayette, the unlucky Francis Barber was wounded at Yorktown for a third time during the war. After the surrender, Lafayette exchanged swords with Barber. He wanted, he declared, to take back to France the weapon so often and so gloriously seen in battle. Major Aaron Ogden, who with Barber had served as a member of Lafayette's *Corps d'Elite* during the entire Virginia campaign, also took a prominent part in storming the British redoubts. For his bravery at Yorktown, he received a special citation by Washington.

After the surrender at Yorktown, Matthias Ogden found much to do to occupy his talents. As a member of a committee from the army he hurried to Congress with petitions for back pay before the country forgot all about its obligations. The mission was fruitless. Back with the army in northern New Jersey, he presented

Washington with a plan for capturing Prince William Henry, the future King William IV. Washington consented on the condition that the Prince, if captured, would be treated with respect. Ogden's plan was to cross the Hudson in flatboats and set fire to the suburbs of New York. During the confusion attending the conflagration, he and his raiders would steal into the city, seize the Prince, and carry him to their boats. To Ogden's disappointment the raid had to be called off after the British discovered his boats before they reached New York. Years later when William IV heard that Washington had ordered Ogden to treat him kindly, if captured, he remarked: "I am obliged to General Washington for his humanity, but I'm damn'd glad I did not give him an opportunity of exercising it toward me." [44]

Since the beginning of the war Elizabethtown had been a center for the exchange of prisoners and for the passing of persons from one side to another under flags of truce. In March, 1782, General Henry Knox and Gouverneur Morris met with General O'Hara and Colonel Abercrombie in Elizabethtown for the adjustment of accounts relative to prisoners of war. But not all the intercourse between belligerents at Elizabethtown was of a legitimate nature. In reality Elizabethtown became notorious as a center for smuggling goods between the British and American lines. Most of the illegal trade was under cover of flags of truce with some officers of either army having a hand in it. So flagrant did the smuggling become that Abraham Clark, in May, 1782, wrote that unless it were stopped the country would be drained of specie.

Washington did all in his power to stop the illegal trade, to little avail. Finally he ordered that no flags could be given or received at Elizabethtown. His orders, however, generally went unheeded. People in Elizabethtown said that even Captain Jonathan Dayton, son of Brigadier General Elias Dayton, was involved in the illegal trade. Colonel Sylvanus Seely and other officers who held command at Elizabethtown during the war were also accused.

At the landing at De Hart's Point the military had a guard-post where sentries watched for illegal trading. It was here in 1781 that the Reverend James Caldwell met his death. The pastor had come to the Point in a carriage to help Miss Beulah Murray on her way to visit her sister in Elizabethtown. After the pastor had helped Miss Murray into the carriage, he went back to the boat to get a package. As he was returning, a guard, one James Morgan, shot him in the back. Captain David Woodruff, standing nearby, caught the minister as he fell. Afterward Woodruff testified that Morgan was not on duty at the time and that he had been bribed to kill the minister. Another soldier swore that he heard Morgan say he intended to "pop" the pastor off at the first opportunity. This testimony is not without support, for Morgan apparently had been recently in contact with Tories. Morgan's defense was that Caldwell did not stop when he ordered him to halt with the package. *

Having been a pillar of the Revolution in New Jersey and a greatly beloved man, Caldwell's death was deeply lamented. A middle-sized man with a kindly face and pleasant voice, he was known for his boundless energies and undaunted courage. In the pulpit he was often known to break out in sobs over the miseries of mankind. At home he loved to work in his garden at the parsonage, which stood back of the church and over the river.

Naturally Mr. Caldwell's funeral was attended by a great throng from near and far. The coffin rested for awhile on the large sandstone step in front of Mrs. Noel's house † for all to view his remains. After the funeral sermon, Elias Boudinot found homes for Caldwell's nine orphans. He himself took one. Another, John Caldwell, was taken to France by Lafayette and educated.‡

For killing the Reverend James Caldwell, Morgan was given a swift trial. His attorney was Colonel William De Hart. The judges were Dr. William Barnet and John Cleves Symmes. Morgan was found guilty of murder. The execution day was cold and there was some delay. Finally Morgan spoke up and said: "Do your duty and don't keep me here shivering in the cold." [45]

Elizabethtown lost another worthy citizen near the end of the war in the death of Lieutenant Colonel Francis Barber. At the

---

* Captain William C. De Hart who thought that the shooting of Mrs. Caldwell was accidental also suggested that the killing of the Reverend Caldwell was not premeditated murder. *NJJr.*, July 11, 1845, April 25, 1848.
† Elias Boudinot's house, now Boxwood Hall.
‡ John Caldwell became a Catholic in France but reverted to Presbyterianism upon his return to America. *NJJr.*, July 1, 1845, March 13, April 14, 1846.

time of his death he was carrying a despatch for Washington, who had just received word of the signing of the preliminary treaty of peace. As he was passing a spot where some men were felling a tree, a warning shout from the men came too late. The tree came crashing down, instantly killing both Barber and his horse.

Not long after the death of his friend Barber, Matthias Ogden left for France. With the war ending, Ogden hoped to strike up a trade with French merchants through his connection with Lafayette. His brothers, Robert and Aaron, had agreed to be partners in the venture, although Aaron entertained misgivings as to the sale of French merchandise in America. Whether or not Matthias made out well business-wise in France, he made a hit socially. In August, he wrote to Dr. Franklin asking the old philosopher if he would care to introduce him to the King since Lafayette had secured an invitation for him at a reception. He also asked the favor of riding in Franklin's carriage from Passy to Versailles. Ogden apparently did not know what honor Lafayette had in store for him at Versailles. On being presented to Louis the Sixteenth, the young American was awarded *Le droit du Tabouret* for his services in the War for Independence.

When Matthias Ogden returned to the United States in October, 1783, he carried with him the first report of the signing of the Treaty of Paris ending the War for Independence. Great was the rejoicing at Princeton when he laid the good news before President Elias Boudinot and the Congress. The long contest had at last ended. Elizabethtown and all the other American communities could now repair the ravages of war and look forward to life in the new country born of the American Revolution.

IX

A Place in a New Nation

When the veterans came home to Elizabethtown after the War for Independence, they found the town much changed from the old pre-war days. Governor Livingston thought that it was full of "unrecommended strangers, guilty-looking Tories, and very knavish Whigs." Many former residents including Colonel Barber, Jonathan Hampton, Parson Caldwell, and Stephen Crane, the elder, had died. Others, like William Peartree Smith and Robert Ogden, Sr., had moved away. Still others, such as the Reverend Chandler and Cavalier Jouet, had been compelled to leave the country for their loyalism. What Livingston overlooked, though, was the fact that many distinguished citizens were returning to lend a hand in repairing the losses and helping the town adjust to post-war conditions.

Most of the veterans returning to Elizabethtown were farmers and mechanics. Since many of the shops and most of the farms had suffered from the war, there was much to be done before the scars were removed. A few of the returning men were merchants, owners of stores and warehouses and in some cases of schooners which docked along the river below the Stone Bridge.

Most distinguished of the Elizabethtown merchants returning from the war was the fifty-year-old Brigadier General Elias Dayton, New Jersey's highest ranking officer since the death of Lord Stirling and the resignation of General Maxwell. Besides his wife Hannah, the female members of Dayton's family were his two charming and witty daughters, Polly and Sally. His oldest son, Jonathan, an officer of the Continental Army, would soon become a leading New Jersey politician. His other sons, Elias B. and William, would make names for themselves locally in the years to come.

After the war, Elias Dayton enjoyed a long and distinguished

Looking up Broad Street from the Stone Bridge, 1795 and after.

career as a public official and dignitary. Until his death in 1805, he was Major General of the Second Division of the New Jersey militia. For the last nine years of his life he was mayor of Elizabethtown. Very properly, too, he became the first president of the New Jersey chapter of the Society of the Cincinnati, an office he held until his death. Under the name of E. Dayton and Son, he carried on an extensive wholesale and retail business. His warehouse and wharf were located on a tract not far from the Court House fronting on Water Street (the old King's Highway) and extending to the river. He also had a store on the south side of East Jersey Street near Broad. At Dayton's dock, schooners would load for the West Indies and other parts of the world. Incoming ships often brought shingles from Virginia and merchandise from American and foreign ports. General Dayton enjoyed keeping store and directing the work at the wharf and warehouse. He also took pleasure in working his farm lots, some of which lay within the Borough. Through his agricultural skill he succeeded on one occasion in raising sixty bushels of corn to the acre, twenty-five being the ordinary yield.

After the Revolution Elizabethtown once again became a center for the practice of law. Among the returning lawyers was Elias Boudinot, who resumed his extensive law practice at his home near the Belcher Mansion. Matthias Ogden whose study of law was interrupted by the war, obtained a license and opened a law office soon after his return from Paris. Meanwhile, his brother Aaron took up the study of law with Robert, the older brother who had intermittently carried on his practice during the war. Aaron Ogden was twenty-eight when he received his license to practice law in 1784. Three years later, as a rising young lawyer, he married Elizabeth Chetwood (daughter of Judge John Chetwood), a charming lass who under the direction of Dr. Robert Halsted had nursed him back to health after he was wounded during the British raid in 1779.

Most of the Continental officers returning to Elizabethtown had belonged to the Continental Army chapter of the Free Masons (Military Lodge, Number 19). The old St. John's Lodge in Elizabethtown, founded by Jonathan Hampton before the war, did not survive the Revolution. For some unknown reason the St. John's chapter was not revived, and it was not until 1818 that

Elizabethtown had another lodge. In 1787 interest was shown in organizing a chapter when Aaron Ogden and Jonathan Dayton petitioned the New Jersey Lodge for permission to found a lodge in Elizabethtown. The request was granted but apparently not enough interest was shown to make it worthwhile. During the years ahead, some men in Elizabethtown were affiliated with lodges in neighboring towns. One of these doubtlessly was David Ross, the bellsmith who learned his trade from Aaron Miller before the Revolution. In one of his record books he copied a rhyme about an awkward lover who after becoming a Freemason became a polished gentleman and straightway won a maiden's heart. It was sung, he noted, to the tune of "Flowers in Edinburgh." [1]

Of inestimable value to post-war Elizabethtown and to the surrounding country was Sheppard Kollock's decision to publish a newspaper in the borough. Kollock was a well-known figure in the state before he moved to Elizabethtown in 1785 to set up his print shop. During the critical years when people were growing tired of the War for Independence, he had published a newspaper at Chatham, New Jersey, which had been a potent force in keeping the spirit of liberty alive.

Kollock was raised in Maryland where, after studying law, he went to work at the age of sixteen as a printer for his uncle, William Goddard, publisher of the *Philadelphia Chronicle*. A few years later he went to St. Croix where he worked as a journeyman printer for the *Danish American Gazette*. While there, he printed a description of a hurricane by a bright lad of fourteen, one Alexander Hamilton. When the news reached the West Indies of the revolt of the American colonies, Kollock hurried home to become a lieutenant in the Continental Artillery. At the Battle of Trenton, during which General Knox's artillery played an important role in winning the momentous victory, one of Kollock's fellow officers was Alexander Hamilton, whom he remembered as the author of the vivid description of the West Indian hurricane.

After the war, Kollock published a newspaper in New York as well as New Brunswick before coming to Elizabethtown to publish a newspaper under the wartime title, *The New Jersey Journal*. His shop was in the old White House built for Philip Carteret. The next year he moved to his father-in-law's house on Golden

Hill, as the elevation was called where East Jersey meets Broad Street. About a dozen years later, Kollock had a large three-story building constructed for his print shop and home opposite the Elizabethtown Academy on Broad Street. Carrying foreign and national news as well as some local items and much advertising, the weekly *New Jersey Journal* cost the subscriber only one dollar and a half a year. Post riders who carried the newspaper to outlying towns and farms gave the publication a wide circulation in northern New Jersey.

Not long after Kollock set up business in Elizabethtown he bought the old paper mill on the Elizabeth River about a mile west of the borough. Presumably this was the mill built by William Bradford about 1728; it produced paper for many books and almanacs as well as for newsprint.

Not much can be learned about the men and boys who worked for Sheppard Kollock. In 1793 he advertised for two boys who would be boarded and given schooling in return for their work at the mill as apprentices. At the print shop he had several apprentices as well as journeymen printers. Matthew Greene, a printer and cartographer from England, lived and worked with Kollock until his death in 1803. Another, Joseph Cree, worked as a journeyman for fifteen years and died during the yellow fever epidemic in 1798.[2]

When Sheppard Kollock moved to Elizabethtown at the age of thirty-five, he already had a sizeable family. One of his sons, destined to become a Presbyterian minister, was Henry Knox Kollock, born at New Providence during the Revolution and named in honor of Henry Knox, commander of the Continental artillery. Another was named after Kosciusko, the Polish engineer. After the collapse of the Polish war for independence, the crippled Kosciusko, on a visit to America, came to Elizabethtown where he was introduced to his namesake. Deeply touched, Kosciusko took from his coat a jewel awarded him for the defense of Poland and gave it to the boy.

Among the many books coming from Kollock's press was the first edition (1789) of Jedidiah Morse's *The American Geography,* one of the most celebrated publications of the day. Governor Livingston, to whom the book was dedicated, helped prepare the manuscript by supplying data on New Jersey and New York and reading it for errors and improvement of style. However, before the volume appeared, Morse became peeved at the delay attending its publication. "Mr. Morse is at Elizabethtown printing his geography. His printer treated him scurvily by appropriating paper intended for him to another use, and thus had delayed his work," wrote a friend of the author.

Most of Kollock's publications were books and tracts of a religious nature, which found a ready market throughout the country. Among the religious publications, the writings of the Reverend Jonathan Dickinson, founder of the College of New Jersey, went through several editions. He also published the third edition of the popular biography of Washington entitled *A History of the Life and Death, Virtues and Exploits, of General George Washington* by the Reverend Mason Locke Weems. The winter of 1802 saw this indefatigable writer and peddler of books and almanacs corroborating with Kollock in printing his life of Washington and doing some salesmanship on the side.

One of Kollock's publications of special interest was the story of Mary Kinnan's captivity and escape from the Indians. Mary Kinnan was born near Basking Ridge about 1763. After the Revolution she moved with her husband to western Virginia. During an Indian raid her husband was killed and she was captured. Kollock is said to have written the story as it was told to him by Mary Kinnan after her escape.

Sheppard Kollock was a religious man with a marked dislike for Deistic literature. When Thomas Paine, whom he had known and respected during the American Revolution, published his *Age of Reason* in 1794, Kollock wrote an "exposé" of the book in his newspaper. His dislike of attacks on orthodoxy by Paine and Voltaire, however, did not deter him from selling their books at his bookstore in the front room of his print shop.

One of Kollock's best selling items was his almanac, which he published year after year. A compilation of practical and curious information, this early "paperback" was eagerly read in every household. Like the lawyers, doctors, and everyone else, Kollock received little cash from his local customers and was satisfied to receive his pay in "country products" including firewood, butter and eggs, or anything which could be used or sold.

Civic-minded Sheppard Kollock, like his brother craftsman,

Benjamin Franklin, did much for his adopted town. In 1792 he helped organize a circulating library, of which Isaac H. Williamson, lawyer and future governor of the state, was for several years the librarian. He also helped the ladies of Elizabethtown organize their Female Humane Society, which saw a long and fruitful life.

For thirty-five years Kollock was a judge of the Court of Commons Pleas for Essex County. In 1822 as a reward for his long service as a leader of the Jeffersonian party in New Jersey, he became the postmaster of Elizabethtown. He sometimes served in the state assembly but was always an important figure at the political rallies, caucuses, and conventions.

Like many another who had fought in the War for Independence, Kollock was ready to forgive all but the most obnoxious Loyalists. America, he felt, could ill-afford to lose many gifted citizens. Hundreds had paid a high price for their loyalism by the loss of properties confiscated by the state. Now that the war was over and they had paid for their mistakes, Kollock asked that they be allowed to return and begin over again.[3]

One of the first of the Loyalists to return to Elizabethtown after the war was Dr. Thomas Bradbury Chandler, who had fled to England in 1775. His son, William, who stayed in America, became a captain in the loyalist New Jersey Volunteers. When the Reverend Chandler returned in 1785 after an absence of ten years, there were some people in Elizabethtown who wanted to put him on a ship and send him back to England. Dr. William Barnet and David Lyon who, Aaron Ogden thought, had not been as zealous for the cause as they should have been during the war, were shouting for revenge against the returning Loyalists. But moderation prevailed and Dr. Chandler was allowed to remain and even to resume his pulpit at St. John's. He was getting old, however, and his health soon became so impaired that the services were usually conducted by an assistant. Five years later he died.

Another Loyalist whose return to Elizabethtown excited little opposition was James Ricketts. Although he had joined the Royal Americans during the Revolution, he saw service in the West Indies rather than fight his old neighbors in New Jersey. Ricketts took over his father's farm on the road to the Point. He died there in 1824. The Ricketts farm was part of the land originally belonging to Philip Carteret. After the land was acquired by Richard Townley by his marriage to Carteret's widow, a marker was placed on the line dividing his property. The stone bearing the date 1694 still stands in front of the library on First Street. Sally De Hart, it is said, called the old farm Abyssinia after Samuel Johnson's *Rasselas, the Prince of Abyssinia,* a name that clung to this section of Elizabethtown for many years.

Another Loyalist to return to Elizabethtown was Cavalier Jouet. Since Jouet had actively assisted the enemy during the Revolution, feeling ran high against him. During the war, Cavalier was captured on Staten Island and brought to Woodbridge where he was allowed the freedom of the town on parole. The people treated him with civility. Consequently, at the close of the war in 1783, Jouet left New York with the intention of settling in Woodbridge. But to his surprise and mortification the very people who had shown him no discourtesy during his captivity were now ready to hang him from the nearest tree. At his first appearance on the street, a mob gathered. "Let's give Jouet a 'Continental Jacket,'" some shouted. Justice Henry Freeman and General Nathaniel Heard, who presently appeared, were no kinder. "What do you intend to do with the 'damned rascal'?" the General asked. Freeman shouted "Hang him, hang him!" More moderate men, however, soon arrived, among them Joseph Bloomfield, the future governor. Someone then spoke out and told how one of Jouet's sons had befriended him while he was a prisoner in British hands. At this the mob let the culprit go. Jouet soon returned to New York and sailed for England, not to return to America for another decade.[4]

When Cavalier Jouet returned to Elizabethtown in 1795 at the age of fifty-eight, he found the townspeople still cool, although they offered him no harm. All his property save that owned by his wife had been confiscated. It was now twenty years since Jouet had lived with his wife and younger children, who had remained in Elizabethtown during his long absence. Fortunately, Mrs. Jouet had been left with a sizeable estate by her father, Jonathan Hampton, when he died in 1777.

In England Jouet studied at Oxford while living on a pension from the British government. He returned to Elizabethtown an

Elias Boudinot. Courtesy Princeton University.

ordained Episcopalian minister seeking a pulpit in America. The heads of the Church realized, however, that this was quite impossible. The American Episcopal Church was weak enough without having ministers who would excite division in the congregation. Jouet finally went back to England where he died in 1810. So bitter was the feeling against him that it was many years after his death before a font (reputed to be of Roman origin) which he had given to St. John's before the Revolution, was brought back into the church.[5]

Though Cavalier Jouet was disliked by the people of Elizabethtown to his dying day, he was never hated like Cornelius Hatfield, the leader of so many vengeful raids on his hometown. Not until nearly thirty years after the war did Hatfield dare to return to lay claim to the property left by his patriotic father. Then no sooner did he appear than the whole town blazed with anger and indignation. However, before violence befell him, Hatfield was arrested for murders committed during the war and brought before Judge Pennington at Newark. Aaron Ogden, Isaac H. Williamson, and William Chetwood, Jr., all Elizabethtown lawyers, appeared for the culprit. Hatfield was finally discharged for the reason that the Treaty of Paris made him not answerable for his crimes during the Revolution. With his life unsafe in America, Hatfield left for England, where he lived the remainder of his days.[6]

Joining Sheppard Kollock, Aaron Ogden, and others favoring forgiveness of the Loyalists, was Elias Boudinot, the president of Congress at the close of the war. Boudinot was a very serious man who wrote long sermonizing letters to his only daughter, Susan Vergereau. Repeatedly he reminded her that she should never forget that her parents had taken the utmost care of her spiritual welfare. "Our baptismal vows for you were public and formal, and they have been daily renewed before God, from that day to this," he wrote.[7] In 1784 Boudinot's "little Eve Lamb" married William Bradford, a noted Philadelphia lawyer and friend of Washington. Parting with her naturally filled Boudinot's heart with sorrow.

Boudinot lived in Elizabethtown for about a decade after the war before retiring to his country seat, Rose Hill, in Burlington. While at Elizabethtown he kept up a correspondence with Washington, with whom he exchanged seeds and agricultural information. During this time he became a member of the Philadelphia Society for the Promotion of Agriculture, to which he contributed an article in 1787 on the Hessian fly.

Although Elias Boudinot is chiefly remembered for his services as Commissary of Prisoners during the Revolution and one-time president of the Continental Congress, he deserves recognition also for his numerous literary endeavors. Most of his writings were confined to the subject of religion and were published after he moved to Burlington. In 1801 appeared his *Age of Reason shewn to be an Age of Infidelity,* one of the many attacks on Thomas Paine and on Deism to appear about this time. In 1816 was published his *Star of the West, an Humble attempt to discover the long lost Ten Tribes of Israel.* The theory that the Indians were descendants of the lost tribes of Israel, which he expounded, was nothing new; it had been proposed by New England writers at a very early date.

During his lifetime, Elias Boudinot accumulated a large fortune, most of which was invested in lands in New Jersey, Pennsylvania, New York, and Ohio. Long before his death he began making lavish gifts to worthwhile causes. To Princeton he gave a cabinet of books on natural history, valued at three thousand dollars. Princeton also received two grants for fellowships that are still extant. To the Presbyterian Church in Elizabethtown he gave a set of handsome chandeliers.* Frequent grants were made by Boudinot for the support of the American Bible Society of which he was the founder and president for many years. His namesake, Elias Boudinot, the famous Cherokee Indian, was educated at an Indian school at Cornwall, Connecticut, which was founded and endowed by Boudinot. In his will he left land to a society for improving the welfare of New York Jews, for educating the Indians, for foreign missions, for the American Bible Society, for the poor of Philadelphia, and for missionary work in the hospitals and prisons of the country.

After the Revolution, as during the long conflict, William Livingston remained the most revered man in the state of New Jersey. Each year until his death in 1790, he was reelected governor. At

* One of the chandeliers saved from a fire which destroyed most of the church hangs in the vestibule. The chandeliers in the church are replicas.

William Livingston. Courtesy Sons of the Revolution in the State of New York.

View of the Livingston Mansion, Elizabethtown.

one time or another Elias Dayton and Abraham Clark received some support for the gubernatorial office but each time they were soundly defeated by the old war governor.

Like Washington and Jefferson and so many distinguished men of his day, Livingston enjoyed tending his garden and orchards. Brissot, the French traveler, called him a skillful writer, a great governor, and a plowman. The latter appellation, he noted, pleased Livingston most of all. Without affectation, Livingston called himself a New Jersey farmer.

On visiting Liberty Hall one would discover without looking far what Livingston enjoyed most. Scattered about his workshop were fishing tackle, garden tools, and books that he had taken from his library of more than five hundred volumes. One day while working in his shop, he called his daughter Susanna to come and see how rich he was in real estate. On entering she found his bench covered with wren houses, a kind of property that gave her father more pleasure than all the real estate one could own. As an agriculturalist, Livingston experimented with seeds from all over the world. To his son, Brockholst, serving as secretary to John Jay in Spain, he wrote in 1780 asking him to send to Liberty Hall all the seeds of flowering shrubs, melons, and other plants growing in Spain which were likely to thrive in New Jersey.

During the years following the War for Independence, Liberty Hall was frequented by many distinguished visitors who came to pay their respects to the old philosopher. British and French officers came to call before going home. Among these were Sir Edmund Assleck and Monsieur de Barbé Marbois. George and Martha Washington also called on the Governor several times during this period. Most looked for of all his visitors, however, was Livingston's little grandson, Peter, son of John Jay and Livingston's daughter Sarah. Peter "brightened the gloom" of the aging man as he helped the youngster through his lessons and took him rambling about the farm. John Jay came with his wife and children as occasion permitted. The two men enjoyed going down to the mill dam behind the house to fish and talk politics. Sometimes, since his father-in-law was fond of seafood, Jay brought from New York a mess of lobsters "notwithstanding their British uniforms!"

During the period of the Confederation, Livingston lent his voice and pen to educating people on the need of a stronger central government. In 1787, as one of New Jersey's delegates he had the satisfaction of attending the Constitutional Convention in Philadelphia. After the Constitution was drafted, he helped to secure its early adoption by the New Jersey legislature. Back home again, Livingston had the help of his "principal secretary of state," as he called his daughter Catherine. Washington once remarked that it was fortunate Livingston had Catherine to write for him since no one could ever decipher his handwriting.

In an age noted for its philosophers and thinkers, William Livingston stands high among the men of vision. In his political philosophy, he believed that sovereignty rests with the people. He was critical, however, of too much democracy since the uneducated masses might not properly understand the issues. Like Franklin, he believed that education should prepare for life and not be primarily cultural or ornamental in character. Society, he thought, had a right to set goals for its education which to him was the cultivation of the individual as a useful member of a free society. He was a believer in academic freedom. "As a person," he wrote, "who resolves to hear but one side of a Controversy, can never be said to be seeking the truth, so no Student can make an advantageous Progress in Knowledge, when he is not freely indulged—both in Conversation and Reading."

Nominally a Presbyterian, Livingston believed that no sect had a monopoly of God's favor. It was not necessary, he said, to be a church member to be a good Christian. He disliked all pomp and ritual, feeling that religion should be simple, based purely upon a trust in God. Naturally he distrusted hierarchies and churches established and supported by the state. "All the Religious Establishments in the world are manifest violations of the right of private judgment in matters of religion," declared the sage of Liberty Hall. With Deism he had little in common, believing, as he did, in revealed religion and in the customary Christian doctrines. Lines from a poem written in his youth sum up his belief in immortality.[8]

> And when with age thy head is silvered o'er,
> And cold in death, thy bosom beats no more,

Thy soul, exulting, shall desert its clay,
And mount triumphant to eternal day.

Two years before his death in 1790, Livingston's alma mater, Yale, conferred upon him the degree of doctor of laws, with President Ezra Stiles officiating. During his last year, shortly after the death of his wife, Livingston had a ray of hope that his son, John, supposedly lost at sea on the *Saratoga* during the Revolution, was alive and a prisoner in Algeria. It happened that a sailor came to Liberty Hall with a story that, as a captive in Algiers, he had met John who was kept at hard labor on the city's fortifications. His description of the young man did not seem true. But it nonetheless raised hope in the breast of the old man at Liberty Hall. John Jay was skeptical but he promised to write and ask the French and English counsels in Algiers to investigate. Six months later Livingston was dead. The home and the life he loved can be appreciated through the lines of his poem written more than forty years before.

Full in the centre of some shady grove
By nature form'd for solitude and love—
On banks array'd with ever-blooming flowers,
Near beauteous landscapes, or by roseate bowers,
My neat, but simple mansion would I raise.

Oft would I wander through the dewy field,
Where clustering roses balmy fragrance yield;
Or, in lone grots of contemplation made,
Converse with angels and the mighty dead.

Unfortunately William Livingston did not live to see his daughter Susanna marry Judge John Cleves Symmes, the noted land speculator. With Susanna's marriage, Liberty Hall in the early years of the 1790's once again became a lively place; it was then owned by Livingston's son, Henry Brockholst Livingston. Not long after Susanna and Symmes were married, his daughter, Anna, by an earlier marriage, eloped with William Henry Harrison, a young army officer who had recently fought the Indians with General Wayne in Ohio. According to tradition, Anna made her escape to join the future president of the United States by climbing out one of the first floor windows of Liberty Hall.

In 1798, Henry Brockholst Livingston sold Liberty Hall to the Englishman, Lord Bolingbroke (known in America as Belasise) who had run away from his wife with a school girl, Isabella Charlotte Antoinette Sophia, niece of the last grand master of Malta. The Bolingbrokes lived in the house until 1806 when they went back to England to live, following the death of Bolingbroke's first wife.

With the departure of the Bolingbrokes, Liberty Hall after being owned successively by Thomas Eddy and Thomas Salter was purchased in 1811 by Susan Niemcewicz, a niece of the Governor's, who had married Count Niemcewicz after the death of her first husband, John Kean of Charleston. After Niemcewicz had returned to Europe (he resided for most of the remainder of his life in Paris), his step-son, Peter Kean, renamed the house Ursino in honor of the Count to whom he had been much attached.

Count Julian Ursyn Niemcewicz who lived in Elizabethtown from 1797 to 1807 was a renowned Polish patriot and playwright. Born in Poland in 1758, he received his education at a military school near Warsaw. Following his graduation he was sent to Paris by the King of Poland as an attaché with the diplomatic corps. Here he met Thomas Jefferson and other Americans, from whom he imbibed a strong love for democracy. As an avowed liberal, after serving in the Imperial Diet, Niemcewicz became the editor of the first Polish republican newspaper. Meanwhile he acquired a reputation as a poet and dramatist. His *The Deputy Returns* is considered the most original Polish comedy of the eighteenth century. In 1794 Niemcewicz joined Kosciusko in his fight for Polish liberty. Both were captured and, after serving three years in prison, banished to America.

After traveling about America for a time, Niemcewicz settled in Elizabethtown. Here he gave French and history lessons to the twelve-year-old Peter Kean, prior to his matriculation at Princeton. This led to a friendship between the Count and the mother; eventually the widow asked the penniless Count to become her husband. It was not, however, until it was agreed that the Count would have no claim to Susan's fortune that her brothers and sisters would consent to the marriage.

Following the marriage, the Count spent his time in gardening, tutoring Peter, and occasionally taking a trip to see more of the country and its people. At first the couple lived for about a year at Hampton Place, the house which had been purchased from the heirs of Dr. William Barnet by an Englishman named Hampton. Thereafter they lived in a small house on the north side of Water Street which Susan purchased from Jonathan Dayton.*

Niemcewicz never seemed to have become attached to life in Elizabethtown or to his thrifty wife, who was about fifty and far from beautiful. In 1802 he returned to Poland to settle his father's estate. When he returned to Elizabethtown two years later, he evidently expected to stay for he procured his citizenship through the good offices of his friend, Aaron Ogden. Hoping, however, that he could help Poland regain its independence with the help of Napoleon, he went back to Europe in 1807, never again to return to America. In Europe he was for many years deeply involved in war and politics. Later in life he once again resumed his interest in music, poetry, and drama. Susan died in 1833, leaving her penniless husband a small annuity. Niemcewicz died in Paris in 1841 surrounded by a circle of friends numbering among them the great writers and composers of the day.[9]

Many prominent men of Elizabethtown, including Elias Boudinot, Jonathan Dayton, and Matthias and Aaron Ogden, held shares and took an active interest in western land speculation, especially in the Ohio tract belonging to John Cleves Symmes and his associates. Matthias Ogden served as attorney for many stockholders of the Symmes's tract before his untimely death in 1791. In Congress, Jonathan Dayton, who became speaker of the Fifth Congress, kept a close watch over the interests of the company. In 1790, he reported to Symmes that only after great effort was a bill defeated which would have reduced the price of public land to the detriment of the land companies.

Matthias Ogden's association with western land speculation was but one of his many business interests. As his war record shows, he was a man of unusual talents and boundless energy. After becoming a member of the State Council in 1785, he received a contract for transporting the mails between New York and Philadelphia by a stage line in which he held an interest.

* The house had been previously owned by Elias Boudinot and still earlier by Abraham Clark. A theater now occupies the site at 1119 Elizabeth Avenue.

Not long after receiving the mail contract, Ogden pushed through the legislature a bill for the coining of three million copper coins to relieve the money shortage in New Jersey. When the contract for minting was made, Ogden became one of the principals in the enterprise. The coins were minted in Rahway, Morristown, and Elizabethtown. Those made in Elizabethtown were stamped in a woodshed off the kitchen of the old house Matthias had inherited from his father. Known as the horsehead pennies, on one side there was a horsehead with the date 1788 and the words *Nova Caesarea*. On the other side was a shield and the *E Pluribus Unum* which, it is said, the Federal government borrowed when it adopted the motto for its silver coins.[10]

After the Revolution Matthias Ogden and his brother-in-law, Colonel Oliver Spencer,* who owned a large house on the corner of Spring and Water streets, took over the tannery which had been handed down in the family since the days of John Ogden, the founder. It was a large tannery processing as many as fifteen hundred hides a day. Bark was ground in a mill consisting of two large wheels fitted with iron teeth and powered by two horses. The vats in which the hides were placed with ground bark and water were emptied with wooden buckets on long poles. One journeyman and five apprentices made up the work force at the tannery. One of the workmen, William Edwards, was a nephew of Ogden's who complained bitterly that his employers overworked and underfed him. The poor lad finally became so sick from over-work and undernourishment that he quit his job and went back to his home in Connecticut.[11]

When in 1791 Matthias Ogden died of yellow fever at the age of thirty-six, his passing was deeply mourned. The New York chapter of the Cincinnati asked all members to wear a mourning ban for three weeks in honor of the hero who fought so gallantly in the War for Independence. Years later when Lafayette visited Elizabethtown, he walked through the old Presbyterian cemetery arm-in-arm with Sheppard Kollock. At Ogden's grave he lingered long in reminiscence of the days when Matthias was one of his closest friends.

Matthias Ogden was survived by his older brother, Robert, and

* Spencer sold out and moved to Ohio in 1790.

by Aaron, his younger brother. Robert, the crippled brother who had stayed at home during the war, became a resident of Sparta by inheriting a farm from his father. He was one of the founders of the Cliosophic Society at Princeton and was known far and wide as the "Honest Lawyer." Before moving to Sparta, he lost a six-year-old son who drowned in the Elizabeth River. "Yesterday noon I had all the dear little Flock around me, at dinner, in health peace & Love," he mournfully wrote.

Great was the rejoicing and splendid the occasion when Washington came to Elizabethtown in April, 1789, on his way to New York for his inauguration as president of the United States. With him was an imposing entourage including such celebrities as Henry Knox, Charles Carroll, John Langdon, and Theodorick Bland. Though in poor health, Governor Livingston rode out with Elias Boudinot, Elias Dayton, Aaron Ogden and others to meet the president-elect. Matthias Ogden and Matthias Williamson were in charge of the long line of militia and light horse which escorted the procession to the Red Lion Inn near the Court House where welcoming speeches were made. After the reception at the Inn, Washington and his party rode to the home of Elias Boudinot where they were joined by the town fathers for a sumptuous banquet. At his spacious home, Boudinot could entertain royally. The serving was on beautiful china embellished in bright colors with the Boudinot coat of arms. The luxurious silverware was made in Paris, London, and New York, some, perhaps, by Boudinot's father, a noted silversmith.

After the banquet, Washington and his party were escorted to De Hart's Point to take passage for New York. Elias Boudinot and many of Washington's Elizabethtown friends went along to witness the inauguration. As the flotilla sailed out into the channel, the militia on shore fired a parting salute. Other boats joined the fleet of little vessels as the President's sloop, porpoises swimming nearby, sailed through the bay to the crowds waiting at the city's wharves.

Washington had been in Elizabethtown many times before and would come again on his travels between Virginia and New York. But on this occasion the new president doubtlessly met the last president of the old Congress who for a short time was making Elizabethtown his home. The out-going president was Cyrus

Griffin, a Virginia lawyer who in his youth had married and run away with a daughter of the Earl of Traquair. Sometime after the inauguration, Washington appointed Griffin a federal judge for Virginia.[12]

Ever since the close of the Revolution, discussion had turned upon the question of a suitable location for the capital of the United States. In 1783, Elias Boudinot told General Dayton that he thought Elizabethtown should "make an offer of their Township for the Seat of Congress, if they think it an object worth obtaining." If chosen for the capital, the township, he thought, should become a district separate from the state and under the jurisdiction of Congress. Elizabethtown as well as Trenton and New Brunswick continued to be considered as possible sites for the nation's capital. However, after Hamilton submitted his plan for the assumption of state war debts by the Federal government, northerners conceded to southern demands for placing the capital south of the Potomac in order to secure the adoption of the assumption bill.

With the adoption of the United States Constitution and the emergence of the party system, Elizabethtown with its aristocratic families became a stronghold of Federalism in New Jersey. From the beginning, however, there were some political leaders in Elizabethtown who opposed the Constitution and became associated with the Jeffersonian party. Foremost among these was Abraham Clark, signer of the Declaration of Independence and an influential member of the Continental Congress.

Born in Elizabethtown township (Roselle), Abraham Clark was as a boy too frail for hard work. A precocious youth, he in time acquired a good knowledge of surveying and the law. Fortune smiled on the industrious young man, for by 1773 he was the owner of fulling mills in Elizabethtown * and Rahway. By this time, too, he had gained a substantial law practice. Never asking legal fees from those who could not afford them, Clark became known as the "poor man's lawyer." His fame as the champion of the rights of the common man grew in 1784 when he pushed through the legislature measures known as "Clark laws," which restricted the power of lawyers and lessened court costs.

* Probably Trotter's Mill.

Succeeding in their purpose, the new laws according to Clark tore "off the ruffles from the lawyers' waists."

Abraham Clark began his political career as high sheriff of Essex County in 1767. At the outbreak of the Revolution he was secretary for the New Jersey Council of Safety. After the war, when the question of amending the Articles of Confederation arose, he attended the Annapolis Convention in 1786. The next year he was elected to the Philadelphia Convention that framed the Constitution, but ill-health prevented him from attending. Fearing the loss of liberties, Clark opposed the Constitution until the adoption of the Bill of Rights removed his objections. He served in the Second and Third Congresses and in 1794, the year he died, sponsored a strong resolution to force Great Britain to recognize American rights on our western borders and on the high seas. Next to William Livingston, Abraham Clark was the most outstanding statesman from Elizabethtown during the Revolutionary period.

When the Revolution ended, the principal families of Elizabethtown continued to own slaves. A traveler in 1794 noted that the slaves had separate little houses behind the mansion house since they stole too much to be allowed to live in the big house. Despite the prevalence of slavery in Elizabethtown, the Revolutionary spirit had brought a change in the thinking of the inhabitants toward slavery. Already many were freeing slaves or providing for their freedom in their wills. Hannah Ogden, widow of Colonel Matthias Ogden, freed her mulatto slave, Michael Hardman, age twenty-six, in 1797. Earlier Governor Livingston freed his two slaves out of respect for "the natural liberties of mankind, and in order to set an example." Cavalier Jouet freed his slave Lucie when he returned to America in 1795, since it was inconsistent "with the Precepts of Humanity & of the Christian Religion to hold in Vassalage any of the Human Species." Abraham Clark also freed his slaves before he died. In 1805 the Reverend Thomas Morrell advertised for a black couple who were promised their freedom after a term of service. In 1792, Elias Boudinot took steps to break up a ring of slave traders when it was discovered that Negroes were being purchased in Elizabethtown for sale in New Orleans. Although manumission was going forward, there were slaves in Elizabethtown for many years to come. Aaron Ogden, for instance, had one or two slaves until he met with bankruptcy in the 1820's.[13]

After the Revolution Elizabethtown grew very slowly. It continued to have its rural setting with its large lots, its well-cultivated gardens, its orchards, and its open fields in sight of the center of town. William Dunlap, the noted playwright and artist, left an impression of the beauty and delights of pastoral Elizabethtown. "This is the Hay Harvest, where the Mowers have passed we see the Bobolink, Blackbird, Robin, Meadow Lark & other birds very busy among the grass stubble.—The wild rose yet blooms in the fields & along the fences where it in some places almost forms a hedge. The Catalpa is in full bloom & the number of trees about this place not only add to the beauty but to the fragrance of the town." [14] No wonder wealthy New Yorkers and Émigrés from the West Indies were choosing Elizabethtown as a country home and a place of retirement.

X

Elizabethtown: The Early National Period

In September 1790, there passed through Elizabethtown a Mr. Spiller, an officer captured with Burgoyne's Army during the Revolution. Spiller was a renowned walker, having walked through most of the countries of Europe and North Africa. In North America he had already walked 1,100 miles; he was in fact on his way to New Orleans when he came through Elizabethtown. Other matters, too, there were to talk about in Elizabethtown besides the everyday occurrences. One day, Colonel M'Gillivary, the Creek Indian, came through town with about thirty braves on his way from Georgia to New York to make peace with the United States. Elizabethtonians marveled when Captain Obediah Meeker raised an ox weighing 2,284 pounds. With smiles and chuckles they read a newspaper advertisement inserted by Mrs. Reynolds offering five dollars to anyone returning her runaway husband. In those days townspeople were singing "Yankee Doodle," "Queen Mary's Lament," and songs about the death of Major John André. Frenchmen were amused whenever an American girl essayed to sing. She put on a grave face, drew down her features, sat rigid in a chair with her eyes on the floor, and then began to sing as though petrified. Otherwise the girls were lively enough. For the young women, church-going appeared to be more an occasion for the display of their finery than a desire to worship.[1]

In 1793 the yellow fever, which was terrorizing the larger cities, caused Elizabethtown to take measures to protect the lives of the people. At a town meeting it was decided that infected travelers would be hospitalized in a house in an isolated spot. A health committee, consisting of General Dayton, Jeremiah Ballard, and doctors Halsted, Morse, Williamson, and Clark,* was appointed

* Dr. Clark died, 1794, age 36.

to carry out the resolutions of the meeting. Any house with a patient was to be quarantined and a sign posted on the door.[2]

By the 1790's most of the older doctors of the Revolutionary generation had died and new ones had risen to take their places. Dr. William Barnet died in 1790. Young doctors, men like Matthias H. Williamson, perhaps were no better than their predecessors but they at least possessed the energy and buoyancy required of their calling. Dr. Williamson, a son of General Matthias Williamson, received his degree in 1793 with a thesis on yellow fever attended with ulcerated sore throat.[3] Opening an office opposite Meeker's store, Williamson offered free service to people too poor to pay the customary fee. With a fortune in outstanding bills and little money coming in, Williamson was happy to be chosen sheriff for Essex County in 1801. Another young doctor soon appeared from one of the town's leading families. This was Dr. John Chetwood, whose long period of service began when he opened an office opposite St. John's Church where he sold the usual line of drugs and medicines.

Probably the best qualified doctor of the 1790's was Dr. Paul Micheau, a graduate of the University of Edinburgh and one time fellow at the London School of Medicine. Not long after he came to Elizabethtown, Micheau opened a medical school, supplying, it seems, all of the instruction. On one occasion he lectured to a large audience on surgery in the long room of the Wales Tavern. With some of the doctors and members of the New Jersey Medical Society critical of his methods and theories, Micheau gathered a group of followers and formed a new medical association. Not long after he came to Elizabethtown, he married Maria Vergereau. She was a daughter of widow Abigail Vergereau, owner of much real estate, including an "oil mill." * Maria soon died; he (who himself was to die not long after) composed a touching tribute for her gravestone.

> Closed are those eyes in endless night,
> No more to beam with fond delight, or with affection roll;
> Eternal silence seals that tongue,
> Where sense and soft persuasion hung,
> To captivate the soul.

* Linseed oil.

Besides the regular practitioners, Elizabethtown had its share of quack doctors. One who came to town in 1799 was a Dr. Baldwin who claimed a cure through the use of his healing salves for lameness and distorted bones and muscles. Even his eyewater was guaranteed to strengthen the eye nerves. Very popular was Dr. Hamilton's "Grand Restorative," an elixir guaranteed to cure coughs, colds, hysterical affections, inward weakness, violent cramps, indigestion, gout, rheumatism, and almost any other affliction. Lee's "Ointment" for the itch was also in great demand. Hopkins' "Genuine Eye Water" was advertised to clear the eyes and improve vision. It would also keep the teeth from falling out by tightening the gums. Other standard "cures" were Dr. Atkinson's "Genuine and Infallible Worm Destroying Lozengers," Dr. Hunter's "Genuine Antibilious Pills," Dr. Bardwell's "Genuine Ague and Fever Drops" and his "Animating Silver Tincture or Pablum of Life," "Aromatic Lozengers of Steel," and "Anodyne Essence" for headaches.

Not all the traveling doctors and dentists were purely quacks. Dr. Loga from New York, an occulist and dentist, had an office at the Union Hotel for several days in 1813. This was long enough to extract the teeth of those in sufficient pain to cause them to seek his services. During his stay the Doctor also sold eye-glasses. Most of the traveling dentists and doctors as well as the local ones, made and sold false teeth (made from hippopotamus ivory), an article in demand by almost everyone over thirty.

For those who preferred to do their own doctoring, family medicine books could be purchased at Sheppard Kollock's book store or at one of the stores in town. William Buchan's *Family Physician or Domestic Medicine* was one of the most popular medical books. Experienced women continued to be called upon for midwifery and nursing. Not uncommon were newspaper advertisements such as the one offering the services of a "well recommended" wet nurse with "a young breast of milk." [4]

Not until 1790 did the people of Elizabethtown feel able to rebuild the Court House and jail burned during the Revolution. In January, following the reactivation of the Charter by a legislative act, the newly appointed mayor, John De Hart, met with the Aldermen and Common Council at the Red Lion Inn and voted to raise £1,250 by taxation for a Court House and jail. A planning committee consisting of Mayor De Hart, General Dayton, Jeremiah Ballard and several others was appointed. At the next meeting of the Corporation, the resolution for raising the funds by taxation was rescinded following complaint by the taxpayers. At another meeting the town fathers decided to try to get the money from Congress as a compensation for war losses. This failed. The Corporation then went bravely ahead and ordered stone and lumber for the Court House. Apparently it was agreed that the money would be raised by a lottery. Accordingly by a legislative act Elizabethtown was permitted to raise £2,500 (in terms of New York currency) by lottery. The lottery, the tickets for which were printed by Sheppard Kollock, was conducted by General Dayton, Jeremiah Ballard, and Mayor De Hart. Lottery receipts came in slowly but since the builder and suppliers were willing to operate on credit, the construction proceeded rapidly.

Supervision of the construction of the Court House and jail was entrusted to Job Haines, a prominent merchant and treasurer for the Borough. When finished, the Court House was a handsome three story brick building with a belfry holding a large brass bell made by David Ross.* On the first floor were three or four court rooms. A large room, presumably on the second floor, was used for public meetings. Other rooms were reserved for the caretaker or were rented. The jail, in the basement, was used to house run-away slaves, the poor, and the insane.

The people had just settled back to enjoy their Court House when it burned to the ground in 1808. The fire was set by a demented boy who was locked in the jail and who perished in the flames. This time the Corporation acted promptly by voting a tax for a new building. When ready for occupancy in 1810, the new Court House with its bell cupola resembled the former structure. For many years the third floor was rented to the Washington Chapter of the Masonic Lodge, which was organized in 1818.[5]

The year the Court House burned, Elizabethtown and Newark nearly came to blows, so heated was the rancor which found its way into the newspapers. The dispute arose over the location of a Court House for Essex County. Newark, which had far out-

* The bell is now in the possession of the Elizabethtown Historical Society, Elizabeth, N.J.

stripped Elizabethtown in population, was determined that the Court House should stay in Newark where it had been since the creation of Essex County in the seventeenth century. Elizabethtonians jealously favored Day's Hill at Camptown * for the site of the county building. In the election on the issue, Newark won. When the result of the election was known all Elizabethtown was ablaze with indignation. A town meeting was called with Dr. Robert Halsted in the chair and Thaddeus Mills acting as secretary. The meeting rightfully resolved that since 13,000 votes had been cast in a county with a population of only 22,000, the election was a fraud and should be re-run. Elizabethtown, however, got little support from the other towns and was compelled in the end to accept the decision that the Court House be in Newark.[6]

One of the principal duties of the Corporation was the regulation of the public market. The market pavilion, erected by the Borough, in this period stood on the east side of Broad Street next to the Stone Bridge. Market days were prescribed for every month except January, February, and March. As was the custom in America, the ringing of a bell on the Court House or nearby church announced the opening and the closing each day. The clerk of the market was a very important man. He let out stalls, collected the rents, and saw that the place was kept clean. Fines were imposed for disobeying the rules, such as the one against throwing refuse into the river. Market hours were early, from daylight until nine in the morning. While the market was open, no meat, fowl, butter, cheese, or eggs could be sold within one mile of it.[7]

As usual, town ordinances for the protection of health and property rights occupied the attention of Borough officials. Ordinances were passed and amended from time to time against throwing garbage in the streets or allowing geese and swine to roam the town. Cows and horses, as well as sheep and swine, continued to get loose and wander away. In 1801 Poundkeeper Job Haines advertised horses for sale which had fallen into his hands. At this time there were over one thousand cattle, four hundred horses, and several hundred sheep within the boundaries of the Borough. Daniel Ogden, the village herder, asked all persons not wishing to have their sheep put into the village herd to keep them properly confined.[8]

* Now Irvington.

Other town ordinances were passed as the need arose. Bakers had to have their names and the weight stamped on the bread they sold. No one could hunt quail or partridge within the limits of the Borough from February to October. There was no law, however, against killing or catching the countless passenger pigeons which, when caught and fed for a few days, became as tender to eat as any domestic fowl. The town could have had an ordinance, too, against speeding, especially the racing to the salt meadows, scythes and pitchforks bouncing in the open carts. One man was killed while racing another farmer to the meadows when his cart turned over. Out in the meadows the Corporation kept the great ditch well-dredged for drainage. In town it continued to hire a watch to patrol the streets by night.

As a national holiday the Fourth of July was a great occasion for celebrating and rejoicing. It was a day, too, when fervent speeches were made lauding the principles of the American Revolution. One of the finest speeches given in Elizabethtown was made in 1793 when Elias Boudinot gave an oration dedicated to President Washington. The Constitution, he told his audience assembled in front of the Presbyterian Church, was founded on the rights of man. Men are not equal in ability, he reminded his hearers, but in America they are equal before the law. "Every man," he declared, "has a natural right to be governed by laws of his own making, either in person or by his representative, and that no authority ought justly to be exercised over him, that is not derived from the people, of whom he is one."

Elias Boudinot had come a long way in his political thinking from the days before the Revolution. From a most conservative man he had become a liberal Federalist. "The meanest citizen of America," he went on to say, "could educate his beloved child with the hope that he might someday command armies, or even fill the president chair." This birthright was unique among nations, he said, and the whole world was watching the American experiment as it unfolded. Boudinot perceived, too, that the standards for women were changing in America. "The Rights of Women are no longer strange sounds to an American ear,—and I devoutly hope the day is not far distant when we shall find them dignifying, in a distinguishing code, the jurisprudence of the several states of the Union." Sensing that the country would soon launch upon a great program of internal improvement, Boudinot saw canals connecting the east and the west by scores of waterways.[9]

Another inspiring Fourth of July speech was delivered the next year by Isaac Watts Crane, who later became the first master of the Adelphian Academy. The speaker asked the people to pray for the success of the Jay Treaty which he hoped would prevent war with Great Britain. He then extolled the American militia, the bulwark of the country's defense. In closing he asked all to stand behind the Federal Constitution, the "palladium" of our liberties. People, he said, should not let the jarring interests of individuals undermine the country.[10]

In planning the Fourth of July celebration it was usual to call a town meeting for choosing a program committee. As many militia companies as possible were enrolled for the parade. The town's own units, consisting of Captain William Crane's Grenadiers, Captain Matthias Williamson's Light Troops, Captain Obediah Meeker's Light Horse, and Captain Williams' Artillery, were seldom absent. All militiamen with complete uniforms were expected to turn out. At the head of the militia General Dayton had first honors, followed by General Matthias Williamson. The parade ended at the Presbyterian Church, rebuilt in 1786. Here prayers were said, speeches delivered, and songs sung. After the service those who had participated in the parade were given refreshments at the town's expense. During the day the members of the Cincinnati had a banquet. Late in the afternoon the town's leading men and their wives gathered for refreshments under a bower erected for the occasion. All during the day the town was crowded with people from near and far. All appeared bent upon enjoying the festivities to the fullest. On one Fourth of July, Ford Cutter served a forty-four pound turtle as a special attraction at the Red Lion Inn.

When the French Revolution and the revolts in the West Indies shook the French nation to its foundations, many refugees sought a haven in the United States for their lives and property. In all about twenty-five thousand French came to the United States in the 1790's. Many of them fled without anything but the clothes on their backs and thus were forced to be the recipients of charity in scores of American towns and cities. For its size, Elizabethtown with an estimated 120 refugees was an asylum of considerable importance. Most of the Elizabethtown émigrés came with money and bought farms and town properties with elegant houses for the gracious living of their class.[11]

In Elizabethtown the French exiles found old Huguenot families who made a special effort to help them. Elias Boudinot, for one, did all in his power to make the newcomers feel at home. In Congress, he made a speech reminding Americans how much the nation owed to French aid during the American Revolution.

But more than to the Huguenots, refugees turned to native-born Frenchmen who had settled in America. In Elizabethtown they had a friend and advisor in the aristocratic Chevalier D'Anterroches. With so many Frenchmen settling in Elizabethtown, D'Anterroches was a busy man. For the wealthy Monsieur Paul de Malherbes of Martinique he supervised the building of an elegant mansion near the Wheatsheaf Tavern on the road to Rahway.

Even among people of English extraction, the exiles found that most of the men with a college education had a fair command of French. Many of those who knew no French were soon busy endeavoring to learn enough of the language to be able to converse with the newcomers. In Elizabethtown lawyer Thomas P. Johnson, who spoke French fluently, became the favorite legal advisor for the refugees. With the town rapidly assuming a cosmopolitan complexion, Dr. George Ross saw fit to advertise his medicines in both French and English.

Many of the French waited for the time to come when they could return to their former homes; they did not care to engage in any line of business in America. Others found employment for their talents. Those who purchased or rented farms worked the land with slaves brought from the West Indies. One of these was Mrs. Perrier, who advertised in 1804 for three runaway slaves who spoke little but French. Some few, especially in the larger cities, were merchants with business houses; others were hairdressers, milliners, dressmakers, etc. Many became teachers, vying with one another for students for their classes in music, painting, dancing, fencing, and in the French language.

Although few of the émigrés remained in America for more than a decade, they left an indelible impression on American culture. With their coming a wave of enthusiasm for French culture swept the country. French fashions, furniture, food, drink, jewelry, music, art, etiquette, and amusements became the vogue. In Philadelphia the people even became accustomed to seeing a French bishop parading the streets with a mulatto mistress.

If Elizabethtown had no French bishop of the kind found in Philadelphia, it at least had an array of French aristocrats almost as interesting. Townspeople could never refrain from smiling when they saw Frenchmen embracing and kissing on the streets. Everyone was fascinated by the elegance of their living. Paul de Malherbes' mansion had fourteen rooms with twelve fireplaces, Venetian blinds, and lavish furniture. Beautiful, too, was the furniture and equipage belonging to Jean Gabriel Prevost Touchimbert, who lived in the large mansion formerly owned by John Nutman opposite General Dayton's residence on East Jersey Street. Touchimbert, one of the wealthiest refugees, dealt in real estate and made loans to less fortunate émigrés. Out in the township (Springfield) lived Monsieur La Croix with his "tawny, elegant black-eyed Creole" wife.[12]

One of the most prominent of the French refugees in Elizabethtown was Lady Anne Renée du Verger de Maupertius, widow of the Governor of Guadaloupe. This worthy lady soon died and lies buried in St. John's Cemetery. Another distinguished émigré was Elie Joseph Trigant de la Tour, formerly lieutenant governor of Port au Prince. Like Malherbes he lived on the Rahway Road until his death in 1801.

Still another former office-holder in the West Indies who came to live in Elizabethtown was Jean Louis Jauvin, a wealthy planter who served under Barbé Marbois when he was governor of Santo Domingo (Hispanola). Jauvin lived near Touchimbert with his wife and two daughters, both of whom were married in Elizabethtown. The elder daughter, Jean Louise Margarite Josephine De Sires Jauvin married a Frenchman from New York. Her dowry was $6,500. The contract was witnessed by Barbé Marbois and a score of other prominent Frenchmen. The other daughter, Marie Denise Lucie Cherie Jauvin, was married with a dowry of $3,636 to Francois Vincent Paule de Gorse de Terrafort of Elizabethtown. Again among the witnesses were Marbois, Trigant de la Tour, Duclaud, and de la Verrioniere.[13]

Barbé Marbois was a noted Frenchman who had been secretary of the French legation to the United States during the American Revolution. In 1783, he became Chargé d'Affairs to the United States. Two years later he became governor of Santo Domingo. When the French Revolution began, he was presently forced to flee Paris. Biographers do not mention Barbé Marbois' sojourn in America during the French Revolution. Essex County records in Newark, N.J., however, show that he lived in Elizabethtown for some time during this period.

Another interesting Frenchman who lived in town was Abraham Du Buc Marentille from Martinique. While living in Elizabethtown, he invented an unsinkable boat designed to save lives at sea. In May, 1803, Marentille's boat was launched in the Elizabeth River near the Stone Bridge and taken out in the Arthur Kill for testing. After every effort was made to sink it, the invention was declared a success.[14] When Marentille moved away he left a quaint and sad reminder for his Elizabethtown friends. On his sister's gravestone was carved a request for the kind people of the town to care for the grave of his sister, Demoiselle Julie Du Buc Marcucy, who had died at the age of fifty-nine. The stone which lies in St. John's Cemetery reads:

> *Son frere Abraham Du Buc de*
> *Marentille recommande le respect et le*
> *soin de cette Tombe aux hospitaliers*
> *habitants de cette Ville*

On the south side of the Stone Bridge, one of the refugees, P. F. Le Breton, ran a store specializing in perfume, silks, jewelry, and other articles of French manufacture. He also owned a farm; and for a time his wife conducted a French school for young ladies. Another French merchant, Lorenzo Da Pont, had a whole-sale-retail grocery and dry-goods store on the corner of Broad and East Jersey streets where he took in exchange flaxseed and other products grown by his customers.[15]

With the rage for French culture, French schools flourished in Elizabethtown. Among those who gave lessons in French, the piano, music, and dancing were Monsieur Dufort, Monsieur Alexander Quesnay, Monsieur St. Aivre, Monsieur Trigant de

Beaumont, Madam Capron, and Madam Tapray. Among the French artists in Elizabethtown was the miniature painter, Charles de Saint Memin. Another painter was Monsieur DuBuc whose portraits could be had in gilt frames for as little as five dollars.[16]

A partial listing of other refugees in Elizabethtown includes many prominent names. From Santo Domingo there was Alexander De Sassier, Claude Francois Valentine De Cullin, formerly attorney general, and Rene Le Roy, a New York merchant with holdings in Elizabethtown. From Guadaloupe there was Francois Desize Goet, and from Martinique the wealthy Jean Etienne Fontanielles. Other French residents were Mrs. Perrier, Monsieur Duclaud, Jean Thibaut, John Robert Boyen St. Lauver, Mareu De la L'Aistre, Joseph Nicholas Michel Juigneron Marolles, Alexander Desbonne, Honoré Chardon, Francis de la Croix, Monsieur Le Grand, Monsieur Montaran, Monsieur Le Saffier, Mademoiselle gere de la Motte, Gobard Pretre, Monsieur Lavignais, Dr. L. Le Cesne, and Dr. John A. Michel.

Some of the French left the United States during the Undeclared War with France between 1798 and 1801, when public opinion turned against any who took exception to American foreign policy. Others left for France after Napoleon came to power. Some, like Monsieur Touchimbert, moved back to the West Indies when it seemed safe to return.

During their sojourn in America, French refugees entertained many visitors as their countrymen roamed over the United States in search of friends and relatives. Le Comte de Colbert Maulevrier on a visit to Elizabethtown noted that it was a *joli* village. Moreau de St. Mery thought the road leading to Elizabethtown had great charm with its *jolies fermes* (pretty farms). If some Americans did not care much for the French ways, the feeling was reciprocated. Generally the French thought that Americans were vain, greedy, talkative, uncultured, and devoid of spirit. Furthermore, they smoked too much and overly indulged in card playing and the consumption of strong drink. The feeling of equality and the extent of democracy in America were to them appalling. Even servant girls wore fancy dresses and sat with the family at the dinner table! But what the French detested most was the American Sabbath. Chastellux wrote that the men "bored with having read the Bible to their children, assembled around a joyless bowl, at the bottom of which there is nothing but drunkenness." [17]

Having nearly recovered from the war by 1790, Elizabethtown once again became an educational center. In 1789, the Elizabethtown Academy, where Francis Barber and Aaron Ogden had taught, was rebuilt by the Presbyterians with funds from a lottery; it was built on the site of the old Academy which had burned during the Revolution. For a short time after the two-story Academy with belfry was finished, Patrick Murdock, a graduate of Edinburgh, was headmaster and Latin Grammar teacher. He was followed by Colonel John Taylor, a Princeton man who served in the Revolution. On the Board of Trustees were town leaders, including Governor William Livingston, Jonathan Dayton, Aaron Ogden, Matthias Williamson, and Mayor John De Hart. These men faithfully attended the quarterly exercises and watched the students display their learning and accomplishments. Most of the students came from local families, although some from far away places boarded in town.

Private schools, which unlike the Academy, operated for a profit, were common in Elizabethtown after 1790. Not all who started a private school managed to succeed but some of the better ones lasted for many years. Among the men and women who conducted private schools during this period were Fanny Byrant, James Stevenson, George Kinne, Mrs. McGregor, and Mrs. Rankin. The private schools conducted by the French Refugees specializing in dancing, music, and art, were favored by the young ladies in town. However, not a few men and boys signed up for the dancing and fencing. Men and women of all ages took courses in the French language.

The variety of talent among the French gave students a wide choice. Madam Capron, who came to Elizabethtown before the French Revolution and whose husband played the base viol for the Philadelphia orchestra, stressed needle work, dancing, and French. Her dancing master was St. Aivre. To attract students he gave balls at which he exhibited the latest dances. In 1791 at one of his balls, he had sixteen young ladies perform the "Bow Dance," the "Minuet de la Cour," "la Gayette" and "Allemande." In 1795 Madam Tapray, an Émigré from Paris, opened a school in the home of Abigail Vergereau * for the harp and piano. More often classes were held in the taverns or the Court House. Trigant de Beaumont in 1806 used the Court House, while in 1809 Louis Susay and Mademoiselle Gevais offered dancing at the Union Hotel.

With the popularity of French culture at high tide, nearly all schools offered the French language and sometimes hired a French teacher. James Stevenson, headmaster of the Elizabethtown Academy in 1794, set up a French department for after school hours. The refugees also found competition from James Mitchell, a native of Scotland who taught in Elizabethtown for nearly thirty years. As a special attraction he taught dancers the "Caledonian Trip" and Aldridge's "Highland Laddie."

In 1806 an important educational institution was founded in Elizabethtown: the Adelphian Academy was erected on Water Street (Elizabeth Avenue) where Scott Place now joins the avenue. The funds for the Academy were provided by stockholders, most of whom resided in Elizabethtown. Dr. Matthias H. Williamson was the first president of the Board of Trustees. The first headmaster was Isaac Crane, the man who gave the Fourth of July oration in 1794. He was followed by Joseph Periam, Jr., whose six years at the Academy were terminated when he was sent to prison for debts. After a life of about fifty years, the Adelphian Academy was used as a public school for a few years. In 1865 the two-story brick building was torn down to make room for a City Hall.[18]

Though only a one-room elementary school, the North End School on the outskirts of Elizabethtown continued to serve the children of the community. Funds for running the school were provided by subscription until it became a public school in the 1840's. Sometime before this, the aged Sheppard Kollock, it is said, taught there before moving to Philadelphia to live with his son-in-law, the Reverend John McDowell. Not many years ago the old bell of the North End School was found and returned to Elizabeth.

In 1792 a library association was formed in Elizabethtown similar to the one founded by Benjamin Franklin in Philadelphia

* The Vergereaus were Huguenot.

at an earlier date. The more wealthy citizens, especially those with a college background, had their own private libraries, but it was felt that a membership library with a large assortment of books would prove useful. Dr. George Ross, a veteran of the Revolution and a vestryman of St. John's, was chosen librarian. Succeeding librarians were Isaac H. Williamson, Abraham Clark, and Smith Scudder. Although it was at first well patronized, interest in the library waned after about twenty years and it was discontinued.

With increasing frequency, Elizabethtown witnessed traveling entertainments, many of educational value. In 1798 a Mr. Bates from Philadelphia gave descriptions, recitations, moral tales, and comic songs at the Red Lion Inn. From New York in 1793 came a man with trained monkeys for exhibition at the Red Lion. Two years before at the Elizabethtown Academy some players presented in two acts "The Morristown Ghost" to "burlesque the force of credulity." * Another play was given the same evening entitled "The Anatomist or the Sham Doctor." [19] In 1803, a traveler advertised that he would make "likenesses" of people at the Red Lion Inn at a price of four for twenty-five cents. The "likenesses," readers were told, were made with a new invention called a "Patent Physiognotrace." Elizabethtown, near New York and on the main line of travel, was particularly favored by all the peripatetic attractions of the day. For special attractions Elizabethtonians often visited New York or Philadelphia. At the Quaker city in 1793 people gathered from all over the country to see the first balloon ascension in the new world, by the Frenchman, Jean Pierre Francois Blanchard.

During the early Federal period, Elizabethtown's small scale manufacturing recovered from the disruptions attending the Revolution. The number of businesses increased and some had expanded to meet rising demands. Most of the shops, however, continued to be operated by the proprietor with the help perhaps of one or two apprentices. A listing of the trades and proprietors reveals the character and extent of manufacturing in Elizabethtown near the turn of the century.

* The play was presented prior to the publication of the *Morristown Ghost* by John Wood, in 1792.

Trade	Proprietor-craftsman
Baker	Joseph Craven
Blacksmith	John Hamilton (specialized in making printing presses)
Brickmaker	Aaron Hatfield
Cabinetmaker	John J. Austin
	Richardson Gray
	John Mann
	Abraham Rosset and Abraham Mulford
	Butler and Meeker
	Brittin and Meeker
Carriage and Coach Painter	Thaddeus Mills
	Jacob Williams
Clockmaker	Isaac Brokaw (before 1790)
	Kennedy Miller
	Samuel Miller
	Samuel Gamage
	Dawes and Woodruff
Coach, Carriage, and Wagonmaker	Elias Wade
	Moses Chandler
	David Whitehead
	Joseph C. Ogden
	Nehemiah Wade
Cooper	John Pert
Cotton Cloth Manufacturer	John Wedderburn and James Love
Harnessmaker	Daniel Day
Hatter	Caleb Blanchard
	George Price
	Luther B. Hendricks
	John Shute
	Jeremiah Ballard
	David Miller
Nailer (Nailmaker)	F. Black
Potter	John Durell who sold to Willis and Steele, 1797
	Ichabod B. Halsey
	Robert Hunt (1780)
	Jesse Pitts and Edward Griffiths (after 1820 owned by Keen Pruden)
	Thomas and Nathaniel Boyston
Saddler	Joseph Stevens
	Isaac Ayres
	Thomas B. Cahow
Shipwright	Benjamin Scudder
Shoemaker	Joseph C. Ogden
	Benjamin Wade
	Samuel Morris
	William Ogden
Silversmith	Matthias and Benjamin Halsted
	Aaron Lane

Trade	Proprietor-craftsman
Silversmith	Kennedy Miller
	Dawes and Woodruff
	Samuel Gamage
	James Byrne
	James Ridway (specialized in silver plating on carriages, harnesses, etc.)
Tanner	Jonathan Wade (fifty vats)
Tailor	Thomas Mann
Tinsmith	John Le Grange
	Stephen Burrows
Weaver	Joseph Nesbit
Wheelwright	Phineas Moore
	Nathaniel Mitchell
Wiremaker	Ogden Woodruff *

The town's stores and warehouses were located along Water Street and Old Broad Street on the south side of the river where the shops of craftsmen were also found. Some of the stores specialized in certain items, although they otherwise served as general stores with almost anything to sell. All merchants did most of their business by barter, taking over the counter country products in exchange for dry goods, hardware, and so forth. As late as 1804 accounts were still kept in pounds, shillings, and pence rather than in the new Federal decimal system. In the stores and shops one heard the latest gossip and news. In 1814 Peter Lacour advertised the names of several persons who, on a Friday night in Aaron Woodruff's store, exercised "slanderous tongues." Lacour, they falsely said, was penniless and his property about to be sold.

Most of the stores were in business for many years although some survived but a short time. Dating from 1772, Jonathan Morrell and his son, Thomas, had a general store on Water Street near the White House. In the 1790's Job Haines and William Shute (son of Barnaby Shute and a veteran of the Revolution) ran a general store which did a large business. No store, however, rivaled the one belonging to General Dayton and Sons which had its origin before the Revolution. Other stores in existence before 1800 were owned by Jeremiah Ballard, Thomas Lovell, Edward Thomas, and George Robertson. The latter, for a while, ran a

* This list is made from advertisements in the *New Jersey Journal* and the *Federal Republican* and is admittedly not complete.

store on Old Broad Street near the Stone Bridge. Later he opened a paint store near Graham's Tavern. Enos Woodruff had a boarding house and general store with a livery stable.

After 1800 the number of stores multiplied. In 1801 a fruit store was opened by G. L. Grapin from New York. John Smylie ran a tobacco store selling cuts of pigtail, plug, and ladies' twist, as well as Spanish and American cigars. James Chapman's tobacco store was located two doors down Water Street from the Union Hotel. Aaron Lane's store and silversmith shop was next east of the White House. By 1815 wood and coal stoves were coming into general use. Aaron Lane carried a full line of stoves, stove pipe, and sheet iron. Other stores opened during the first decade of the nineteenth century were run by H. R. Dayton, Thomas Baldwin, John Wheeler, James Oliver, Thomas Price, Ichabod Williams, Thomas Crowell, James Wilson, Stephen H. Woodruff, Isaac Kipp, and John M. Meeker. Stores run by partners were those of Tunis and Woodruff, Johnson and Ayres, Price and Mulford, Schmidt and Steinfeldt, and Burrows and Howell. Abraham Efraimowicz, a Jew, was the junk collector.

At the turn of the century the old grist mill by the Stone Bridge was owned by Benjamin Scudder, whose father had purchased it from Barnaby Shute. By 1809 it was taken over by Jacob Geiger who installed a mill for making linseed oil. Farther up the river stood Crane's Mill, afterward known as Harris Mills. Above this was Trotter's Mill, near Ursino, which was still a fulling mill. Kollock's paper mill was located at the next dam, above Trotter's Mill near the old stone quarry.

After the turn of the century Elizabethtown's principal taverns continued to be the three which had long been the main inns within the Borough. The old Marquis of Granby of pre-Revolutionary days was now called the Red Lion Inn. As the Red Lion Inn it was successively operated by Samuel Smith, Jacamiah Smith, Richard Lyon, Francis Witt, Ford Cutter, Samuel Dow, Henry Freeman, and Joseph Gibbs. Between 1798 and 1800, when it was run by Richard Lyon, it was known as the Sign of the Artillery and Light Infantry. When Gibbs ran the tavern between 1805 and 1807 it was called the Sign of the Gate. The signboard read: "The Gate Hangs Well But Hinders None, Refresh and Pay and Travel On." After 1807 when the tavern was named The

Indian Queen it was run successively by Samuel Owen Smith, Mr. Webb, and others.

When Richard Lyon ran the old tavern as the Sign of the Artillery and Light Infantry there occurred a sensational incident that provided a topic for gossip for a long time to come. It started when three officers of the regular army got into a fight with some of the civilians loitering in the tavern. Getting the worst of the fisticuff, the officers drew their swords and made at their antagonists. When Innkeeper Richard Lyon tried to stop the fighting, he was chased out of his tavern by the soldiers. In the street a crowd soon had the officers surrounded. Fortunately for the officers, town magistrates arrived just in time to save them from the fury of the mob. The officers were brought to trial in the local court but were soon dismissed. As reported in the newspaper, the bruises sustained by Mr. Lyon were so well-plastered with paper dollars that the case was quietly dropped.[20]

Vying with the Indian Queen was the old inn on the corner of Broad and Water streets built by Matthias Williamson for a home before the Revolution and successively used as a tavern by Joseph Crane, Samuel Sayre, and Mr. Wales, during the 1780's and 90's. In 1801 it was acquired by Major Edward Clark and named Union Hall. The tavern, as described earlier, was a large three-story frame building with an adjoining barroom and kitchen facing Water Street. After 1809 the Union Hotel, as it was then called, was owned by Thomas Gibbons, a very wealthy planter from Savannah. When Gibbons bought the tavern it was operated by Stephen Halsey, who quarreled with the new owner and left. Between 1810 and 1818 it was successively operated by Stephen Burrows, Peter Coryell, Ephraim Clark, and James C. Sayre. From 1818 to 1820 it was rented by Miss Emma Hall for her private school for girls.

Following its use as a school, the building once more became the Union Hotel under a succession of managers. William Craig, who entertained Lafayette in 1824, ran it until 1829. He was followed by David Sanderson, the noted horseman, who married the beautiful daughter of Innkeeper Ellis Noe. In time Sanderson became the subject of criticism for having a basement bar called the Diving Bell where customers were known to have a "high time." Finally, the Borough refused to renew his license

J. M. GAYLORD'S

U N I O N   H O T E L,

CORNER OF BROAD & WATER STREETS, ELIZABETHTOWN, N. JERSEY.

    This well-known establishment (formerly kept by D. SANDERSON), IS NOW OPEN for the accommodation of the Public. The situation is healthy and agreeable, and every attention is paid to the comfort of Travellers. The Cars of the *New Jersey Rail-Road & Transportation Co.* from New York to Philadelphia, (*via* Newark, Elizabethtown, Rahway, New Brunswick, and Princeton,) stop within a few rods of the house every trip, to and from the above places.

*   An extensive LIVERY STABLE is attached to the establishment, where first-rate Horses and Carriages can be obtained.*

and he sold out. J. M. Gaylord took over the Union Hotel in 1838. Eight years later it was in the hands of a Mr. Waters. The tavern renamed The American Hotel burned down in January, 1867.

After 1810 the old Graham's Tavern on the northeastern corner of Broad and East Jersey streets became known as the City Tavern. This long low tavern with its two acre plot faced East Jersey Street. In 1793 Captain Joseph Lyon, a brewer, rented the tavern from the Widow Graham who had married Robert Forrest. Lyon probably continued to use the name Sign of the Two Lions which Morris Hatfield had adopted in 1788. After purchasing the tavern in 1796, he operated it until 1807 when he rented it to Robert Ratoon of Perth Amboy. In 1809 the tavern was purchased by Captain "Count" Lewis Rivers. Rivers rebuilt it in brick and renamed it the City Tavern. The new tavern with its fourteen rooms became the show place of Elizabethtown. It was here that Captain Henry Van Dalsem, who rented the tavern from Rivers, shared the honor of entertaining Lafayette during his visit. After 1828, when it was owned by Edward Price, the building became a boarding house.

Another important Elizabethtown tavern of the early days of the nineteenth century was the Steamboat Hotel, renamed the Mansion House about 1830. This tavern was the house built by Barnaby Shute in 1762. It stood on Broad Street facing Water Street, between the Court House and the Indian Queen Tavern. It was a two-story building with eight rooms, each room with a fireplace. The back of the house had a double piazza overlooking the river. After 1771 the building was owned by Samuel Smith, who also owned the Red Lion Inn next door. Smith lived in the Shute house and at times used it as a boarding house or a tavern. Henry Freeman ran a boarding house there around 1800. In 1817, when it became known as the Steamboat Hotel, it was run by Ephraim Clark, who had a reputation for adding a little water to his whiskey and rum. In 1820 William Vanderpool took over the Steamboat Hotel. In the 1830's, when it was called the Mansion House, it was successively operated by Ellis Noe, B. C. Chamberlain, and Joseph Lyon, Jr. For a few years it was the residence and office of Dr. G. R. Chetwood. At the time of the Civil War it was called the Sheridan House. In 1866 it burned.

During the early days of the nineteenth century there were other taverns in Elizabethtown of less importance than the Union Hotel, the City Tavern, the Indian Queen, and the Steamboat Hotel. Often the smaller, less frequented inns did not remain in business for long. At the turn of the century there was a tavern opposite the Two Lions (City Tavern) on the south corner of Broad and East Jersey. It was called the Sign of the Grenadier and Light Horse and was successively operated by William Van Arsdale, Benjamin Mills, and Thomas Lawrence. Both before and after its use as a tavern, the building was used as a store. The building was distinguished by four large willows which dominated the premise with their sweeping branches.

Another well-known inn was the Carteret Arms, erected by Colonel Edward Thomas on the site of an older building in 1795. The old building was doubtlessly the long low inn kept by John Dennis as early as 1728. Edward Thomas, Sr., acquired it about 1730 and used it for an inn. During the Revolution it was a favorite haunt for soldiers of both armies when they occupied the town. The new building, the Carteret Arms, stood nearly opposite the Indian Queen on the houselot acquired by Abraham Shotwell in 1665. Carteret Arms was first kept by Robinson Thomas, son of the colonel. After 1837 it was at times used as a school, a factory, and a residence. From 1860 to 1872 it housed an orphanage, and from 1903 to 1912 it was the home of the city's public library.

Postmasters were usually businessmen who received their appointment through politics. After the Revolution, Samuel Smith, owner of the Red Lion Inn, was the postmaster. He was followed by Lewis Woodruff, who was succeeded in 1792 by James Chapman, owner of the tobacco store on Water Street. Chapman had charge accounts for those who paid their postage bills regularly. For this service he received a small commission from his patrons. After Chapman, Sheppard Kollock was postmaster from about 1810 to 1829, when he was succeeded by Thomas B. Dayton.

In 1786 Elizabethtown's Methodists were organized as a congregation by the Reverend Thomas Morrell, a well-known circuit rider. Morrell was the captain who raised a company and marched off to fight in the battle of Long Island many years before. After recovering from a severe wound received at Long Island, the young soldier had fought at Brandywine and Germantown. Thereafter he was mustered out of service because of poor health. He then returned to Elizabethtown where he helped his father, Jonathan, run his store on Water Street. After being converted to Methodism, Morrell became a circuit rider for ten years. In 1804 he retired from the circuit and settled down in Elizabethtown as the minister for the Methodist Episcopal Congregation. The Meetinghouse, a small frame building near the Adelphian Academy, was erected in 1795. Here for thirty-four years, Pastor Morrell preached his hell-fire sermons. After he died, the Methodists built a large brick church on the east side of Water Street near Broad.*

William Dunlap, the noted playwright and artist, often visited Elizabethtown and on one occasion went to hear the dynamic clergyman Thomas Morrell. The latter, he was told, had been an ungodly man given to strong drink before being "Plucked as a brand from the burning." The sermon Dunlap heard was about a man who became purified after being in the possession of the devil for some time. When the devil returned, he brought back a stronger devil who took possession of the poor man, then worse off than before. "The preacher," wrote Dunlap, "told his ignorant Audience (for ignorance was written in every countenance of the small number of people there, and stupidity in most, except some youth) that in those days God suffer'd Devils to take possession of the bodies of men, that he might manifest his power through Christ in testing them out. He said this was not common now tho' there were many people at this time sorely afflicted by disorders for which physicians could find no names, which disorders were occasioned by some devil having enter'd into the bodies of such people. Usually, now, however, the devils, according to the Reverend Morrell, enter'd men's souls and made themselves at home." [21]

About the time when William Dunlap was observing the Reverend Thomas Morrell, the camp meeting craze swept America. Soon New Jersey was the scene of huge camp meetings. At Long Hill, near Chatham, the Methodists held camp meetings that

* This building, at the present time (1964) in very bad condition, is used for a warehouse.

often lasted a week or more. People came many miles with their tents and covered wagons to hear the impassioned sermons of the ministers preaching in relays from early morning until late at night. Many of their listeners were sent into paroxysms of religious frenzy, shouting and wailing and rolling on the ground. Critics found that camp meetings were conducive to immorality, especially among the young. Years later Thomas Nast, the cartoonist, pictured a lad at a Civil War recruiting station being asked the name of his father. The young man answered that he did not know since he was a "camp meeting baby."

At the time Methodism was taking root in Elizabethtown, the Presbyterians rebuilt their church which had burned during the Revolution. To start construction, the trustees mortgaged the land on which the parsonage had stood. Most of the money for the church, however, was raised by a lottery. Built of brick, the building was sixty feet square with galleries supported by pillars on the sides facing the pulpit. As formerly, most of the pews were rented to the members. The free pews were four in front of the pulpit, four next to the door, and four in the gallery. A square pew near the pulpit was reserved for visitors. Three side pews near the door were for Negroes. Although the church was ready for services by September, 1785, the beautiful spire atop the belfry was not added until a decade later during Mr. Austin's pastorate. All Elizabethtown boasted of the height and beauty of the spire on the Presbyterian Church, covered as it was with tin which sparkled in the sunlight.*

The first minister in the new church was the Reverend William A. Linn, who stayed but four months. He was followed by the Reverend David Austin, who purchased the Belcher House for his home. Austin was a man of considerable talent. Soon after he came he published a religious journal called *The Christian's, Scholar's and Farmer's Magazine* (first issue, April 1789), designed "to promote Religion, to disseminate useful Knowledge, to afford literary Pleasure and Amusement, and to advance the Interests of Agriculture." He also published a four-volume set of sermons by outstanding ministers, irrespective of denomination, entitled *The American Preacher.*

* The spire blew down in 1899. Rebuilt in 1901, it burned in 1946.

While preaching in Elizabethtown and living in the Belcher House, Austin was caught up in the Millennium movement that was sweeping America. Presently he undertook to set a date for the personal return of Christ to establish his Kingdom and rule the world. He supported his predictions by writing a book called *The Millennium*. This was followed by another entitled *The Voice of God to the People of these United States*. When the appointed day arrived in May, 1796, "Prophet" Austin was ready to receive the Lord. All day he waited in the Presbyterian Church with a crowd of devoted followers. Young ladies, dressed in white ascension robes, sat with folded hands and uplifted faces for the first appearance of their Saviour. But the day passed and the disappointed Believers returned home. The next Sunday, the Reverend Mr. Austin preached a sermon entitled "The Lord Delayeth His Coming."

When the "Prophet" finally announced that he was called by the Lord to found a church of the Millennium, Jonathan Dayton, Aaron Ogden, Jeremiah Ballard, and other trustees (most of whom had been skeptical about his teachings from the first) asked the Presbytery of New York to dismiss him. Their petition was granted and the Reverend David Austin henceforth became an itinerant preacher carrying his message of the Second Coming as an independent missionary. In 1804, he reappeared in Elizabethtown and succeeded in getting admirers to rent space in the Methodist Church for Millennial services. Failing, however, to obtain enough support, Austin presently left town, not to return again.[22]

During Washington's administration and for many years thereafter, Elizabethtown was a stronghold of Federalism in New Jersey. As controversy developed over Alexander Hamilton's proposals for strengthening the Federal government and funding the national debt, Aaron Ogden and other prominent citizens of Elizabethtown took the lead in supporting the Secretary of the Treasury. Unlike aristocratic Elizabethtown, Newark became a Jeffersonian stronghold with many of its most prominent citizens coming out against the administration. Although they were few in number, Elizabethtown had some Jeffersonians of its own. The most prominent of these was Sheppard Kollock, whose newspaper became an oracle of Jeffersonian Republicanism for New Jersey.

The Federalists, it should be noted, did not argue that wealth and social position alone entitled them to rule the country. Rather, it was by their experience and education that they were entitled to govern, they maintained. They did not deny that all men were equal before the law or that they should have qual opportunities once the prerequisites for leadership were met. As Elias Boudinot said, all Federalists admitted that "the first great principle established by the Revolution, is the rational equality and rights of men." [23]

In 1793 Elizabethtown Federalists led by Aaron Ogden gave Washington their unqualified support in his neutral policy toward the French Revolution. At a mass meeting with Elias Dayton in the chair and Elias Boudinot the secretary, it was resolved that Washington should be fully supported. A similar resolution was adopted at a meeting for all Essex County at which Elias Dayton presided. Sheppard Kollock, as a Republican, did not approve of neutralism and wrote an editorial entitled "The Cause of France is the Cause of Universal Liberty." [24]

When the Whiskey Rebellion broke out in western Pennsylvania, Federalists accused Republicans of encouraging the rebels in not paying the excise tax. Again Kollock came to the defense of the Jeffersonians who were, he said, defending the principles of the American Revolution and the rights of man. In general, however, New Jerseyans agreed that the Federal government must be supported and the whiskey tax paid if the union were to endure. When called upon to provide its quota of militia for putting down the rebellion, the state responded promptly.

On orders of Governor Richard Howell, Major General Elias Dayton called out the required number of men and began preparations for marching. William Chetwood, the future judge, became a major on the staff of General Henry Lee, in command of the expedition. Aaron Ogden was made a colonel and assigned to Governor Richard Howell's staff. Among the first to be ready to start for Pittsburgh were the Elizabethtown Grenadiers and Light Infantry Company (the Fourth Regiment, N.J. Infantry), commanded by Colonel William Crane, hero of the attack on Quebec in 1775. With Crane were Major Robert Ross, Adjutant

David Lyon, Quartermaster John Hendricks, Paymaster Robinson Thomas, Surgeon Isaac Morse, and Surgeon Mate Jacob Halsted, all of Elizabethtown.

Another officer from Elizabethtown was Joseph Lewis Chevalier D'Anterroches who as a young man had run away from a school in France to join the British Army during the American Revolution. Having become a prisoner of war, he was allowed to live in Chatham on parole. Here he fell in love with a local girl named Mary Vanderpool. In spite of her father's dislike for Frenchmen, even though this one happened to be related to Lafayette, the two were married. Thereafter D'Anterroches' future lay in America. The D'Anterroches settled on a farm in Elizabethtown on the road to Rahway, where the couple enjoyed the respect and admiration of their neighbors and friends. In the march against the whiskey rebels, D'Anterroches was aide-de-camp for Brigadier General Jonathan Walton White in command of the New Jersey cavalry and of the entire cavalry after the army began to march.

Elizabethtown's Light Dragoons were included in White's brigade. The company was officered by Job Haines, a local merchant, John Wood, the printer, William Dayton and Richard Lyon, the innkeeper. Dr. Matthias H. Williamson was the surgeon for the dragoons.

During the Whiskey Rebellion and the crisis arising from Hamilton's financial measures, Jonathan Dayton, son of General Dayton, was a member of Congress and gave the administration his firm support. Elected speaker of the House in 1794, Dayton was instrumental in softening the attitude of Congress toward the Jay Treaty. In New Jersey, too, his influence brought wider support for the treaty.

Although members of the ruling gentry, men like Jonathan Dayton were close to the life of the common man. When at home in Elizabethtown, Dayton was a farmer as well as a merchant, a lawyer, and a land speculator. Whether at home or abroad, he always had concern for his farm. In a letter to his father from Philadelphia, Dayton asked for the loan of the General's oxen for drawing manure. Jonathan had his team of oxen carting manure but he wanted to hurry the work so that the plowing could begin. Most people, whether aristocrats or not, still had their milk cows in Elizabethtown. In 1797, Aaron Ogden advertised for his two brindle cows and red heifer which had strayed away on the road to Springfield.[25]

Realizing that they were beginning to lose ground politically under the attacks of the Republicans, Elizabethtown Federalists in 1795 organized a "Constitutional Association" for the defense of federalism. At a meeting early in the year, the society resolved that the Constitution of the United States must be preserved as the bulwark of the union and of national liberties. President Washington, the resolution declared, deserved the thanks of the whole nation for successfully taking the country through difficult times occasioned by the wars arising from the French Revolution.[26]

After the election of President John Adams, the Jeffersonian party made rapid gains throughout the country. In 1797, for the first time the Republican ticket carried Essex County. As in all elections, little attention was paid to the property or other qualifications for voting. Even the French Refugees who had no intention of becoming citizens often voted without being challenged. In general the average freeholder was an indifferent voter, many of them seldom going to the polls unless to sell their votes.

By a quirk in the state constitution, women were allowed to vote at this time. Apprehensive of defeat, the Elizabethtown Federalists scurried about and brought seventy-five ladies to the polls as well as a large number of Negroes of both sexes. But their votes were more than offset by the large number of women in Newark and elsewhere who voted Republican. Federalism was dying in New Jersey.[27]

With the rising tide of Jeffersonianism, many Federalists forsook their party and joined the more popular organization. Staunch Federalists such as Aaron Ogden, however, refused to compromise and even opposed the Louisiana Purchase as being of little value to New Jersey. Jonathan Dayton, who became a United States Senator in 1803, nonetheless saw fit to trim his sails and vote for the treaty for acquiring the new territory.

After his term in the Senate, Jonathan Dayton came perilously close to being scorched by the intrigues of Aaron Burr. A life-long friend of Burr's and a noted speculator in western land, he became involved in Burr's Mississippi venture. Apparently Burr used funds advanced by Dayton and intended for land speculation to further his designs in the Mississippi Valley. When treason charges were brought against Burr in 1807, Dayton was one of five others indicted for high treason and brought to trial at Richmond, Virginia. Just before Dayton left Elizabethtown for Richmond to stand trial, the *New Jersey Journal* voiced the opinion that his actions and motives were misunderstood and that he would be proved innocent. The prediction was correct for, when he appeared before the Circuit Court of Virginia, the United States attorney dismissed Dayton for lack of any specific charges.[28]

In 1798, the United States became involved in an undeclared naval war with France when the latter sought to bend America to its will by depriving it of the freedom of the seas during one of its wars with Great Britain. As a defense measure in case the French should attempt an invasion of the country, the War Department ordered the recruitment of a provisional army. By presidential appointment Alexander Hamilton became major general in command of the emergency army north of the Potomac. On orders from Hamilton, New Jersey raised the Eleventh Infantry Regiment. Aaron Ogden, by Governor Howell's appointment, became second in command of the regiment with the rank of lieutenant colonel. For a time the New Jersey regiment camped near Scotch Plains with the Twelfth New York Regiment. Together they were known as the Union Brigade. Soon after the Union Brigade was organized, Ogden became Deputy Quartermaster General for the outfit. When President Adams brought the controversy with France to a close by a judicious treaty with Napoleon, the Provisional Army was disbanded in June, 1800.

While the Provisional Army was being formed by the War Department, militia all over the country were turning out for training with a zeal not seen for many years. In Elizabethtown the militia could be seen drilling regularly on the parade ground in front of the Court House. They were officered by Chevalier D'Anterroches, William Crane, and other veterans of the Revolution. During the crisis, Mayor Elias Dayton and the Common Council sent President Adams a note voicing their approval of his foreign policy. The note was presented to President Adams by Jonathan

Dayton, who received in return an answer thanking the town for its support.[29]

During the crisis attending the Undeclared War with France, there were critics, chiefly Republicans, who thought that Hamilton and like-minded men desired to create a large standing army to be officered by Federalist gentlemen. One of those accused was Aaron Ogden. Whether or not there was any truth in the assertion, Ogden and the other emergency officers retired from the army as soon as peace was made. There is no doubt, however, that Aaron Ogden, like Hamilton, coveted military glory. The year after he resigned from the Provisional Army, Ogden found satisfaction in being made Governor Bloomfield's aide-de-camp, although the office was purely honorary.[30]

Although Colonel Ogden suffered from the growing unpopularity of his political party, he continued to enjoy favor in Elizabethtown as the recipient of many elective and appointive offices. From 1785 until 1801, he held the post of clerk of the Court of General Quarter Sessions for Essex County. Upon being elected to the United States Senate in 1801, however, he was forced to relinquish his clerkship after a bitter controversy with Republican leaders who maintained he had no right to hold both offices.[31]

In Elizabethtown, Sheppard Kollock continued to be the leading figure in Republican circles. His newspaper extolled the virtues of democracy and strongly supported all Jeffersonian candidates. "What is Democracy?" he asked in an editorial. "It is a government," he wrote, "formed by the general voice of the people—a government wherein the will of the people alone predominates. It is the great source from which all free government is derived." [32] All over the state the common man was flocking into the Methodist and Baptist churches for religion and into the Jeffersonian party for political inspiration. The Presbyterians and Episcopalians, drawn mainly from the educated and propertied class, were ordinarily Federalists.

In 1801, New Jersey elected Joseph Bloomfield as its first Republican governor. But in the following year Aaron Ogden and the Federalists gained enough in the legislature to keep Bloomfield out of the governor's chair. For a year New Jersey had no governor. At this time the Federalists were also able to deprive Essex County (with its strong Republican majority) of any new seats in the legislature by blocking efforts to achieve a reapportionment. Such control on the part of the Federalists, however, was but temporary. The change was apparent in the township of Elizabethtown and even in the Borough where the rise in Republican voting was significant. Sheppard Kollock maintained that the Federalists could no longer hold the Borough if it were not for the votes of minors, non-residents, slaves, paupers, and old Negro women.[33]

When the Federalist legislature in 1801 sent Aaron Ogden to fill out the unexpired term of Senator James Schureman in the United States Senate, he was considered an "Argus" sent to watch President Jefferson. Republicans, naturally, did not appreciate Ogden's presence in Washington. At the first session he arrived in Washington only two days before the Senate adjourned. As the Republicans put it, he said "aye" four times, collected $144 for mileage and $24 for "watching Mr. Jefferson." [34]

On returning to Washington the next year, Ogden delivered a cogent speech before the Senate against abolishing the judgeships for the United States Circuit Courts and for maintaining the independency of judges. A masterful debater, he stirred the halls of the chamber with his eloquence. "Save us from the injustice, the oppression, and the miseries of dependent tribunals, by preserving to us, forever, the entire independence of our national judges," he pleaded. As it turned out, the Republicans did not succeed in undermining the independency of the judges but they abolished the tier of circuit court judges created by the Federalists after the defeat of President Adams. In the Senate the vote was close, with Jonathan Dayton joining his fellow townsman, Aaron Ogden, in the unsuccessful fight against repeal.[35]

As the contest grew hotter between the rival political parties in Elizabethtown, Sheppard Kollock lost no opportunity to praise the Jeffersonians and censure the Federalists. He defended Thomas Paine, who was attacked by a mob in Trenton in 1804, as "the ablest politician of his day, the firm supporter of the rights of man." When a William Bradford made an attack on democracy in a Philadelphia newspaper, Kollock labeled men like him enemies of the people. Bradford's article had denounced democracy as a sinister concept which would lead to civil war, desolation, and anarchy. In answer, Kollock called this charge a libel against the great mass of patriots who had supported the American Revolution with the belief that it was founded upon the principles of the rights of man.[36]

With the aim of strengthening the Federalist party in Elizabethtown and vicinity, Aaron Ogden and other Federalists helped John Wood, formerly editor of the *Newark Gazette* and more recently publisher of the *American Farmer* at Poughkeepsie, to found a newspaper in Elizabethtown. The newspaper called the *Federal Republican* first appeared in January, 1803. Although it was well subscribed, it failed to attract enough advertising and was discontinued after about a year.*

During the titanic struggle between Great Britain and Napoleon, Federalists were sharply critical of Jefferson's neutrality in the face of constant infringement upon American rights on the high seas. For a time, however, all parties united when the British frigate *Leopard* attacked the *Chesapeake* within American waters. Elizabethtown's Mayor Caleb Halsted sat as chairman of a town meeting called to consider the outrage. A committee, consisting of Aaron Ogden, Jeremiah Ballard, Sheppard Kollock, and others, was appointed to draft a resolution. As adopted, it asked the national government to take appropriate steps to safeguard the interests of the country.

One episode the same year turned out quite differently from the sensational *Leopard-Chesapeake* affair. It happened when Dr. Isaac Morse of Elizabethtown, while transporting a load of hay by boat, came alongside the British frigate *Chichester*. Somehow his boat got tangled in the ship's rigging. "Cut away!" shouted a British officer. Hearing the order, Dr. Morse called out that he would not cause his boat to be damaged in the least. When the British officer paid no heed and ordered his men to ply their axes, Dr. Morse swore that he would fire the hay at the first stroke. At this instant the commanding officer appeared on deck and ordered the ship to be freed without damage to the Doctor's boat. He then asked Dr. Morse to come aboard and share a bottle of wine with him. Morse accepted and, after being royally wined and dined, returned to town with his load of hay.

Dr. Morse was a man noted for his kindness and good humor.

* Rutgers University has the only complete set of the *Federal Republican* in existence.

People declared that patients owed their convalescence more to his sympathetic treatment than to all his drugs and prescriptions. He was also a man of remarkable patience and forbearance. One day his hogs got into a neighbor's field and were shot by an irate farmer who loaded up the dead pigs and sent them home. Later when the farmer's pigs got into the Doctor's garden, he had them tied up and carted home. Such was the Doctor's practice of doing good for evil.[37]

In 1807 when President Jefferson resorted to an embargo against France and Great Britain as a step short of war, his party firmly backed his pacific program. In New Jersey the call went out for all farmers, merchants, and mechanics to turn out and vote for the Republican standard-bearers if they preferred peace to war. In Elizabethtown the Republicans put up a ninety-five foot liberty pole with the motto "May the Embargo continue until European Despots respect our rights." [38]

With the failure of the embargo and the policy of sealing off American commerce from world trade, President James Madison eventually took the path to war with Great Britain in 1812. The decision was denounced by Federalists generally who considered war with Great Britain contrary to the political, economic, and national interests of the country. A war with Great Britain, they argued, was unnecessary and unrealistic since the real enemy to liberty was Napoleon.

In June, they called a meeting in Elizabethtown in the interest of preserving peace. Aaron Ogden, Caleb Halsted, and other prominent Federalists made speeches condemning the course of the Administration. Within a few weeks, another meeting was called at which Aaron Ogden and Deputy Mayor William Crane were chosen to represent Elizabethtown Federalists at a party convention in Trenton for nominating candidates. Ogden, for one, was selected to run for the State Legislative Council and for presidential elector.[39]

As the 1812 campaign progressed, the political struggle became heated and bitter. The Republicans reminded the people that the American Revolution had its Tories espousing peace and submission. Republican warning, however, went unheeded. Indeed, the desire for peace was so strong that the party of Jefferson went down to defeat for the first time in more than a decade. The

Federalists elected thirty representatives and the Republicans but twenty-three. New Jersey's failure to support the war is understandable. It had little trade to protect on the high seas and its people were not interested enough in conquering Canada or Florida or crushing the Indians on the frontiers to be won over by the arguments of the "War Hawks."

Following the election, the Federalist legislature chose Aaron Ogden as governor of the state. Elizabethtown at once prepared a celebration for its favored son. During a meeting of leading citizens at the City Tavern, a committee was chosen to wait on Colonel Ogden and request his presence. At the appointed time Ogden arrived at the City Tavern, where he was greeted by a salute fired by militia drawn up in front of the tavern. After a banquet there were the usual toasts and speeches. Aaron Ogden was a good scholar and a master of oratory: his words sparkled with Latin quotations and allusions to Shakespeare. The next day he left for Trenton escorted by the Elizabethtown and Newark Light Horse and many admirers.[40]

After convening, the New Jersey legislature passed a resolution condemning the involvement of the country in a war with Great Britain. The war, the resolution said, was "inexpedient, ill-timed, and most dangerously impolitic." Everything the nation had gained so far was put in jeopardy, the Federalists asserted. If the Administration attempted to make an alliance with the despot, Napoleon, such action, the resolution stated, could lead to the dissolution of the union. Going even farther, the Federalists dared to say that it was impolitic for the United States to question England's right to impress their own seamen found on American ships.[41]

Although Governor Ogden agreed with his party's stand, he was not the man to withhold support once the country had declared war. In response to President Madison's request for each state to meet its quota, he issued orders for raising a regiment for immediate duty. In recognition of his military experience, the War Department offered Governor Ogden a place as major general in the United States Army. He, however, declined the honor believing that he could be of greater service to his country by remaining governor of New Jersey. With so many inhabitants opposed to the war, Ogden, no doubt, did right in staying at his post and serving as a war governor.

In late November, he came to Newark to inspect the militia assembled under the command of Brigadier General Gould. After the review, the Governor urged all young men to consider volunteering for active service. Until peace came, he told his audience, everyone must strive for victory. In Elizabethtown he was pleased to find the people rising to the occasion and girding themselves for war. Major Thaddeus Mills, the coach painter, had his militia drilling regularly on the grounds in front of the Court House. A company of riflemen, smartly dressed in green jackets and red-fringed overalls, looked especially military to the Governor. He was also pleased to find that recruiting for the regular army was rapid at the City Tavern. Since there was a shortage of arms, he ordered that damaged muskets and rifles be sent from a Federal arsenal to Elizabethtown where gunsmiths under the direction of Stephen Dod soon had the arms in working condition.[42]

Aaron Ogden was not reelected governor in 1813. Continued opposition to the war by the Federalists had the effect of lessening the popularity of the party in the state as a whole. Ogden himself had earned high praise for his support of the war but the people would not elect the men who would insure his reelection. If Ogden had aligned himself with the Republicans at this time his reelection would have been certain. The kind regard of all for Governor Ogden was no better expressed than by his old political foe, Sheppard Kollock. "Had the pious Federal governors in other states," wrote Kollock, "followed the praise-worthy example of Governor Ogden, and shown a similar disposition to aid the operation of the General Government in a vigorous prosecution of the war, we should not have met with the sad reverses of fortune which we have experienced, nor would England have rejected the honorable and pacific overtures which have been offered by Mr. Madison." [43]

With the threat of a large-scale invasion of the United States by Great Britain growing imminent after the defeat of Napoleon, a mass meeting was held at the Elizabethtown Court House in September, 1814. It was decided that all able-bodied men over forty-five who could not qualify for the army, should organize as a home guard. As a result a company of older men was organized with Jonathan Dayton, the fifty-five-year-old veteran of the Revolution, as captain. Obediah Meeker, a captain of the light horse during the Revolution, was named first lieutenant. Jeremiah Ballard, a captain in the Third New Jersey Regiment during the War for Independence, became second lieutenant. With fears rampant that the British might try to invade New Jersey, beacons were set up on the heights above Springfield and other high points for calling out the militia.[44]

While Elizabethtown was preparing for what might come, many of her sons were fighting in distant places and on the high seas. Most distinguished of those in the Navy was Commodore William Montgomery Crane. Born in 1776, Crane was the son of Captain (General) William Crane who accompanied General Richard Montgomery on the ill-fated attack on Quebec in 1775. Made a midshipman in 1799, Crane served on the *United States* under Captain John Barry in the Naval War with France at the close of the Century. Promoted to lieutenant in 1804, he commanded *Gunboat Number 7* in Captain Edward Preble's heroic but unsuccessful bombardment of Tripoli. Four years later he was an officer on the *Chesapeake* when, without provocation, it was attacked by the British ship *Leopard* in American waters. At the opening of the War of 1812, he commanded the Brig *Nautilus* which was run down and captured by the *Shannon* after an exciting six-hour chase. A court of inquiry found that Crane had done everything possible to prevent capture by the larger and swifter vessel. From 1812 to 1814, he served with distinction with naval units on Lake Ontario. In 1815, during the campaign against Algiers, he was given command of Commodore William Bainbridge's flagship, the *Independence*.

After 1815, Commodore Crane served as commandant of naval operations in many waters. His last service was as Chief of the Bureau of Ordnance and Hydrography. As Chief of Ordnance he opposed the installation of the big cannon called the "Peacemaker" on the battleship *Princeton*. When in 1844 the gun blew up and killed Secretary of State Abel P. Upshur and other observers, Crane felt that he was partly to blame for the accident. Brooding over the tragedy, he committed suicide in 1846.

With Commodore William Crane on the ill-fated *Nautilus* in 1812 was another career officer from Elizabethtown. The young

man was midshipman Charles L. Williamson. After he was exchanged, Williamson served on several other ships during the
War of 1812. At Lake Champlain he distinguished himself while
serving on Captain Thomas Macdonough's flagship, the *Saratoga*,
in the battle off Plattsburg Bay. After the battle he was thanked
by Congress for his heroism and presented with a sword of
honor. Williamson next served under Bainbridge in the war
with Algiers. His career ended in 1842 when he was for some reason cashiered by the Navy Department. He died in Elizabethtown four years later.

Fortunately war never touched the shores of New Jersey during
the second war with Great Britain. Elizabethtown, which had
suffered much during the War for Independence, remained far
removed from the battlefields. When peace came, it seemed to
vindicate the stand Aaron Ogden and the Federalists had taken
at the outset of the war. It had been a costly and disruptive war.
However, notwithstanding the country's failures during the war,
a new sense of nationalism emerged from the contest which carried over into the postwar era, the age of the steamboat and the
railroad, in which Elizabethtown would play an important role.

An Age of Altruism

In 1820, Elizabethtonians could walk down to Joseph Crane's store on Water Street and buy soda water and ice cream.[1] This cosmopolitan luxury, however, did not prove that Elizabethtown was growing or changing very rapidly. Quite the contrary, the growth of Elizabethtown for the ten or fifteen years following the War of 1812 was slight and the town changed but little in appearance. Except in the business section on Water and Old Broad streets, it maintained its country-like setting of gardens and orchards and widely-spaced houses. In the business section where change was most common, streets and sidewalks were improved from time to time and new buildings erected to take care of commercial needs.

As street commissioner, Elias Wade, the leading coachmaker, had charge of Elizabethtown's highways and sidewalks. Occasionally he was obliged to compel delinquent property owners to lay sidewalks or plant shade trees prescribed by Borough ordinances. Most of the businessmen, however, needed little urging and often went beyond the requirements of law, vying with one another in making improvements. Brick and flagstone sidewalks took the place of wooden walks or gravel paths as one proprietor after another followed the example of his neighbor. Under Commissioner Wade's charge there were some town street-lamps in front of public buildings. Most of the lighting, however, was done by the owners of stores and shops who wanted lights in front of their places of business. On most of the streets there were no lamps at all, with consequent danger of fast driving at night. In 1817, Samuel Wilcox, son of the Elder James Wilcox, ran into another carriage in the dark and died a few days later from his injuries.

Borough expenditures continued to be very small during the

early years of the nineteenth century. In 1822, a new market pavilion with a brick roof supported by stone pillars was erected on the site of the old market near the old Stone Bridge on Broad Street. As amusing as it was typical of the times was the way the town fathers handled the matter of repairing the town clock on the Court House. Samuel Miller, a local clockmaker, offered to repair the clock, but Mark Lane, another clockmaker, convinced the Common Council that it would be better to have a new one made. Thereupon the Council voted to have Lane make the clock. This decision was not well received by the townspeople. Lane was then informed that the town fathers had reconsidered and decided against having him make a new clock. The question was finally settled when the Common Council voted to have the clock repaired for $200 by a New York clockmaker.[2]

Until 1808, Elizabethtown depended entirely upon the bucket brigade for fire-fighting. Every householder, as in former days, was required to have one or two leather buckets ready at all times. Every able-bodied man was obliged to turn out to help fight fires at the sound of the gong. For water the town depended on private wells and a few town pumps maintained by the Borough on Broad and Water streets.

In 1808, the Common Council purchased a fire engine and voted to lease land next to the Court House for a building to house it and the town's artillery, consisting of two Revolutionary War cannons. The engine called the "peppermill" was simply a rotary pump mounted on a truck carrying a wooden water tub. A team of firemen manned the handles and supplied the power which sent a twenty or thirty foot stream of water from a hose attached to the pump. The waterbox was kept filled by a chain of men who passed buckets of water along the line from the well to the fire engine.

Although the engine improved fire protection in Elizabethtown, it was too inefficient and cumbersome to be much of an advance over the old-fashioned bucket brigade. Fires continued to take a heavy toll of property. After a large fire in 1811, agitation arose for more fire fighting facilities. Nothing was done, however, until 1825 when a new and better fire engine was purchased.[3]

During the second quarter of the nineteenth century, Elizabethtown's fire fighting facilities steadily improved. The year 1828 saw the organization of a hook and ladder company, known as Lafayette Number One. The cost of the equipment was met by subscription and a sum voted by the Corporation. For the first four years the hook and ladder cart was probably housed in a barn near the Court House. In 1832, however, space was provided for it when an addition was constructed on the rear of the Engine House alongside the Court House. Other expenditures were also made for fire protection in 1828. Fifty feet of hose were purchased by the Borough for each of the fire engines. Large brick cisterns were constructed at appropriate locations for reservoirs.

By 1841 the Borough had spent nearly six thousand dollars on fire protection since the purchase of the first engine in 1808. Doubtlessly fire protection was the largest civic expense during this period. It now had three fire engines, seven hundred feet of hose, a hook and ladder cart, three buildings for housing the equipment, and four brick cisterns. One of the fire chiefs was David Sanderson, the noted tavern keeper and stagecoach driver. After 1830, the Borough had a fire warden for each district and a chief engineer to supervise the fire department. The chief engineer for many years was Keen Pruden, a wealthy merchant and owner of a large earthenware factory located between Water Street and the river.[4]

Beginning in 1845 the Borough hired a few regular firemen for around-the-clock service. Most of the fire fighting, however, continued to be done by volunteers who took great pride in their particular company. The forty-eight members of Fire Company Number Three lovingly called their engine "Old Gal." All the companies turned out in full dress for the Fourth of July parades and on similar occasions. As was customary, firemen drew all their equipment with ropes. Horses were not used until a later date with the advent of heavier equipment. One exception occurred in the 1854 Fourth of July Parade. That year Protection Engine Company Number One put their engine on a wagon which was drawn by six horses led by a groom in Moorish costume.[5]

Police as well as fire protection became a growing need in Elizabethtown during the early years of the nineteenth century. A complaint often heard was that gardens were raided during the night. In 1800 Horatio R. Dayton sought relief from prowlers by advertising in the newspaper that he had set some wolf traps in his garden since these animals had become very troublesome.

Men and boys roamed the streets by night committing acts of vandalism and other offenses. With the multiplication of servants, apprentices, free Negroes, and day laborers, trouble of this nature increased with time. Gangs were especially destructive of lamp posts, fences, trees, and orchards. Elizabethtown had a curfew and a Watch but the curfew often went unenforced and the Watch could not alone keep the culprits in control.

By 1811 the noisy street gangs were getting quite out of hand. Presently Jonathan D. Skinner was knocked down and severely injured when he attempted to disperse some disorderly Negroes. The next morning the town was in an uproar. Mayor Halsted acted promptly by calling a town meeting. That night a mob of whites roamed the streets looking for Negroes to assault. Before morning the mob had demolished the house of one Negro and ransacked another. Sensing that the situation required immediate action, the Corporation increased the Watch and ordered the jail to be enlarged.[6]

Trouble from street gangs kept occurring. Bent upon saving money, the town fathers reduced the Watch as soon as the streets became quiet and disorders became infrequent. The trouble then would blaze anew. Action was taken in 1822 to curb disorders when Thomas Salter complained that a gang had broken the new ornamental fence in front of his home. Agitation arose again five years later with a new wave of vandalism. This time the Corporation decided to try to enforce the curfew. Twenty dollars was voted for ringing the Presbyterian Church bell every night at nine for the ensuing year.

Throughout the next quarter century, street disorders and petty crimes continued to increase. By 1845 it had become so dangerous to be out on the streets at night that the Corporation appointed fifty volunteer watchmen in a concerted drive to put an end to the trouble. As before, the lid was kept on only so long as the streets were well-patrolled. Consequently it was not until the City government was established a decade later that the problem was brought under proper control by the creation of an adequate police force.[7]

Care of the poor saw little improvement during the early years of the nineteenth century. As in earlier days the pauper was "sold" to the lowest bidder for board and lodging. In most cases the lot of the pauper was understandably miserable. The cost of medical care for the poor was likewise kept at a minimum. In 1826, Dr. George R. Chetwood was appointed Borough physician for the poor with an annual stipend of twenty dollars for his services. Finally in 1847 a new plan for care of the poor appeared when a building was purchased to house them; thus began the era of the "poor house." [8]

Elizabethtown's early start as an educational center came to full bloom after 1815, for it was now noted for its excellent private schools. By that time the popularity of French culture had faded. Otherwise there was little change in the kind of instruction offered. One of the most successful boarding schools for girls was conducted by Miss Eunice Hall. In 1814 the *New Jersey Journal* noted that Miss Hall's school was an excellent institution, the girls neat and well-mannered. When examined by the town fathers the young ladies stood up admirably under severe testing. One of the leading supporters of Miss Hall's school was the civic-minded Reverend John C. Rudd, pastor of St. John's.

Unfortunately Miss Hall's school came to an abrupt end after a student from Georgia became sick and died. Following her death, a friend of the girl's father, Dr. Robert Grant, also from Georgia, accused Miss Hall of causing the girl's death by negligence and mental cruelty. Soon all Elizabethtown became divided over the accusation. Some people defended Miss Hall: others sided with the Doctor.

To try to save herself from impending ruin, Miss Hall sued Dr. Grant for slander. At the trial Dr. John Chetwood testified that he believed the charges were false and that Miss Hall had given the girl good care. Susan Chetwood, the Doctor's wife, collaborated with her husband and added that she believed Dr. Grant had a grudge against Miss Hall for her refusal to loan him her piano. The Reverend Rudd swore he had always found the school well run. He had visited the school three times a week during the past five years and had never found cause for criticism. During the trial it was shown that the dead girl had been a problem. She had shown no respect for her elders and had laughed at Dr. Rudd with his pious manners and his lectures on morality and Christian virtues.

In the end Miss Hall won the suit and collected damages of $250. But the scandal had done its work and her school had shrunken to a handful of students. Dr. Grant had sworn that he would see to it that no more students ever came to the school from the South and his threat had already been proven effective. Not long after the trial, Miss Hall closed her school and moved to New York where she was able to begin over again.

Among the supporters of Dr. Grant was Jonathan B. Dayton, son of Senator Dayton. Dayton took up a collection for the $250 which was offered to the Doctor to show the people of the South that there were men in Elizabethtown who had respect for what was right. Dr. Grant, however, graciously declined the money.[9]

Private schools for boys in Elizabethtown were as popular as those for young ladies. One of the best of the boys' schools was conducted by the Reverend John C. Rudd, the rector for St. John's. Another excellent boys' school was opened on Chilton Hill by the Reverend John T. Halsey. After a few years this school was run by the Reverend John Taylor under whose auspices it became very popular. With no reflection on Mr. Taylor, it may be noted that one of his students was William Marcy Tweed whose rule as "Boss" Tweed in New York City would become the classic example of city corruption in the nineteenth century. Between 1834 and 1854 James C. Nutman conducted a popular boys' school first on Broad Street and later on Meadow Street near General Scott's house.

As a church-sponsored private school, the Elizabethtown Academy continued serving its patrons until sometime in the 1830's when the trustees decided that the popularity of the Adelphian Academy and other schools made it impractical to maintain the school any longer. The building was remodeled and thereafter served as a lecture hall for the First Presbyterian Church.

During the golden age of the private schools in Elizabethtown many of the larger old houses were used for schools. Among those which at one time or another became schools were Boxwood Hall and the Belcher House on East Jersey Street, the Old Chateau on Rahway Avenue, Carteret Arms, and the Union Hotel. It was after Aaron Ogden had lost the Belcher House for debts that the building for a time became an exclusive girl's school under Miss Clarissa D. Spaulding.

Not all the schools in Elizabethtown in the first half of the nineteenth century were private schools catering to the wealthy. There was, for example, the Manual Labor School sponsored by the Reverend John McDowell and the Reverend David Magie. The philosophy underlying this school was that it would develop a well-rounded individual by combining manual labor with book learning. Although stressing manual labor, the school was not vocational in its aim, since all students were assumed to be preparing for college or the seminary. In addition to attending his academic classes, each student was required to devote three hours a day to some manual labor in a workshop provided by the school. This would take the place of "frivolous boyish sports," build character, and cultivate thrift and industry, it was thought. By working in the shops, the students were expected to earn most of the cost of their schooling; thus it was possible for poor boys to get an education. At the start it was estimated that it would cost a student no more than sixty dollars a year to attend the school, after his earnings were deducted.

Unfortunately the Manual Labor School had a short life. A rented two-story building served for the workshop, and the upper floors of Kollock's print shop for the academic studies. William H. Burroughs, formerly head of the Germantown Manual Labor School in Pennsylvania, was hired as principal. Soon, however, financial difficulties forced the trustees to close the school. The managers, it appears, paid the students too much for their work. Many students wasted material as well as their time in the workshops. Better business methods, perhaps, could have made the school a success.[10]

The inspiration for many educational and eleemosynary endeavors in Elizabethtown came from its ministers, especially the Reverend John C. Rudd. Rudd came to Elizabethtown in 1805 to fill the pulpit left vacant by the resignation of the Reverend Samuel Lilly. At one time he edited a journal published in Elizabethtown and known as *The Churchman's Magazine*. After serving St. John's and the community for twenty-four years, Rudd moved to Auburn, New York.

One of the charitable societies sponsored by the Reverend Rudd

The Reverend John McDowell

The Reverend David Magie

The Reverend Nicholas Murray

The Reverend John C. Rudd

Early nineteenth century Elizabethtown ministers.

was the Female Humane Society, founded in 1810. During the life of that Society, most of the prominent women of Elizabethtown became members. Among them were Mary Jouet, Ann C. Williamson, Ann Barber, Mary C. Ogden, Harrietta McDowell, Jane Dayton, Molly Mills, Elizabeth Ogden, and Susan Niemcewicz. In all, over one hundred and twenty women became charter members. The first meeting was held shortly after Christmas, 1810, in the Adelphian Academy. Dues were one dollar a year. Ann Dayton, wife of William Dayton, was elected First Directress, an office she held for many years. Her successor was Elizabeth Ogden, wife of Aaron Ogden.[11]

The Elizabethtown Female Humane Society experienced a long and useful career. To get the Society off to a good start many of the men of the town made contributions to it. During succeeding years, Elizabethtown churches customarily held annual charity sermons for the Society. In 1812, the Reverend John McDowell collected over one hundred dollars at his charity service, while Dr. Rudd at St. John's collected forty-five dollars and Mr. Morrell twenty-one dollars at the Methodist Church. That year the Society spent about two hundred and fifty dollars for poor relief and education, having started an elementary school in a room at the Elizabethtown Academy. About thirty pupils under eleven attended the school. During the year the Society collected clothing for the poor. In 1817 the students at Miss Hall's boarding school contributed a large bundle of clothing for the Society's poor relief. Another service of the Society consisted in supplying needy women with flax and yarn to enable them to help support themselves by spinning and weaving. The names of the women receiving aid show that nearly all were of the old Elizabethtown families. Charity in Elizabethtown consisted of caring for poor relatives since nearly everyone was related. Some of the women receiving aid from the Society in 1811 were Mrs. Hatfield, Mrs. Crane, Mrs. Sayre, Mrs. Ross, Mrs. Foster, Mrs. Edwards, and Mrs. Johnson.

Another charity organization, founded in 1816, was the Elizabethtown Free School Association, sponsored by the Reverend John McDowell of the First Presbyterian Church. McDowell, who married Henrietta Kollock, daughter of the printer, came to Elizabethtown in 1804. After twenty-eight years of service to his church and town, he moved to Philadelphia to become the minister for the Central Presbyterian Church.

The purpose of the Elizabethtown Free School Association was to furnish education for Negroes and poor white children in Sunday schools. Having been originated in England by Robert Raiker about 1781, the Sunday School movement had finally found its way to America and in Elizabethtown John McDowell went ahead with plans to start Sunday schools at his church. He became the president and Jeremiah Ballard the vice president of the Sunday School Association. Soon the membership of the society numbered over one hundred men and women.

The first school started by the Association was a Sunday School for Negroes. Soon there were eighty Negroes of all ages attending classes which began after the church services and lasted all afternoon. The teaching was done by volunteers. Finding their efforts meeting with success, the Association opened another Sunday School for white girls. A third school, for white boys, completed the system. Within a few months over two hundred pupils were enrolled in the Sunday schools.

Until the public schools were founded, charity and Sunday schools filled a real need in Elizabethtown. In 1819 Miss Mary Dow became superintendent of the girls' Sunday School with an enrollment of over one hundred. She was assisted by fourteen volunteer teachers, all leading women of Elizabethtown. One of the most enthusiastic of the young teachers was Miss Ann Chetwood, daughter of Judge William Chetwood. Mr. Edward Sanderson was superintendent of the Sunday School for white boys. He had eight men teaching four classes. Oliver Nutman was the superintendent of the colored school with five women and seven men for teachers. Bibles and other books for study were donated. In 1819 the Elizabethtown Bible and Tract Society, the Elizabethtown Auxiliary Tract Society, and the Elizabethtown Female Tract Society gave books and Bibles. With almost everything donated, the Association spent only thirty-two dollars that year on the schools. In commemorating the fiftieth anniversary of Robert Raiker's Sunday School movement, the Association held a big celebration in 1831. Teachers, pupils, and sponsors all gathered in an orchard for a picnic which lasted until sundown.[12]

While the Sunday School movement was flourishing, interest

turned upon the Lancastrian system of education that was sweeping England and America. In 1818, Joseph Lancaster, while on his American tour, lectured on the monitorial system at the Elizabethtown Court House. By this time the New Jersey legislature had belatedly passed a feeble act for the encouragement of education. Elizabethtown, however, took no action to implement the law or experiment with the Lancastrian system until 1825 when a meeting was called at the Union Hotel for considering the question of public education. It chose Moses Chandler, coachmaker, for its chairman and then voted to rent rooms in both the Elizabethtown and Adelphian academies for instruction by the Lancastrian or Monitorial system. To implement the plan, an organization known as the Elizabethtown Public School Association was created, the Reverend John C. Rudd, president, and the Reverend David Magie, vice president. The trustees were Peter Kean, Edward Kellogg, and Stephen P. Brittin, three leading business men. Since the instruction was given by the more gifted students under the direction of a teacher, schooling by the Lancastrian system was inexpensive. In addition to a small amount raised by the Association, about one hundred dollars was appropriated by the township of Elizabeth for the school.[18]

Another step toward a public school system came in 1830 when the Township of Elizabeth created nine school districts including the Borough. Trustees were appointed for each district with the power to rent buildings and hire teachers. The trouble was that no money was appropriated for the schools by the township. All the money that the districts could depend upon was $411 of state aid. When apportioned among the districts according to their school age population, the aid ranged from $17.76 to $82.31. If the district were to have a school the rest of the money must come from charitable organizations or private donors.

With public schools classified as pauper schools, all who could afford the cost continued to send their children to private schools, which in turn did all in their power to impede the establishment of a public school system. Sentiment, however, was gaining in favor of a true public school system. Already New Jersey was far behind more progressive states like New York and Massachusetts with their tax-supported public schools. New Jersey, declared the proponents of public education, needed a state board of education and more state aid for common schools. What free schools existed were usually found on side streets, in rundown houses, staffed with incompetent teachers.

Progress was slow until the New Jersey legislature passed an act in 1838 which provided more state aid and empowered the local governments to raise additional funds by taxation. In 1845 the trustees of the Elizabeth township school fund reported that the township had five schools with an enrollment of about eight hundred pupils. For the quarter session the cost of instruction amounted to $2.05 per pupil. Small as this sum was it represented a sizeable increase in school expenditures. In addition to the five free schools, there was still the school sponsored by the Female Humane Society, attended by about one hundred pupils.[14]

The year 1850 is the date usually assigned for the beginning of public education in New Jersey. That year the Borough became district number two in the township with six public schools, one of which was for colored children. The Borough at this time had a population of about four thousand with slightly over one thousand children of school age. Out of this number about four hundred and fifty pupils attended the six public schools. The others went to private institutions or failed to attend school. One of the public schools under Miss Susan M. Stiles was on Harrison and Crane streets. Another was on Washington Street, while one was housed in the old Adelphian Academy. The cost of running these schools came to two thousand dollars. Two years later school appropriations had risen to three thousand dollars for the Borough.

Public education advanced steadily in Elizabethtown during the following years. By 1856 appropriation for schools had risen to eight thousand dollars. For the improvement of instruction the schools were divided into the primary, the intermediate, and the grammar departments. It was not until 1887, however, that the City of Elizabeth established a High School. Two years later, Joseph Battin gave his two hundred and fifty thousand dollar mansion for a High School building. The Battin High School accommodated nearly five hundred students and was considered the best high school in New Jersey at the time.[15]

For many years Elizabethtown Presbyterians saw the need for another church since the old First Church could no longer accommodate all its members. As minister of the First Church, the

Reverend John McDowell consequently proceeded to form another congregation. Through his efforts the Second Presbyterian Church was organized in 1820. The twenty-five-year-old Princeton graduate David Magie who would serve for forty-five years, was selected for its pastor. Services were first held in the Lecture Room of the Elizabethtown Academy. Soon after a brick church was constructed on Golden Hill on East Jersey Street for Mr. Magie and his congregation.

The American Bible Society, founded by Elias Boudinot after he moved to Burlington, assumed an important role in the religious life of nineteenth century Elizabethtown. In 1816, the Auxiliary Bible Society was founded with Aaron Ogden the president and the Reverend Thomas Morrell, vice president. The same year saw the founding of the Female Auxiliary Society with Susan Niemcewicz, the First Directress. So popular were the Bible societies that a branch was organized for the young ladies with Miss Elizabeth Halsey the First Directress. The function of all the local societies was to raise money which the American Bible Society could use for buying and distributing Bibles and religious literature to schools, churches, and the poor.[16]

The Elizabethtown African Colonization Society was another enterprise classified as a charitable organization. Elizabethtown was late in organizing a society for helping free Negroes colonize in Africa. The chapter was founded in 1854, long after the movement had taken hold in many other communities. At the organizing meeting in the First Presbyterian Church, leaders of the state society declared that it was the duty of all Christians to help Negroes get to Africa. Included in the Elizabethtown chapter of the Colonization Society were people from all the religious denominations, including the rapidly growing Roman Catholic congregation. Contributions raised in Elizabethtown went to the state chapter which among other things was endeavoring to establish an iron industry in an African colony which it was sponsoring.[17]

One of the most popular crusades of the nineteenth century was the temperance movement. Nearly every town in America became the scene of temperance activity. Foster Day, owner of the old Trotter's Mill, was president of the Elizabethtown Temperance Society of which Dr. Charles Davis (who lived in the Belcher House), the Honorable William Chetwood, and many other leading citizens, were members. During this period the *New Jersey Journal* carried articles extolling temperance and reciting the bad effects of alcohol. Fourth of July speeches were turned into lectures on temperance and one Elizabethtown tavern even discontinued the sale of liquor and became a temperance house.

In an effort further to help the poor and underprivileged, Elizabethtonians considered the need of a library for the poor. The Library Association established in the 1790's had not been very successful but it was thought that a library entirely free would be patronized. In 1812 the subscription library was moved from Chapman's tobacco store and post-office on Water Street to the home of Smith Scudder, the librarian. But by this time, the library was in trouble. Books borrowed were not returned. Furthermore, funds could not be raised to replace them. Soon the Association voted to close the library in view of the lack of interest. Subsequently thoughtful people voiced their concern that a community known for its wealth and culture had no public library. Quoting Benjamin Franklin, one writer reminded readers that "A nation of well-informed men, who have been taught to know and prize the rights which God has given them, cannot be enslaved." [18]

Men like the one who quoted Franklin met and formed the Elizabethtown Apprentices Library Association in 1821. Peter Kean was elected president and Stephen S. Brittin vice-president. Lawyer John J. Chetwood, son of Dr. John Chetwood, was the secretary. When the first meeting was held, following the organization of the society, President Kean delivered a speech in which he set forth the aims of the Association. The Library, he said, should help keep the youth of Elizabethtown from idleness and make them more useful and better citizens. "Our safety, happiness, prosperity, and honor, depend upon the intelligence of the people," he concluded.

Peter Kean, who died at the age of forty in 1828, was a man of unusual talents. His father, John Kean, a South Carolina patriot in the Revolution and one time member of Congress, died when Peter was a child. From his mother, Susan, an astute business woman and manager of the family investments, Peter gained much of his practical education. From his step-father, Count

Niemcewiz, Peter gained his fluent use of the French language as well as a foundation in the liberal arts. After graduating from Princeton, he took a leading part in the civic affairs of Elizabethtown and the state at large.

Not long after the organizational meeting, the Elizabethtown Apprentice Library became a reality. Space was obtained in the Elizabethtown Academy. Soon nearly five hundred volumes were collected and placed in the custody of J. F. Randolph, the librarian. From the start the use of the library by the laboring class was not encouraging. During the first year the library had but eighty-five readers. The library was given six or seven hundred volumes by the defunct Library Association. But the result was the same. Few apprentices wanted to read. In 1835 the disappointed sponsors closed the library. Not until after the Civil War, when the demand for books and learning had grown, did Elizabethtown have another library, this one destined to become a permanent public institution.[19]

During the early part of the nineteenth century, Elizabethtonians were favored with a variety of lectures and performances. At the Indian Queen Tavern in 1811, a Mr. Morris delivered a lecture on the advantages of a scientific education. Science was an increasingly popular subject and in 1820, David Young gave four lectures on astronomy at the Adelphian Academy. A year later, a Mr. Hazelton, dressed in a Grecian costume, lectured on the moral influence of memory. The lecture began at "early candle light" and cost the listener twenty-five cents. Some years later Captain Symmes expounded his theories on the nature of the earth at the Court House. The earth, he thought, was not solid. It was hollow, with large openings at the poles for light and heat to enter. The inner regions of the earth, therefore, were inhabited, he maintained. Symmes won a few converts in Elizabethtown but most of his audience attended out of curiosity or to ridicule the "scientist" who wanted Congress to send an expedition to the North Pole to test his theories. If few Elizabethtonians found Professor Symmes' ideas plausible, many were eager to learn about phrenology, a fad that was sweeping the country. At "early candle light" on a July evening in 1838, a lecture on the subject was given at the Court House for all those interested in explaining mental faculties by the formation of the head.[20]

The founding of singing schools, choirs, and glee clubs in these early years of nineteenth century Elizabethtown reveals a genuine interest in good music among the townspeople. For more than twenty years Elias Thompson ran a popular singing school. Mr. Thompson would allow no spectators in the hall or brook any distractions during the practicing. In 1812 singers had the opportunity of receiving instruction in a musical academy which lasted for a few months. In 1819 selections from Handel were sung by a mixed choir under the direction of Ebenezer Shaw at St. John's Episcopal Church. Musicians from the outside also performed. From New York came the American Conservatorio to sing at St. John's. From the city also came a Mr. Lewis with his four gifted children between the ages of four and ten, who gave a concert with the pianoforte, harp, violin, and violincello.[21]

Of the traveling dispensers of culture none were more sought after than the portrait painters who set up studios in the taverns. In 1822, N. K. Brown was in Elizabethtown painting miniatures at Craig's Union Hotel. Another painter who had a studio at the Hotel was John J. Baker, a student of Thomas Sully.[22]

Exhibitions of one kind or another attracted throngs of the curious. Egyptian mummies excited great interest when they were exhibited in 1825. Statuettes in wax were another attraction. Stowell and Bradley's "Elegant Museum" was on exhibition for four days in 1817. The collection had thirty-six figures of famous men displayed on a "grand mechanical panorama" painted by well-known American artists.[23]

In an age when oratory was considered a fine art, Elizabethtown had its literary and debating societies dating back to the 1790's. The first literary club, known as the Philamatic Society, apparently had a short life. The second club, called the Philanthropic Literary Society, was organized in 1802. After a few years, interest lapsed and the society broke up. In 1816, however, the Philanthropic Literary Society was revived when Oliver S. Halsted was elected president and Jabez Crane vice president. The society aimed to improve oratory, facilitate reading and reasoning, and promote social graces and correct principles.[24]

The first regular meeting of the Philanthropic Literary Society was held at the Court House. The program consisted of four debates. The first question debated was whether or not theatrical plays should be prohibited. Jabez Crane argued that the theater should be outlawed. He lost the debate. President Halsted, however, stated his belief that society would profit by a law prohibiting such forms of amusement. The second question was whether or not banks were beneficial to society. The affirmation won and this time President Halsted agreed with the verdict. The third debate was on the question of whether or not representatives should be bound by the will of their constituents. The negative won. The last question on the need of capital punishment was also won by the negative. The Society, however, voted that the affirmative was right since society must have the means to protect itself.

Although the Philanthropic Literary Society got off to a good start, after about a year interest waned and the club disbanded. Another short-lived debating society appeared in 1821. Since the question of capital punishment was exciting interest throughout the world, this topic was again selected for debating. The question, however, was considered objectionable in Elizabethtown. An editorial in the *New Jersey Journal* argued that the question was not debatable since God had settled the question once and for all when he said "Whosoever sheddeth man's blood, by man shall his blood be shed." [25]

Occupational societies in Elizabethtown enjoyed a growing popularity as the nineteenth century wore on. In 1817 the Essex County Agricultural Society was organized by Aaron Ogden and other leaders in the county. Manifestly this was a society for dilettantes rather than dirt farmers. In 1823 Peter Kean became the president. That year at the annual fair at Orange, New Jersey, Kean gave an address before the Society on rotation of crops and the breeding of livestock.

Another society of an occupational character was the Elizabethtown General Mechanics Society, organized in 1808. Thaddeus Mills, the coach painter, was the first president with Elias Wade, the coachmaker, as vice president. From the earliest days the master mechanic had been the most powerful single interest in Elizabethtown but they had never before attempted to form a society as had their brothers in New York and Philadelphia. With the membership including many of the wealthiest citizens and captains of the business community, the mechanics society was a very influential organization. Dedicated to helping the poor as well as serving as a fraternal society, the officers had charge of the benevolent activities of the organization. For many years the Mechanics met at the Adelphian Academy, but in 1832 they built a lodge hall on Bridge Street near the Academy.

Not until 1818 did Elizabethtown have another chapter of Freemasons. By this time only a few people could remember the old Temple Lodge founded by Jonathan Hampton before the Revolution. The new chapter, of which Aaron Ogden was a sponsor, was called the Washington Lodge Number 41. Oliver Hatfield became the first master. The installation of officers took place in the First Presbyterian Church, with prayers by the Reverend John McDowell. For many years the Lodge rented the third floor of the Court House for its meetings. The Lodge broke up in 1833 but was revived in 1854 as Washington Lodge Number 33.

By 1840 Elizabethtown had a chapter of Odd Fellows, known as Franklin Lodge, Number 9. The meetings were held on the third floor of a brick building on Broad Street near the Railroad Station. The main room was elaborately furnished with Turkish carpets and velvet-covered seats. Frescoes on the seventeen-foot walls were painted by two Italian artists whose identity is unknown. Quite understandably, the Odd Fellows Hall was something for Elizabethtonians to boast about.[26]

Naturally light forms of amusement continued to occupy the leisure hours of most people in Elizabethtown. On entering a home, the caller often found a pack of the popular "courting cards" with the American eagle boldly stamped on the back of each card. "Courting cards" met the approval of even the local ministers since the game was designed to advance the interests of cupid by transforming "the heart of adamant, into a heart of purest love and kindness." Made for the use of "every Beau and Belle in America," the questions and answers on the cards were rendered more alluring by appropriate verse.[27]

During the summer months the young men and boys found much enjoyment swimming in the river at the mill ponds. Jacob Crane's Mill Pond just above the West Jersey Street crossing was the most popular pool. Whether or not the bathers wore any clothing, townspeople objected to swimming during daylight hours. For many years the Corporation tried to prohibit swimming within the Borough but without much success. Finally in 1823, the town relaxed enough to allow swimming during the day if it was confined to pools out of sight of the bridges and highways.[28]

In winter sleigh-riding continued to be a favorite outdoor pastime. In 1836, David Sanderson, owner of the Union Hotel and a former stagecoach driver, drove to Newark and back a sleigh pulled by ten beautiful greys. Newark tried to out-do Sanderson by sending two sleighs, each of which was pulled by twelve horses, through the streets of Elizabethtown. People, however, were quick to note that each of the Newark teams was driven by two drivers while Sanderson handled his reins alone. A little later Sanderson made it clear that Newark could not compete with him when he harnessed sixteen greys and drove them with "ease and dexterity" to Newark with the stars and stripes waving from the sleigh. Everyone acknowledged that Sanderson's horsemanship had never been equaled in the state of New Jersey.[29] He lived to be a very old man. In 1889, more than fifty years after his celebrated drive to Newark, one of the fire companies called out the veteran horseman to take the reins of their fire engine team in the Fourth of July parade.

About a year before Sanderson's famous sleigh ride, people were shocked to learn about a "barbarous and inhuman" prize fight held at Elizabethtown Point. The combatants were two "bullies" from New York, one an Englishman, the other an Irishman. They came on steamboats crowded with nearly two thousand men elated with the prospect of witnessing a bloody fight. Three magistrates from Elizabethtown tried to stop the exhibition, but without success. The men fought for two hours before one was so badly beaten that he could fight no longer. Prodded by Elizabethtonians, the state legislature passed an act imposing heavy fines and a prison term on prize fighters and their sponsors, including the owners and captains of steamboats. Even the spectators became subject to a fine and a year's imprisonment.[30]

The year 1826 saw the fiftieth anniversary of the signing of the Declaration of Independence. For the occasion, Elizabethtown put on a great Fourth of July celebration which attracted people from miles around. Peter Kean was officer of the day in charge of the biggest parade ever held in Elizabethtown. At the head of the line marched a blaring brass band. Next came Captain Brown's Light Artillery, followed by the Light Infantry under Captain

Price and Captain Fielding. Next in line was Hinchman's Rifle Corps. Captain Lawrence's colorful Governor's Guard brought up the rear of the militia. Normally the local Cincinnati and the other veterans of the Revolution would have been in line but they had gone to Trenton for a grand review of the survivors of the War for Independence.

After the militia came an impressive agricultural display with wagons filled with farm implements. Next came floats with men flailing grain, winnowing wheat with a fanning mill, and performing other kinds of farm work. On one float decorated with bunting women were engaged in spinning flax and wool. Although most of the agricultural tools on display were little different from those in use for the past century or more, there was nonetheless a sign of the impending revolution in agriculture. An ingenious horse-drawn mowing machine from Delaware caught the eyes of everyone and made people wonder what would be next!

After the agricultural section there were floats featuring Elizabethtown craftsmen. There was a float for the butchers, one for the bakers, and another for the candlestick makers. A float for the cordwainers had a cobbler engaged in making shoes. Behind the float marched fifty members of the New Jersey Cordwainers Guild. Other floats followed: for the carpenters, bricklayers, masons, stone cutters, potters, cabinetmakers, coopers, coachmakers, coach and carriage painters, bookbinders, even the hairdressers and Mr. Diamond's watch shop.

While celebrating their independence, Americans did not forget others in the world struggling for liberty. In 1824, a house-to-house canvass was made for funds to help the Greeks win independence from the Turks. At a large meeting at the First Presbyterian Church, Jonathan Dayton and Peter Kean made speeches extolling the Greeks. When the collection was taken, it was found that over two hundred and fifty dollars had been given to the cause of Greek independence.

Years later, in 1847, Elizabethtown was again engaged in raising funds for a country in distress. Ireland was having a terrible famine and Americans answered the call for help by sending great quantities of provisions to the starving people. At a large meeting, a committee headed by the Reverend Nicholas Murray

View of Elizabethtown near Lyon's Tavern, 1795.

was appointed to make collections in Elizabethtown. The money raised was turned over to a state committee which presently had two shiploads of provisions on the way to Ireland.[31]

After an absence of more than forty years, the Marquis de Lafayette returned to Elizabethtown to visit old friends on his triumphal tour of the United States in 1824. For the event Elizabethtown was decorated and illuminated as never before. Lafayette landed at Paulus Hook after crossing the Hudson on the steamboat *Chancellor Kent* with his son, George Washington Lafayette. They were met by Governor Isaac H. Williamson and other dignitaries, who escorted them to Newark. After a reception at Newark, the Marquis and his son, escorted by the Elizabethtown Light Horse, left for Elizabethtown in the company of Jonathan Dayton, Aaron Ogden, and others.

Upon arriving in front of the Union Hotel, the procession passed through a triumphal arch covered with evergreens. In the long room of the Tavern, a great banquet was spread and speeches were made by Ogden, Dayton, and others. During the reception, the Freemasons presented Lafayette (who belonged to the Military Lodge during the Revolution) with a gold medal. After the banquet, Lafayette and his son were escorted to the home of Jonathan Dayton where they spent the night.*

The next morning Lafayette visited Aaron Ogden, his aide-de-camp during the Virginia campaign. While they were breakfasting, conversation turned upon the days when they held Cornwallis at bay while Washington and Rochambeau were marching to Yorktown. Eighty years after Lafayette's visit, a granddaughter of Colonel Ogden's told how all the grandchildren belonging to Ogden and Colonel Barber were lined up at the Belcher House for the Marquis' inspection.

Lafayette was especially pleased to meet Mary Vanderpool D'Anterroches and her children. Her husband, Joseph Louis, was no longer living, having died at the age of sixty on a visit to France to see relatives, including Lafayette.

During Lafayette's stay, no one had done more than Jonathan Dayton to make his visit a memorable occasion. But the exertion and the excitement had been too much for the sixty-year-old

* Formerly the home of Elias Boudinot; now Boxwood Hall.

veteran of the Revolution. Within a week after the Marquis had left, Dayton died.

Lafayette passed through Elizabethtown again nearly a year later on his way to embark for home on the United States frigate *Brandywine*. Again the streets were lined by cheering townspeople as he rode with Aaron Ogden and Peter Kean in the latter's handsome coach drawn by four grey horses. Before departing, Lafayette paid his respects to Susan Dayton, wife of the dead senator. He also once more visited the old Presbyterian burying ground where so many of his comrades lay sleeping. Walking arm in arm with Sheppard Kollock, he stopped at one stone after another. Long he lingered at the grave of Matthias Ogden and at those of Parson Caldwell and his wife.[32]

For a long time Elizabethtown had felt the need of a bank. Prior to 1812 when the State Bank of Elizabethtown was founded, there had been some banking conducted by individuals. In 1787, for instance, Jonathan Hetfield had a banking business in the old White House on Water Street. Business such as this was unlicensed and entirely unregulated. After the founding of a bank in Newark in 1804, agitation for a similar institution in Elizabethtown mounted. The wishes of the Elizabethtonians were fulfilled when in 1812 the legislature chartered the State Bank of Elizabethtown with a capitalization of one hundred thousand dollars. Most of the stock was owned by local people including William Chetwood, Caleb Halsted, Jr., James Wilson, Aaron Ogden, Mrs. Susan Niemcewicz and her son, Peter Kean.

The directors of the State Bank of Elizabethtown lost no time in getting banking under way. At a meeting in the Union Hotel, Thaddeus Mills, the well-known coach and carriage painter, was appointed president of the bank. In about a year, Aaron Ogden succeeded him. Elias B. Dayton (Senator Dayton's younger brother) was named cashier, following the resignation of the first appointee. After the selection of officers, the house of Ichabod Williams directly opposite Sheppard Kollock's print shop on Broad Street was rented for a temporary place of business. Soon a lot was purchased (where the State Bank of Elizabeth now stands) and construction of a building was presently begun. In 1813 the State Bank moved into its new home, a stately Georgian building with two massive chimneys at each end. The first floor, raised six feet off the ground, was reached by a double stairway with wrought-iron railings. One of the first services to the community came in 1814 when the Bank, at the instance of the Borough Council, issued forty-five thousand paper notes worth twenty-five hundred dollars for use as small change. The bills ranged in value from two to twenty-five cents.[33]

Ordinarily the State Bank of Elizabethtown operated with a profit. During its first year, its net profit amounted to over six thousand dollars. For a while, however, it was involved in financial difficulty owing to loans aggregating thirty thousand dollars made to Aaron Ogden, the Bank's president. Ogden was finally forced into bankruptcy and the Bank was rescued by Peter Kean, William Chetwood, and some others capable of underwriting its obligations. Naturally Ogden was removed from the presidency of the Bank following the disclosure of his insolvency. With his removal, William Chetwood, a prominent lawyer, became the president. Not until 1837 did the State Bank have a competitor in Elizabethtown, when the Citizens and Mechanics Bank was incorporated and opened its doors for business.[34]

Although the bank stimulated business activity, industrial growth continued to be slow. One new business was the wire shop next to the Methodist Church on Water Street where Ogden Woodruff made fanning mills and screens for sieves, grist mills, and windows. He also made a good wire rat trap. Although in no way rivaling the large boot and shoe industry in Newark, Elizabethtown had several shoe shops employing six or eight workmen. Tucker and Garthwait, opposite the Adelphian Academy, made ladies' shoes of kid, morocco, and satin.[35]

If Elizabethtown could be considered outstanding in any line of business before 1840, it was in the coach and carriage industry. The largest carriage shop was owned by Elias Wade. In 1803 he made an elegant two horse coach with silver molding for the wealthy Georgia planter, Thomas Gibbons. Twenty years later, he made a four horse coach for Gibbons, who had become famous as a steamboat operator. The new coach was painted yellow and striped with black. On each side was painted a steamboat. With his business growing rapidly, Wade in 1816 took in three partners, David Price, Ambrose Williams, and Oliver Stiles. Wade's chief competitor was Moses Chandler, who was widely known for his workmanship. Thaddeus Mills, the carriage painter, also offered competition when he opened a coach and carriage making shop. Elizabethtown had at least three other carriage makers in the early part of the nineteenth century.

The town had several brass foundries in the early years of the nineteenth century. Before the Revolution, it will be remembered, it had brass foundries belonging to Aaron Miller and David Ross, makers of bells, brass instruments, clock works, and other objects. In 1810 Robert Price, Jr., operated a brass foundry on East Jersey Street nearly opposite the Belcher House. Price made brass andirons, shovels, tongs, machinery parts, and clock works. Another brass foundry was owned by Elijah Kellogg in the 1820's. At this time, also, Thomas P. Walworth had a brass foundry in conjunction with a cast-iron foundry.[36]

Walworth's cast-iron foundry, located somewhere along the river back of Water Street, was apparently a business of considerable size. Besides cast iron, his plant turned out malleable castings for machinery. Many castings were made for the Steam Engine Factory next door to the Walworth Foundry. In the cast-iron line, the foundry turned out the usual run of castings, including stoveplate, sleighshoes, wheelboxes for wagons and carriages, plows, kettles, and flatirons.

Of all the industries of Elizabethtown during the period before 1840, the Steam Engine Factory is the most notable. The factory was owned by Aaron Ogden who put up most of the money, and by Daniel Dod whose ingenuity was an asset fully as essential as the capital. Dod had been trained by his father as a clock and instrument maker, the trade which schooled America's first batch of great inventors. After attending Queen's College (Rutgers), Dod started a factory for making cotton cloth. This undertaking failed. It was right after this that Dod, who had patented some of his ideas on steam engines and steamboat machinery, became a partner of Aaron Ogden in his Steam Engine Factory in Elizabethtown.

During the six or seven years that Ogden and Dod were in business together, machinery and engines were made in their Steam Engine Factory for steamboats under construction in many parts of America. Dod's first steamboat, Aaron Ogden's *Sea Horse*, earned for him a national reputation for steamboat designing.

After the *Sea Horse,* which was considered the fastest steamboat afloat, Dod made further improvements in his engines and machinery as one order followed another from near and far. In 1819, he made much of the machinery for the steamship *Savannah,* the first ship to cross the Atlantic with steam power.*

Inventing and improving engines and steamboat machinery were costly; and by 1818, Ogden and Dod were overwhelmed with debts. Soon the State Bank of Elizabethtown took over the Steam Engine Factory as well as Ogden's new steamboat, the *Atalanta.* Ogden had already disposed of the *Sea Horse.* Dod, who was considered a poet and philosopher as well as an inventor, got started again in New York with the help of friends. His life, however, was soon terminated when a boiler burst on a steamboat he was repairing. Ogden struggled on for a few more years before bankruptcy finally took all his worldly possessions. Daniel Dod and Aaron Ogden were pioneers in the advancement of American engineering; they deserve to be recognized in the chronicles of American industry.

* The heavy machinery for the *Savannah* was made at the Speedwell Iron Works in Morristown.

Old Elizabethtown: The Finale

On a day in July, 1816, Thomas Gibbons, fat and fifty-eight, got out of his carriage with labored breath, and with whip in hand, pounded on the door of Aaron Ogden's office in the west wing of the Belcher House. As eccentric as he was wealthy, Gibbons had few friends and many enemies. Not finding the Colonel at home, he tacked a challenge to a duel on the door and went away. The challenge (which Gibbons had taken the pains to have printed) told how he had been arrested in May for not paying a note which Ogden had purchased without his knowledge. "I was—arrested in a Suit at Law, in your name, in the City of New York, after I was on board of the Steam Boat, returning to Elizabethtown," the paper read. Since they lived within half a mile of each other and Ogden had not notified him that he had a claim against him, Gibbons swore that he would teach him to "proceed with Decency." What Gibbons did not know was that Ogden had forgotten to notify him and that he was not aware of his arrest. Regretting the embarrassment he had caused, Ogden at once sent his apologies. This might have ended the affair but for another matter that infuriated Gibbons much more than his arrest. Mrs. Gibbons had gone to Ogden seeking a separation from her husband and Ogden had agreed to help her. "I understand that you have interfered in a Dispute between Mrs. Gibbons and myself," wrote Gibbons on the hand-bill. Then he added as a postscript, "I hope you are prepared to explain yourself for your wanton interference in a case so delicate. If you stand mute, I shall adjudge you as pleading guilty, and treat you as a convict." *

* Handbill addressed to Aaron Ogden, July 26, 1816. Gibbons claimed that Ogden ran out the back door when he saw him stopping at his house. This story seems unlikely since it does not fit Ogden's character. Ogden maintained he was not at home when Gibbons called.

Thomas Gibbons. Courtesy of William L. Hopkins, Jr.

The Gibbons-Ogden controversy grew out of a long quarrel between Gibbons and John M. Trumbull, his son-in-law. Trumbull had persistently prodded his wife, Ann, to get a settlement from her father on a share of an estate she had inherited from an uncle. Gibbons had said all along that he would see to it that she would get what was coming to her and more. Already he had turned over to her his interest in the ferry leased by Aaron Ogden at the Old Point. Trumbull, however, was not satisfied and had sought the advice of Ogden, who counselled Ann to sue, if necessary, for her share of her uncle's estate. So intemperate in his language did Gibbons become during the quarrel over Ann's inheritance that Trumbull finally sued his father-in-law for libel. The trial took place in Newark where Gibbons created a scene by his unrestrained abuse of his son-in-law.

John Trumbull and Ann, in turn, persuaded Mrs. Gibbons to seek a legal separation from her husband. Gibbons, John charged, kept a harem of both white and colored women at his home in Elizabethtown. He asserted that Ann and her mother were not going to maintain a brothel for Gibbons. Stung by accusations and recriminations, Gibbons struck back by charging that Trumbull had seduced Ann before they were married. As for Ann, so her father said, she was a little devil with a poisonous tongue. Believing perhaps that he could make himself appear a little better by comparison, Gibbons ranted about his wife's father who, he declared, had one affair after another with dozens of married women and widows in Georgia.[1]

Thomas Gibbons had settled in Elizabethtown about the year 1800 after acquiring a reputation as one of Georgia's most astute and successful lawyers. Unlike his father and his brothers, he became a Loyalist during the Revolution. The black sheep of the family, he was arrested in 1782 and confined to his mother's plantation, White Hall. Apparently he had not taken a prominent part among the Georgia Tories, for in 1783 he succeeded in having his name removed from the list of those scheduled to have their estates confiscated. He was, however, among those who lost their political privileges as well as the right to practice law for a number of years. In 1791, Gibbons made a brilliant comeback when he successfully backed General Anthony Wayne for Congress. After that, his wartime sins then quite forgotten, he served as mayor of Savannah for several years. In 1795, too, he was a member of the Georgia Constitutional Convention. By 1800 his law practice earned him upwards of fifteen thousand dollars a year. Having also made a windfall from land speculation, he came to Elizabethtown as one of the wealthiest men in the country.

Before pinning the challenge on Colonel Ogden's door, Gibbons sent Jonathan Dayton (the old Senator whose daughter had married Gibbons' son, Thomas Heyward) to try to persuade Ogden to drop his wife's suit for separation. Seeing the handwriting on the note presented by Dayton, Ogden refused to take it or even to discuss the matter. This action provoked Gibbons into challenging Ogden to a duel. "My friend General Dayton will arrange with you the time, the place, of our Meeting," the handbill stated. Gibbons, however, was disappointed to find that Ogden saw no reason for accepting a challenge arising from his duties as a lawyer. Ogden's refusal to accept the challenge was generally applauded as the only sensible thing to do.

This time it was Ogden's turn to teach Gibbons a lesson. Gibbons was indicted for breaking the law against duelling, but the judge agreed with Gibbons that the word "Meeting" did not necessarily imply that a meeting need be for a duel and the case was dismissed. Meanwhile Ogden sued Gibbons for trespassing at the time he tacked the challenge to his door. The case dragged on until 1823 when the Court awarded Ogden five thousand dollars in damages. A higher court reduced the amount to twenty-five hundred dollars, which Gibbons was forced to pay. Ogden's handling of the whole affair, it was said, did much to end duelling in America.

Gibbons' clash with Ogden had still more important and far-reaching consequences than its effect on duelling. Gibbons, who never forgave his enemies, now resolved to break into the Elizabethtown-New York ferry business for the purpose of ruining his enemy, whose steamboats had laden him with a heavy debt. In his design to destroy Ogden, Gibbons was completely successful, for within a decade Ogden was financially ruined.

As a connecting link in the route between New York and Philadelphia, the Elizabethtown ferry had been in use since the earliest days. With the increase in travel and transportation,

ferries had steadily grown in importance. After the Revolution
the principal ferry between New York and Elizabethtown was
operated by Edward Thomas from Crane's Ferry at De Hart's
Point. After Thomas died in 1795, the ferry was run by General
William Crane until it was sold to Colonel Ogden, Jonathan
Dayton, and Dr. John Stites. The latter soon sold his interest to
his partners. Dayton eventually sold his interest to Thomas Gibbons, who in 1804 leased his share in the ferry to Aaron Ogden
for a period of ten years.[2]

Although passengers generally used the ferry at the Point,
much of the freighting was handled on the wharves at the Landing Place below the Stone Bridge. It was this phase of the ferrying that gave Ogden most of his competition. One of the ferries
at the Landing was operated by Morris Hatfield, formerly the
proprietor of the Sign of the Two Lions (Graham's Tavern). In
1802, he announced the launching of a handsome new ferry
boat called *The Freedom* which would sail between John De
Hart's dock and New York. Soon he had another sailing boat
named *The Friendship*. Merchants owning docks at the Landing
Place also had sailboats which plied between Elizabethtown and
New York. One of these was the *Mary Ann*, owned in 1800 by
William Shute and later by David S. Canfield. Another was Job
Haines' sloop, the *Maria*. Other merchants with sailboats or a
share in them were Elias Dayton, William Crane, Austin Perry,
John Hanyan, and Ogden and Lewis Woodruff.[3]

Steamboat navigation began on the waters of the Hudson in
1807 when Robert Fulton sent his *Clermont* steaming up the
river to Albany. The next year, John Stevens of Hoboken built
his steamboat *Phoenix*. It began running between Elizabethtown and Manhattan as the first regular steamboat service in
America. But the life of his ferry service was short. Before many
months elapsed, Robert R. Livingston and Robert Fulton were
granted by the New York legislature exclusive right for thirty
years to navigate steamboats on the waters of the Hudson.
Finding it useless to fight the New York monopoly, Stevens sent
the *Phoenix* to the Delaware where it plied between Philadelphia
and Trenton. Presently Colonel Ogden made an agreement with
Livingston and Fulton whereby their steamboat the *Raritan*,*

---

* The *Raritan* was the second steamboat built by Robert Fulton.

which ran between New York and New Brunswick, was allowed to use his dock at De Hart's Point for a stop.

An adventurous man, Aaron Ogden wanted to get into the steamboat business himself. Perhaps he felt that his concession would prompt Livingston and Fulton to grant him a license to operate a steamboat between New York and Elizabethtown. His advances, however, proved futile for the New York men gave him no encouragement. New Jersey, nonetheless, in January, 1811, passed an act stating that if any citizen of New Jersey was restrained by the New York monopolists from operating a steamboat, he would be entitled to damages in a New Jersey court. Encouraged by this legislation as well as the advice of lawyers who thought that the Livingston-Fulton monopoly could not hold against a steamboat of superior design, Ogden borrowed to the hilt to have Daniel Dod build the *Sea Horse*, with advanced designs in the engine, boiler, and water wheels. The boat, itself, was built by Cornelius Jorelemon, a noted shipwright of North Bellville. It was seventy-five feet in length, with an eighteen foot beam. When equipped with Dod's twelve horsepower engine and the machinery, the *Sea Horse* could obtain a speed of up to nine miles an hour. On one occasion the *Sea Horse* raced Livingston's *Olive Branch* (the fastest steamboat out of New York) in the Arthur Kill and left her far behind.[4]

By the time the *Sea Horse* was ready for service, Ogden found his New York competitors prepared to prevent his boat from making the run between Elizabethtown and New York. The New York legislature had passed an act authorizing the seizure of any steamboat infringing on the Livingston-Fulton monopoly. Confronted by an intransigent rival, Ogden appealed to the New Jersey legislature for help. In his petition he explained how, with Dod, he had bought the John Fitch patents and had constructed a steamboat with important improvements over existing ones. As a result, a law was passed late in 1813 with provisions similar to those of the New York law, giving Ogden a monopoly of steam navigation in the waters of New Jersey.[5]

When the New Jersey law was passed, John R. Livingston was the owner of the New York monopoly, having purchased it from Robert R. Livingston and Robert Fulton. His steamboat, the *Raritan,* with its copper boiler made in Boston by Paul Revere of midnight-riding fame, could now be forced to discontinue the run to New Jersey. The New Jersey law, however, did not force him to capitulate. Rather it brought steamboat navigation to a halt between New York and New Jersey with the monopolists on either side not daring to send their boats to the opposite shore.

Although neither side dared to send steamboats to the ports of the other state, they did the next best thing. Ogden ran the *Sea Horse* to Jersey City, where passengers took the horse or teamboat, *Substitution,* to New York: the horseboat, probably of Dod's design and manufacture, was made of two boats fastened together with beams; over all, was a deck with a water wheel in the center, powered by six horses on a treadmill. While Ogden operated in this way, Livingston sent his steamboat to Staten Island where passengers could take a teamboat or a sailboat to New Jersey.[6]

As soon as the "Ogden law" was enacted by the New Jersey legislature, John Livingston had his friends in New Jersey start a campaign for repealing the measure. His efforts were rewarded in January, 1815, when with the help of interested parties, especially in Amboy, the "Ogden law" was repealed.

With his own state turned against him, Ogden went to Albany to plead his case before the New York legislature. So well did he criticize the impropriety and ill-effects of the steamboat monopoly that the New York legislature came within one vote of repealing the law. In his argument, Ogden was the first to point out that the New York monopoly violated the commerce clause of the United States Constitution, thus anticipating John Marshall's famous decision in the steamboat case (Gibbons *vs.* Ogden, 1824).

So close did Aaron Ogden come to winning his case in New York that Livingston decided to make a concession, even though it might lessen business on his New York-Amboy-New Brunswick line. Following negotiations, Ogden secured a ten-year permit to operate steamboats between Elizabethtown and New York. For his license, he paid Livingston eight hundred dollars annually. He also gave Livingston the right to use his dock at Market Street in New York by paying one-half the rental. After the papers were signed, Ogden proudly began running the *Sea Horse* between Elizabethtown Point and New York.[7]

While Ogden was struggling against the New York steamboat monopoly, trouble arose with Thomas Gibbons; it led to the challenge and the ensuing controversy with Gibbons over steamboat rights. Gibbons' first attempt to upset Ogden's steamboat interests occurred shortly after the challenge episode when Gibbons demanded that Ogden either sell him his share of the ferry at De Hart's Point or buy him out. Such was the original agreement, Gibbons maintained. Ogden answered that this was not his understanding of the terms. There was one matter, however, that Gibbons failed to take into account. He was no longer the owner of an interest in the ferry, since he had deeded it to his daughter. As it turned out, Ogden renewed his lease through Ann Gibbons, with John Trumbull acting as her agent and advisor.

During the altercation over the Ferry, Colonel Ogden reminded Gibbons that in the first place he had helped him buy the property. He also reminded Gibbons how often he had been entertained by Ogden at the Belcher Mansion. For all his kindness, Gibbons, he said, showed no appreciation. Gibbons retorted that Ogden had been wined and dined just as often at his home at Rose Hill in Elizabethtown. Anyhow, he said, he was not in the habit of keeping score on social calls. Next the two men argued over stock in the State Bank of Elizabethtown, Ogden claiming that Gibbons had tried to get a controlling interest. In answer, Gibbons said that he had bought the stock for his grandchildren, with no thought of trying to control the company. Sensing that he was mistaken about Gibbons' motives in buying the stock, Ogden apologized. This was typical of Aaron Ogden who, notwithstanding the provocation, never lost his sense of equilibrium.[8]

Determined to put as much pressure on Ogden as possible, Gibbons lost no time in purchasing two sailboats for the run between Elizabethtown and New York. When ready for service, his boats sailed from the Rising Sun or Walnut Hill Farm at Halsted's Point, a property he had purchased in 1805. On the farm was a large ferry house with nine rooms, seven fireplaces, and a wide piazza going all around the house, perched as it was on a knoll called Strawberry Hill. The farm, itself, had two hundred and seventy acres with barns and buildings for stables and storage.

Since 1811, Gibbons had owned a steamboat called *Stoudinger* or *Mouse of the Mountain* which had been used in New Jersey waters. If this boat could be put into service against Ogden's *Sea Horse,* Gibbons with his vast resources could soon crush his rival by lowering the rates. With this thought in mind, he went to see John R. Livingston about procuring a license for running his steamboat between the Rising Sun and New York. Gibbons found Livingston sympathetic but bound, he thought, to abide by his contract with Ogden.[9]

Burning with anger at finding Ogden's monopoly seemingly incontestable, Gibbons lashed out against his rival in every conceivable way. To break Ogden's hold of ferrying by his control of the area around De Hart's Point, he demanded that Elizabethtown have a public dock near the Stone Bridge. "I wish to see the Stone Bridge in Elizabethtown," he wrote, "shake hands with White Hall in New York." Not only navigation facilities but the Elizabethtown State Bank, of which Aaron Ogden was president, were run by the privileged few, Gibbons charged. A Jeffersonian Republican, he voiced the sentiment of his party when he declared that monopolies and Federalism went hand in hand. "We the Republicans of Elizabethtown," he shouted, "must rise and assert our rights."

Gibbons' words met the hearty approval of most Elizabethtonians who sent him to Trenton as the champion of the common man to lay his petitions before the legislature. As a result, the legislature empowered Elizabethtown to improve the navigation of the Elizabeth River and to found another bank in the Borough. As it turned out, however, Elizabethtown was not prepared to appropriate the funds necessary to dredge the river or start another bank. Although nothing tangible came of Gibbons' State Bank and Creek Navigation bill, it gained him popularity, as did his announcement that one-half of the receipts from the passenger service on his sailboats would go to the Elizabethtown Female Humane Society.

Early in 1817, while enjoying the plaudits of his townsmen, Gibbons learned that Livingston would not intervene should he run his *Mouse of the Mountain* between the Rising Sun and New York. He accordingly put the *Mouse* on daily trips to New York. His hopes, however, were dashed when Ogden secured an injunction from a New York court prohibiting the *Mouse* from making the run. The battle of the injunctions had begun.[10]

About the time that Gibbons tried to employ the *Mouse* on the run between Elizabethtown and New York, Ogden and Dod completed their new steamboat, the *Atalanta* (named after the legendary fleet-footed Grecian maiden), and put the new boat on the Elizabethtown-New York run. The *Sea Horse* was then put in service between Elizabethtown and Amboy.

It was not long after the launching of the *Atalanta* that the weight of Thomas Gibbons' financial resources began to tell in the steamboat war. Ogden's *Atalanta*, with its handsomely furnished cabins and unique engines served by two copper boilers, had cost a great deal. The first break came in April, 1818, when pressure from creditors forced Ogden to sell the *Sea Horse*. The loss of this boat made it impossible for him to serve the stage running from Amboy to Philadelphia. His failure to meet the terms of his contract freed the stage line and made it possible for Gibbons to step in and sign an agreement for furnishing the ferry service out of Amboy.

More trouble came swiftly to Aaron Ogden. In 1817 he mortgaged the *Atalanta* to the Union Bank of New York for fifteen thousand dollars. Not being able to meet his payments, he was forced to sign over the boat to the Union Bank in 1819. The Bank then leased the *Atalanta* to Ogden for one hundred dollars a week. Since Ogden also owed the State Bank of Elizabethtown a large sum, the Elizabethtown bank purchased the interest owned by the Union Bank of New York and became the sole owner of the *Atalanta*. Thereafter Ogden rented the *Atalanta* from the State Bank, with Peter Kean acting as agent for the Bank.[11]

On the advice of his lawyers, Gibbons decided in 1818 to test again Ogden's monopoly by equipping the *Mouse of the Mountain* with a Federal license for interstate traffic and putting it once more on the Elizabethtown-New York ferry service. For his captain, Gibbons hired Cornelius Vanderbilt, the future railroad titan. Vanderbilt received sixty dollars a month plus one-half of the bar receipts, presumably a rather attractive income for the millionaire-to-be.

As soon as Vanderbilt began running the *Mouse* to New York,

Ogden appealed to the Chancellor of New York for an injunction to stop the service. Lawyers for Gibbons countered by asking the Chancellor to refuse an injunction on the grounds that Ogden's permit did not include steamboats plying out of Halsted's Point. The injunction, however, was issued against the use of the *Mouse* for ferrying between Elizabethtown and New York. A fine of ten thousand dollars was to be levied if the injunction was violated.[12]

So that no customers would be inconvenienced by his inability to operate his steamboats between Elizabethtown and New York, Gibbons employed four sailing boats for the ferry between the Rising Sun and New York. Meanwhile he put his steamboats, the *Mouse* and a new one called the *Bellona*, on the run between Amboy and Paulus Hook. Again Gibbons called upon the governments of both New York and New Jersey as well as the Federal government to rise and break the unholy monopoly strangling steamboat navigation. Ogden, according to Gibbons, asked New Jersey to give up her rights on the Hudson River just to save himself from ruin. "Give me your waters, New Jersey, or I am ruined," were Ogden's words, according to Gibbons.[13]

Early in 1820, New York again came out firmly for its right to control all navigation on the Hudson up to the high water mark on the New Jersey shore. John R. Livingston once more saw fit to enter the contest when he sought and obtained an injunction against anyone but Ogden operating a steamboat south of Paulus Hook. This was aimed at Gibbons' steamboats plying between Paulus Hook and Perth Amboy, which were competing with steamboats under Livingston's ownership or jurisdiction.[14]

Since Gibbons was fighting for the rights of New Jersey, public sentiment remained strong in his favor. With the new and sweeping New York injunction against him, he countered by appealing for retaliatory action by New Jersey. His petition was answered by an act of the legislature which made steamboats equipped solely with a New York license subject to seizure in New Jersey. Acting upon this law, Chancellor Isaac H. Williamson issued an injunction against Livingston's steamboats coming to New Jersey. Livingston again tried to circumvent the injunction by sending his steamboat the *Olive Branch* to Staten Island, where passengers could be ferried to New Jersey in sailboats. But this was stopped when Williamson ordered Livingston to appear before him for violating the injunction.[15]

While John R. Livingston was endeavoring to combat the New Jersey injunction, Aaron Ogden was engaged in trying to stave off an injunction against his steamboats by petitioning the legislature. He stressed the fact that he had risked a fortune for the advancement of navigation. In truth, he could have said that all his troubles arose from the vindictiveness of one man. Ogden's petition had many signers, especially from Woodbridge. Nevertheless, he was playing a losing game. In September, in spite of all, Chancellor Williamson issued an injunction against Ogden and Peter Kean for operating steamboats under a license prejudicial to the interests of New Jersey. By that order, the *Atalanta* must cease running between Elizabethtown and New York.[16]

The battle for steamboat rights, however, was not ended. In October, a lawyer reported to Gibbons that Ogden would try to get the New Jersey "Jurisdictional Law" repealed. Failing to do so, he would go to jail, it was said, to excite public sympathy. In defiance of the New Jersey injunction, Ogden therefore again ran the *Atalanta* to New York. The old fighter, however, saw fit to cease operation when confronted by another injunction from Chancellor Williamson. Thereafter he and Kean employed the *Atalanta* to take bathers and fishing parties to points along the New Jersey coast. It was about this time that Gibbons won another round in the battle by getting an injunction prohibiting the officers of the State Bank of Elizabethtown from extending any more credit to Ogden on the ground that he was insolvent.[17]

One of the lawyers retained by Thomas Gibbons was the rising statesman, Daniel Webster. Webster advised Gibbons to defy the New York injunction and bring the case before the highest court of New York. If the decision went against him, he should then appeal the case to the Supreme Court of the United States. Gibbons acted accordingly. In November, Livingston brought suit against Gibbons for violating the New York monopoly. The case was tried before the Marine Court of New York. The jury found in Livingston's favor. The damage, however, was set at one cent.[18]

During the closing months of 1821 and the early part of the following year, Ogden was still trying to be released from the New Jersey injunction. He was now willing to compromise with Gibbons, but the latter—with plenty of money—was determined upon crushing his rival. In 1822 the State Bank of Elizabethtown took over Ogden's interest in the Old and New Points, thus stripping the Colonel of what remained of his ferry business. The New York license to operate a steamboat between Elizabethtown Point and New York, however, was still in Ogden's name. Consequently when the case was finally brought to the Supreme Court by Gibbons' lawyers in 1824 it was known as Gibbons *vs.* Ogden. Before the case was finally argued before the Supreme Court, Livingston and Ogden made a last attempt to reach an agreement with Gibbons, but the latter remained adamant.[19]

When the case of Gibbons *vs.* Ogden was argued before the Supreme Court, Daniel Webster and William Wirt, two of the foremost lawyers in America, appeared for Gibbons. Thomas A. Emmet and T. J. Oakley handled the case for Ogden. In a famous decision, Chief Justice John Marshall held that Chancellor Kent and Chancellor Livingston of New York were both in error when they declared that the commerce powers granted the Federal government should be strictly construed. In essence, the decision made it clear that the states had no jurisdiction over interstate waters, the navigation of which was subject to the control of Congress and Federal authorities.

After the battle for navigation rights was over, Ogden saw his last piece of property taken from him when the State Bank foreclosed and in 1827 took the Belcher Mansion. During the thirty years that Ogden owned and occupied the Belcher House, it had stood as one of Elizabethtown's finest mansions. Since he had recourse to much traveling during his busy years, his stables were well-stocked with horses and his barn filled with carriages, riding chairs, and sleighs. Two or three Negro slaves took care of Ogden's stables and carriage house and tended the gardens and orchards on the old Belcher property.[20]

Though penniless, Aaron Ogden never lost his prestige or political standing. During the heated election of 1828, when Andrew Jackson was pitted against President John Quincy Adams, some very surprising switches occurred in politics. Colonel Ogden, the staunch Federalist of former times, logically akin to Adams as a Hamiltonian, came out nonetheless for Andrew Jackson. To Ogden, Adams was something of a renegade for having deserted the Federalist party years before. No doubt, too, Old Hickory appealed to the Colonel's martial spirit. In any event, as a reward for supporting Jackson, he was appointed Assistant Collector for the Port of Jersey City at a salary of one thousand dollars a year. The incumbent, who had supported Adams, was removed to make room for Ogden.[21]

The remainder of Aaron Ogden's days were spent in Jersey City, except for a short time in the New York prison. His prison experience at the age of seventy-four arose from his being apprehended and thrown into jail for debts while he was visiting New York. He was discharged after the New York legislature, at the instance of some of Ogden's friends, including Aaron Burr, passed an act forbidding the imprisonment for debt of Revolutionary soldiers. Ogden's prison term apparently was not altogether unpleasant. A constant stream of visitors was allowed to come and go, making the days pass quickly and agreeably for the old soldier.

Life in Jersey City was likewise pleasant for the aging Colonel. Here he had many visitors and good neighbors. For a while, one of his neighbors was Aaron Burr, an old friend of his boyhood days. In 1829, while living in Jersey City, Ogden (who had been elected president of the New Jersey chapter of the Cincinnati in 1824 and vice president of the national organization the next year) became the president of the national Society of the Cincinnati, having been preceded by Washington, Hamilton, Charles C. Pinckney, and Thomas Pinckney. In the days when he lived in it, Jersey City was a secluded little village of country lanes and beautiful shade trees sheltering the homes of wealthy New Yorkers. There he died in 1839 at the age of eighty-three; his children and grandchildren were around him when the end came.

In the year he died another noted citizen of old Elizabethtown passed away. This was Sheppard Kollock, who died at the age of eighty-eight in Philadelphia while he was visiting his son-in-law, the Reverend John McDowell. Kollock retired from the newspaper business in 1818 after selling out to Peter Chatterton. From

1820 to 1829 he was postmaster for Elizabethtown. An appointment of President Monroe, the office came as a political reward for Kollock's long service to the Republican party. For thirty years, too, he was judge of the Essex County Court of Common Pleas. He held other local offices during his long political career. In 1828, however, Kollock felt that he could not support the candidacy of the hero of New Orleans. As a result he was removed from the post office on the election of Andrew Jackson. His successor was Thomas B. Dayton, a capable young man who had supported the winning candidate.* Critics said that though they had nothing against Dayton, it was a shame, to turn out a loyal democrat, especially an old man who needed the money derived from the office.[22]

During the campaign of 1828, supporters of President Adams tried to stigmatize the Jacksonian party as the party of mechanics and day laborers. Although only partly true, the Jacksonians accepted the label and turned it into political capital. There was nothing disgraceful in having the support of mechanics and farmers, they declared. Men such as these were the "bone and sinew of the Country." The Adams party, they charged, was the party of money and "stuffed shirts." At a great mass meeting of Jackson supporters at Elizabethtown, Captain Cyrus De Hart, an old Revolutionary War veteran, took the chair. He was flanked by William Chetwood, Elihu Brittin, John Townley, and other prominent citizens. The meeting closed by resolving that the Adams' administration was making war upon the rights of the people. All lovers of liberty were asked to vote for Andrew Jackson.

During the campaign Sheppard Kollock headed the County Committee for President Adams. The latter, Kollock told the mechanics of New Jersey, stood for a tariff which alone could save them from ruinous foreign competition. Kollock's arguments apparently appealed to the mechanics of Elizabethtown, for most of their votes went to President Adams. When counted, the vote stood 322 for Adams against 152 for Jackson.[23]

In June, 1833, President Andrew Jackson accepted an invitation to attend a reception at Elizabethtown on a trip which

---

* Dayton had the post office in his low brick house on the lot south of St. John's Church.

brought him through the town. Elizabethtown put on its usual parade with the militia and Light Horse in full regalia. The President rode in a carriage with Mayor Stephen P. Brittin behind six grey horses driven by the expert horseman, David Sanderson. At Sanderson's Union Hotel, Jackson was wined and dined and smothered with speeches lauding his political and military achievements.[24]

Three years after his visit to Elizabethtown, Jackson made the State Bank of Elizabethtown one of his "pet banks." The reason for the selection of the Elizabethtown bank for this favor is not difficult to find. Looe Baker, a Jacksonian, was president of the bank while William Chetwood, another supporter of Jackson, was a Congressman and able to pull the necessary strings for the State Bank. As a "pet bank" the State Bank of Elizabethtown became a depository for Federal funds in a move to crush the Bank of the United States. When the great banking and financial collapse came in 1837 following a period of inflation, the State Bank of Elizabethtown, like all the others in the country, was caught in the crash and went through a period of great strain.

With the ever-growing need for better transportation facilities, the craze for turnpikes and canals struck Elizabethtown as well as other towns. In Elizabethtown at the turn of the century, Aaron Ogden was one of the leaders promoting turnpikes for the state. He lobbied for the Morris Turnpike and petitioned the legislature for a turnpike and new bridges between Paulus Hook and Trenton. Since action on the turnpike proposal between Morristown and Elizabethtown was prompt, Ogden was soon deep in the work of organizing a company. The charter for the Morris Turnpike was granted in 1801. Gabriel H. Ford of Morristown became president. Elias B. Dayton of Elizabethtown was chosen treasurer. As one of the principal stockholders, Ogden gave much of his time to the matter of laying out the road. The tollgate at Short Hills, he thought, should charge more than the others since travelers at this point could not easily avoid using the new road. Ogden's belief that the road would prove profitable was well founded. The turnpike, which cut a path straight from Elizabethtown to Connecticut Farms and on to Morristown, was soon earning dividends of over four percent.[25]

As early as 1828 there was talk in Elizabethtown of building a

Governor Isaac H. Williamson. Courtesy Princeton University.

railroad from Elizabethtown Point to Easton, Pennsylvania. Three years earlier, Colonel John Stevens of Hoboken had built the first American locomotive, which puffed and chugged around a circular track at his villa on the banks of the Hudson. After this experiment, interest in railroads became contagious. In 1830 a company headed by Stevens' two sons received a charter for the Camden-Amboy Railroad, destined to be the first railroad in New Jersey. Enthusiasm was so great that the capital stock was sold out within ten minutes after it was offered. Within a year a section of the Camden-Amboy Railroad was constructed and in operation.[26]

In Elizabethtown, railroading was on everyone's lips following the chartering of the Camden-Amboy Railroad. In November, a meeting of citizens for organizing a railroad company met at the Court House. Four men, former Governor Isaac H. Williamson, William Chetwood, Edward Price, and William Starkweather, were appointed to wait on the legislature with a petition for a charter for a railroad from Elizabethtown Point to Somerville. Their request was granted and the charter, dated February 9, 1831, authorized the raising of $200,000 for building the railroad. Before construction was begun five years later, the capitalization was increased to five hundred thousand dollars.[27]

The first president of the Elizabethtown-Somerville Railroad, Isaac H. Williamson, was governor of New Jersey from 1817 to 1829. Born in 1791, he was the youngest son of General Matthias Williamson. After marrying Anne Jouet, a daughter of the old Loyalist, Cavalier Jouet, Williamson practiced law. Very early in his career, Aaron Ogden recognized him as one of the most promising lawyers in the state. Later as governor and chancellor, Williamson laid down precedents which became a foundation for equity law in New Jersey. In 1831 when the Elizabethtown-Somerville Railroad was chartered, he was mayor of Elizabethtown.

By the charter, the Elizabethtown-Somerville Railroad could charge no more than six cents per mile for passengers and six cents per ton per mile for freight. The railroad, the charter read, was a public highway which anyone could use by paying the tolls. According to this clause any citizen could drive his own horse-drawn vehicle on the railroad, providing he took the pains to fit his wagon or carriage with the necessary flanged wheels. Records do not show if any citizens availed themselves of this privilege.

Stock for the Elizabethtown-Somerville Railroad found a ready sale. Little risk seemed to be involved since the railroad was free from any taxation until dividends reached seven percent. Thereafter the tax was limited to one and one-half percent of earnings. Business prospects for the railroad appeared excellent. From the rich farming country in the center of the state the railroad could draw produce to Elizabethtown Point for conveyance by water to New York.

In spite of all the enthusiasm, the Elizabethtown-Somerville Railroad was slow in materializing. Surveying started within a few weeks after the charter was issued but it was halted from time to time for one reason or another. Not until 1835, four years after the charter was given, was actual construction started. Colonel James Moore was hired as construction engineer. Starting at the Point, the tracks were laid beside the road leading to Elizabethtown. Meanwhile the trustees made a contract with Edward Kellogg of the Ferry Company for transporting passengers and freight to New York when the railroad started operating.[28]

When the railroad builders approached Elizabethtown, great excitement prevailed. The news was out that the Railroad Company had been given the right to lay track right up Broad Street through the center of town. This was a horrible thought to the businessmen and residents on Broad Street. Trains, they declared, would hurt business as well as interfere with services in the churches. The Railroad had no right to usurp the principal street, was the universal opinion.

Regardless of public sentiment, the railroad builders began to break ground on Broad Street early on a Saturday morning. That evening a petition from the Broad Street property owners was presented to the Common Council and Aldermen. Having given their consent for laying the track up Broad Street, the town fathers found themselves in a dilemma. After talking with the Directors of the Railroad, the Common Council reported that if the Railroad proved a nuisance, the Company promised to take up the track on Broad Street and relocate it. Apparently this pleased no one.

Sunday passed; the next day track-laying continued on Broad Street. Then one morning townspeople awoke to find that during the night some "mysterious agency" had removed the track. Persons who saw the men at work reported that they were disguised but apparently not as Indians, as at the Boston Tea Party. When the Directors saw what had happened, they decided to give in. Instead of coming up Broad Street, the route followed East Jersey Street, down Jefferson, to its terminus at the Union Hotel on Water Street.[29]

For the maiden run to the Point, a great crowd collected in front of the Union Hotel to witness the event. On a Saturday evening in August, Innkeeper David Sanderson took the reins of the two-horse team harnessed in tandem. The *Town Car* with its open-air deck on top was loaded with excited passengers: town officials and the officers of the Railroad with their wives. As Sanderson cracked the whip, the *Town Car* went rolling over the tracks. A chorus of cheers followed the car as it sped away toward the Point with its jubilant riders.[30]

During the early years of its existence the Elizabethtown-Somerville Railroad Company leased the road to an operator. The first operator was David Sanderson who leased the line from his hotel to the Point. The *Town Car* was owned by the Company while Sanderson furnished the horses and personnel. In 1844 he sold his lease and four horses used on the Railroad to the Elizabethport and New York Ferrying Company. The Ferrying Company operated the two mile Railroad until 1848, when the Elizabethtown-Somerville Railroad Company took it over and replaced the horse-drawn car with steam engine service.[31]

It was not until January, 1839, that the Elizabethtown-Somerville Railroad was completed as far as Plainfield, New Jersey. For the run between Elizabethtown and Plainfield, the Company had a nine-ton engine called the *Eagle*, built by the Baldwin Locomotive Works in Philadelphia. It was a cabless engine with a tall smoke stack. The driving shafts from the cylinders were attached to two sets of large wheels while two sets of small wheels supported the front end of the engine. On the maiden trip from Elizabethtown to Plainfield, Henry Frazer, the engineer, drove the engine with its single passenger car and four boxcars over wooden rails capped with strips of wrought iron. The tickets bore notice that passengers could be called upon to assist the conductor if necessary.[32]

As soon as the Elizabethtown-Somerville Railroad was extended beyond Elizabethtown, the well-known intersection with the New Jersey Railroad (later called the Pennsylvania Railroad) came into being at the west end of Broad Street. Finally in 1893, this dangerous crossing was eliminated when the railroads were elevated through the City of Elizabeth.

In 1840, the Elizabethtown-Somerville Railroad reached Bound Brook. Two years later it reached Somerville, a distance of twenty-five miles from its terminus at Elizabethport. By this time, however, the Railroad was in financial difficulties. After being sold at auction, it came under the control of Commodore Vanderbilt in 1848; he succeeded in reviving it and finally making it into a prosperous enterprise.

When passengers on the Elizabethtown-Somerville Railroad reached Elizabethport, they were ferried to New York in one of the two steamboats then in use at the Point. The older steamboat, built in 1831, was called the *Water Witch*. First owned by Captain Jacob De Groat, it was later acquired by Vanderbilt. The other boat was the *Cinderella*, built for Captain Jacob Van Pelt in 1832. Both steamboats were for a time owned by the Elizabethport-New York Ferrying Company. Elizabethport languished as an important terminal in 1868 when the Newark Bay Bridge was constructed. After that, railroads took their passengers and cargoes directly to Hoboken or Jersey City for ferrying to New York.

Largely owned and directed by men of Elizabethtown and having its eastern terminus at the Point, the Elizabethtown-Somerville Railroad was considered a town project in which everyone had a patriotic interest. Nonetheless, the Elizabethtown-Somerville Railroad was not the first railroad to be built through Elizabethtown. The first one was the New Jersey Railroad, chartered in March, 1832, to run between Jersey City and New Brunswick. By 1834 the New Jersey Railroad was completed to Elizabethtown. The next year it reached Rahway.

The first run on the New Jersey Railroad between Elizabeth-

Depot and Hotel at Elizabethport.

St. John's Church.

Railroad Crossing about 1850.

First Presbyterian Church and Elizabethtown Academy.

Court House.　　　　　　Liberty Pole.　　　　First Presbyterian Church.

town and Rahway was made on December 31, 1835. The little train with its engine and four passenger cars loaded with local and state dignitaries made the trip to Rahway without mishap. But, on the return, one of the passenger cars jumped the track and turned over the baggage car. Fortunately no one was seriously injured.[33]

The coming of the railroad to Elizabethport caused men to view the area as a good location for manufacturing. The first step toward bringing manufacturing to the Point was taken in 1835 when Edward Kellogg and other business men, chiefly from New York, bought a large tract of land adjacent to the ferry and called it the "New Manufacturing Town of Elizabeth Port." The response for locating factories at the Point was prompt. Within a year the Port had a malleable iron works specializing in shears and scissors. Soon the New Jersey Flax and Hemp Manufacturing Company moved from Elizabethtown to the Point where several large buildings were constructed to house the establishment.[34]

Meanwhile houses were built at Elizabethport for workers, who found their labor in demand at the mills and iron works, on the ferries, and by the railroad. A school was constructed for elementary education. Amazingly enough, the promoters also built a Lyceum or public hall with Grecian columns. Apparently they were hoping that the Port would attract people interested in cultural pursuits. Soon travelers could find room and board at the luxurious three-story Elizabethport Hotel operated by a Mr. Gale.

Within ten years after the coming of the railroad, Elizabethport had grown to a town of over eight hundred people. Since most of the residents were Irish immigrants with little or no education, the Lyceum must have seen little use in Elizabethport. In the mills and factories the men worked twelve hours a day, six days of the week. Most of the laborers frequented the bar-rooms after working hours. Here they spent so much of their meager wages for liquor that their families suffered miserably. Ignorant and rough, the Irishmen were as notorious for fighting as for their consumption of alcohol.

By 1850 the manufacturing plants at the Port had steadily increased in size and number. That year the Elizabethport Malleable Iron Works employed nearly one hundred workers. A rope factory employed over fifty men. Another factory making straw hats and bonnets, owned by E. Cummings, hired thirty or forty men. All the factories were powered by steam engines whose boilers were fired with Pennsylvania coal brought to the Port by railroad or canal.

By 1864 Elizabethport had grown like a mushroom. Factories extended all along the waterfront. Back of the factories were rows of streets with drab, poorly constructed, and nearly identical houses for the workers. Before the end of the decade the Singer Sewing Machine Company erected its giant factory where Crane's Ferry had stood at the time of the Revolution. All along the waterfront surrounding the mills and factories were piles of coal, iron, lumber, and other raw materials. Countless smokestacks poured forth clouds of black smoke laying a film of soot over everything within miles. What a contrast to thirty years before when the whole area was still covered with meadows and quiet farms! Such was the price America had to pay for its industrial progress.

Elizabethtown, itself, while generally retaining its aristocratic and residential character, saw some industrialization also during the second quarter of the nineteenth century. The most noted industry in Elizabethtown was oilcloth manufacturing. Indeed, during this period Elizabethtown became the center of oilcloth manufacturing in America. As early as 1833 an oilcloth factory was in operation. Known as the Abro and Hoyt Oil Cloth Factory and owned by James Abro, this factory was the largest of its kind in the world. It was located on the west side of the river beyond the bend on Pearl Street. It was not long before Elizabethtown had another oilcloth factory. Located at East Grand and Meadow streets near the Jersey Central Railroad (the old Elizabethtown-Somerville line), it was called the John Jewet and Son New Jersey Oil Cloth Factory and later the D. J. Edwards and Company Oil Cloth Factory.

Another sizeable factory located in Elizabethtown proper was the pottery owned by Keen Pruden. Located between Water Street and the river nearly opposite Pruden's mansion on Pearl Street, the pottery turned out twenty thousand dollars worth of earthenware a year. The pottery was established about 1811 by Edward Griffith, an immigrant from England. Pruden, who learned the trade in his uncle's pottery in Morristown, took over the earthenware factory in 1820. Rebuilt after a fire in 1826, Pruden's factory turned out brownware, stoneware, and teapots. He also sold imported chinaware.

During his time Pruden was one of the most prominent citizens of Elizabethtown. Long a director of the State Bank, in 1851 he became its president. In 1835 he became a director of the New Jersey Flax and Hemp Manufacturing Company. Nearly twenty years later he helped to found the Elizabethtown Water Company. His mansion on Pearl Street was one of the show places of Elizabethtown.

Along the wharves down from Pruden's Pottery were two large lumber yards and a tannery. In the town were the usual shops and small factories, many of them going back to the post-Revolutionary period. Foremost among these were the old coach and carriage establishments and the furniture and cabinet shops. The old mill built by John Ogden by the Stone Bridge was still in operation although most of the flour and grist was ground at the Elizabethtown Mills operated by F. Harris and Son.*

Broad and Water streets, the main thoroughfares, were slowly changing as old buildings were torn down to make room for new and larger structures. People from miles around came to see the new flagstone sidewalks on Broad Street, said to be equal in size to any in New York. Along Broad Street in 1847 came the magnetic telegraph wires strung on poles with the permission of the property owners who this time offered no objection to so inoffensive an innovation.[35]

During the last decade or two before Elizabethtown became a city, the number of residences or mansions increased rapidly as new fortunes were made in the age of railroads and industrialization. Most of the new dwellings followed the Gothic style which was rapidly supplanting the Georgian. Among the show places of the era was the palatial home of Ex-Governor Williamson on Governor's Lane.† Another was the gingerbread-trimmed house of the merchant, Stephen P. Brittin on East Jersey Street. Other beautiful new homes were owned by such prominent citi-

* Formerly Crane's Mills.
† Now the home of the Elk's Club. Governor's Lane is now part of Westfield Avenue.

zens as Elias Wade, Job Magie, A. Lachaise, William Spencer, Thaddeus Mills, and Keen Pruden.

As in former times, East New Jersey Street was a street of beautiful homes. On this street, next to the Second Presbyterian Church, was the old mansion owned by John Nutman during the time of the American Revolution. In the 1790's this was the house owned by Jean Touchimbert, the French refugee. It was now owned by William Chetwood, a noted lawyer and judge and one-time mayor of the Borough. Eventually the beautiful Boudinot mansion on East Jersey Street became a home for elderly women. The old Belcher House across the way, except for being a school and then a factory for a short time, remained a residence as one owner followed another.

In the middle of the nineteenth century no house in Elizabethtown attracted more attention than the old brick mansion on East Jersey Street built for Dr. William Barnet before the Revolution. This was altogether natural since the house had become the home of General Winfield Scott whenever he found time to relax from his duties. Sometimes, too, the General used the house for his army headquarters. After Dr. Barnet died, the house was owned by a man named Hampton. In 1805 it was purchased by Colonel John Mayo of Richmond, Virginia, who made Hampton Place, as the house was called, his summer home. A man of great wealth, Colonel Mayo enjoyed a reputation as an engineer, having built a famous bridge over the James River near Richmond. The Colonel's wife was Abigail, the daughter of John De Hart, one-time member of Congress and a mayor of Elizabethtown. Long after, people would recall how the Mayos rode into town from the South in a magnificent coach with six outriders and postillions. Following the death of Colonel Mayo in 1818, the property passed to his beautiful and talented daughter, Maria, who had married General Scott.

Near General Scott's house was a pond which fed the little brook that ran down through Horse Hollow into the river. Today, filled-in and altogether unrecognizable, Horse Hollow has become Park Place. At one time, probably when Hampton, supposedly an Englishman, owned the place, an island was formed in the shape of Great Britain in the pond. Trees were planted at the proper places to indicate the sites of important cities of the British

General and Mrs. Winfield Scott at Hampton Place, East Jersey Street.

Isles. There is another story that in the 1790's a Frenchman rented the property and put some toy ships in the pond flying French flags. When schoolboys substituted British flags for the French, he is said to have become so angry that he moved away.

Among General Scott's children was his blond tom-boy daughter who had the whole town talking. On one occasion while she was driving her father's coach the horses pulled off the front wheels while trying to get through the deep mud on East Jersey Street. The girl, however, clung to the reins as she was pulled off the seat and down into the mire. Still tugging at the reins and covered with mud, she brought the team to a halt. Another time, competing with an army officer at slashing at a post with sabers while charging on horseback at break-neck speed, she whirled about and came dashing toward a high fence against which stood a row of taunting boys from Nutman's school. The boys jumped back just before the girl went whizzing by, slicing off a row of pickets from the fence on which they had been leaning.

Not long before General Scott was called to lead the United States Army in Mexico, the memory of patriots of the Revolution was revived when a monument was erected for the Caldwells. Interest in the town's history had been aroused by the publication of *Notes on Elizabethtown* by the Reverend Nicholas Murray, pastor of the First Presbyterian Church. Led by Murray, a subscription was circulated and money raised for a monument for the Caldwells. Robert Eberhard Schmidt von der Launitz, who had studied sculpturing at Rome and had made a name for himself in America for his monuments, was hired to make the memorial.

When the day of the presentation arrived, a large crowd gathered in the old Presbyterian Cemetery for the dedication. At the ceremony were Governor Charles S. Stratton, Ex-Governor Mahlon Dickerson, Ex-Governor William S. Pennington, Chancellor Oliver Spencer Halsted, Chief Justice Joseph Hornblower, and many other dignitaries of the state.[36] The Reverend David Magie opened the service with a reading from James Caldwell's Bible. This was followed by a prayer by the Reverend John McDowell. The oration was delivered by the Reverend Samuel Miller of the Princeton Theological Seminary. When Dr. Miller had finished, the people listened to several selections by the Church choir. Then the Reverend Nicholas Murray dedicated the monument to the memory of the martyred Caldwells. A slab of marble on a granite base, the seventeen-foot monument still stands in the old cemetery.

Nicholas Murray * who succeeded John McDowell as pastor of the First Presbyterian Church in 1833 at the age of thirty-one was a very remarkable man. Born in Ireland of Catholic parents, Murray came to America in 1818 and was quickly converted to Protestantism. With the help of Presbyterians who recognized his ability, he graduated from Amherst College and the Princeton Theological School. He was the minister for the First Presbyterian Church in Elizabethtown for twenty-eight years. During this time he contributed much to the religious and educational life of his adopted town and country. In Elizabethtown he established a Lyceum which drew many of the outstanding speakers and thinkers in America. He also worked diligently for the advancement of the common schools. Murray likewise is remembered for his part in the founding of the New Jersey Historical Society. His writings, other than his history of Elizabethtown, were mainly essays against Catholicism. In 1852, for instance, he wrote a series of letters addressed to Chief Justice Roger B. Taney, who was a Catholic. Although Murray was highly critical of some of the doctrines and practices of the Catholic Church, he was no bigot. In 1845, when the St. Mary's Roman Catholic Church was founded in Elizabethtown, he contributed to the building fund and otherwise encouraged the founders of the church. Much of Murray's success as a pastor and civic leader was due to his attractive, witty, and congenial personality.

During the Mexican War, Elizabethtown took great pride in the victories of its adopted son, General Winfield Scott. People were also proud of Captain William C. De Hart, a native son and grandson of Mayor John De Hart. As a young officer, De Hart served as an aide-de-camp for General Scott in the War of 1812. When the Mexican War broke out, he again became General Scott's aide-de-camp. In this capacity he served with distinction until he contracted a deadly disease in Mexico and was compelled to return home.

* He was the grandfather of Nicholas Murray Butler, President of Columbia University from 1901 to 1945.

The Reverend Isaac P. Howell.

It was not long after Captain De Hart's return to Elizabethtown before the high respect of his townspeople was severely strained following the publication of his articles in which he reasoned that Mrs. Caldwell's death was accidental and that the soldier who shot the Reverend Caldwell may have been acting from a sense of duty. Before the Mexican War, Captain De Hart had published a classic work on military law sponsored by the War Department. His reputation for close reasoning and careful writing, however, weighed little in his favor when it came to questioning the myths and legends surrounding the lives of local heroes. Tempers, especially that of the outraged Dr. Murray, had barely cooled a bit when Captain De Hart succumbed from the disease contracted in Mexico. It was with great sorrow that General Scott returned to Elizabethtown after the war to find his much-beloved aide had died. At the reception ceremony, General Scott took occasion to express his deep sorrow for the loss of Captain De Hart, whom he considered a soldier of unusual talents.[37]

In 1845, the year the Caldwell Monument was raised, the first Catholic Church was erected in Elizabethtown. Named St. Mary's, this church, which architecturally resembles the classic style of American churches with belfry and steeple, still stands on that part of Old Broad Street now known as Washington Street. By 1851 the parish had built a parochial school on a lot next to the church. Just beyond the school on ground now owned by the Church stood an African Methodist Episcopal Church.

The Reverend Isaac P. Howell was selected by Bishop John Hughes of New York to be the first rector for St. Mary's with its one hundred parishioners, the majority of whom were Irish. Isaac Howell was born in Philadelphia where his father, who was Protestant, was an eminent physician. His mother, Mary Elizabeth Rosette, was a Roman Catholic of French extraction. After attending Mount St. Mary's College in Maryland, Howell was ordained by Bishop Hughes in 1844. It is interesting to note that while Howell was the priest, the Mexican general, Santa Anna, who lived at Elizabethport while visiting his old foe General Scott, attended St. Mary's.

For a number of years prior to the transition from a borough to a city in 1853, there had been a growing feeling that the old

Charter was inadequate for Elizabethtown. Critics maintained that the Mayor, Aldermen, and members of the Common Council, who were appointed by the state legislature, obtained office by pulling wires and courting the favor of politicians. Many Borough officials, they said, could never be elected by the voters of Elizabethtown. That the Borough Charter, dating from 1739, was a liberal instrument of government at the time it was adopted, no one denied. But it had been inadequate and archaic, they maintained, since the adoption of the Declaration of Independence and the inauguration of republican government.[38]

With sentiment for changing the form of government gaining rapidly, a meeting for considering the question was called at the Court House in January, 1849. After some discussion it was resolved to petition the legislature for amendments to the Charter which would allow the election of Borough officials by the voters. In addition they asked that Elizabethtown have a free hand in raising public school funds. In answer to the petition, the legislature amended the Charter as requested. Henceforth the Mayor and the Common Council were to be elected by the voters of Elizabethtown. The Aldermen would continue to be appointed by the legislature but they would have no voice in the Borough government any longer. Thereafter their sole duty would be to act as judges on the Court of Common Pleas and General Sessions.[39]

Although the legislature had corrected most of the abuses experienced under the old Charter, sentiment in Elizabethtown soon favored an abandonment of the Charter for a city government. Local pride as much as anything motivated the people. Elizabethtown was growing rapidly and they wanted it to be classed as a city like other communities of its size and importance in the state. In 1854, therefore, the legislature created the City of Elizabeth with a government consisting of a mayor and council of twelve. Three years later, Union County was carved out of Essex County and Elizabeth became a county seat.

In many ways old Elizabethtown was a typical American community as it progressed through its long life of nearly two centuries. In other respects, it was an exceptional town. Elizabethtown was perpetually in the swirl of important events for the state, for the nation, and for the town, itself. Its life story consequently is closely knit with the general course of American history. Stimulated by an involvement in great events, each generation produced an unusually large number of public figures who left their mark on the course of history.

In its pioneer days, Elizabethtown was the focal point in the long controversy with the Proprietors. The end product of the lengthy battle with the Proprietors as led by Elizabethtonians was the advancement of the cause of political liberty in New Jersey. After the Revolution, in which it figured prominently, Elizabethtown continued its slow growth, not sharing very much in the industrial progress of Newark and some other New Jersey communities. During this period it remained essentially a community of small farmers, artisans, professional men, and retired people. It was not until the second quarter of the nineteenth century with its railroads and steam power that it experienced an upsurge of industrialism which eventually transformed it into a manufacturing city with all the unattractive features of industrial towns. Even then (and to some extent to this very day) the industrialization occupied mainly the Port area, leaving the older section, except for the business district, primarily residential. Long after the dawn of the twentieth century, traces of old Elizabethtown still remained in the survival of ancient houses on their large plots with gardens and orchards. A remnant of these, shorn of most of the acreage, still remains.

Three hundred years have passed since the founding of Elizabethtown. In 1764, the citizens roasted an ox in front of the Marquis of Granby to commemorate the one hundredth anniversary of the founding of the town. While they celebrated, many were wont to speculate on what the future held. Two hundred years have passed since that time. What lies ahead is again open to question. But whatever the future holds may we ever be mindful of our heritage built from the labors and ideals of our forefathers. Today there remain but a few ancient houses in Elizabeth. As one of the oldest and most historical buildings in the city and state, the Belcher House stands as a link between the past, the present, and the future. It stands as a constant reminder of that storied past.

References

Chapter Two

1. Edwin F. Hatfield, *History of Elizabeth, New Jersey* (New York, 1868), pp. 22-23.
2. *New Jersey Archives, First Series,* I, 14 (Hereafter cited *NJA*).
3. *Ibid.,* I, 15-16.
4. Charles Philhower, "Aboriginal Inhabitants of Union County," *Proceedings of the Union County Historical Society* (1923), pp. 20-23.
5. *NJA,* I, 17-19.
6. Hatfield, pp. 33-34.

Chapter Three

1. James T. Adams, *History of the Town of Southampton* (Bridgehampton, N.Y., 1918), pp. 71, 88n.
2. *First Book, Records of the Town of Southampton* (Sag Harbor, N.Y., 1877), p. 162.
3. G. R. Howell, *Early History of Southampton, Long Island* (New York, 1866), p. 27; Adams, p. 230n.
4. *NJA,* I, 504-506.
5. *Ibid.,* I, 49-50; James Alexander to Robert Hunter Morris, Jan. 21, 1756, Stevens MSS, #7833, Stevens Institute, Hoboken, N.J.
6. Elizabethtown Records, p. 6, Princeton University MSS; Hatfield, p. 58.
7. George J. Miller, *The Printing of the Elizabethtown Bill in Chancery* (Perth Amboy, 1942), p. 7.
8. See Town Records, Ear Marks, 1714 and after, Rutgers University Library.
9. Jasper Danckaerts, *Journal of a Tour Through Several American Colonies, in 1679* (Brooklyn, 1867), p. 36.
10. *NJA,* XXI, 29.
11. Danckaerts, pp. 75, 163.
12. Hatfield, p. 120.
13. See *Records of the Town of Newark, New Jersey* (Newark, N.J., 1864), p. 12, for a typical meeting house.
14. Hatfield, pp. 206-207.
15. *Ibid.,* p. 123; *The Minutes of the Board of Proprietors of the Eastern Division of New Jersey, 1725-1744, with an Introductory Essay by George J. Miller* (Rahway, N.J., 1960), II, 136.

Chapter Four

1. Hatfield, p. 51; *An Answer to a Bill in Chancery of New Jersey* (New York, 1752), p. 20.

2. Philip Carteret to the Proprietors, August 2, 1666, Stevens MSS, #2886.

3. Joseph Atkinson, *The History of Newark* (Newark, N.J., 1878), p. 14.

4. *NJA*, I, 42; *Bill in the Chancery of New Jersey* (New York, 1747), p. 34.

5. *Bill in the Chancery of New Jersey*, p. 39; *Answer*, p. 20; *Minutes of the Board of Proprietors*, I, pp. 19-20.

6. Hatfield, p. 134.

7. *NJA*, I, 83-87.

8. *Records of the Town of Newark*, p. 43.

9. *NJA*, I, 58-61.

10. *Ibid.*, I, 89-91.

11. *Ibid.*, I, 88.

12. *Ibid.*, I, 101-103.

13. *Documents Relative to the Colonial History of the State of New York* (Albany, 1858), II, 571.

14. *Ibid.*, II, 582; *NJA*, I, 129-130.

15. Documents, *op. cit.*, II, 595, 600, 603; *NJA*, I, 130-137.

16. Aaron Leaming and Jacob Spicer, *The Grants, Concessions and Original Constitutions of the Province of New Jersey* (Somerville, N.J., 1881), pp. 51-52; *NJA*, I, 176-177.

17. *Records of the Town of Newark*, p. 65.

18. Preston W. Edsall, *Journal of the Courts of Common Right and Chancery of East Jersey, 1683-1702* (Princeton, N.J., 1937), p. 170.

19. *Minutes of the Board of Proprietors*, I, 19.

20. Hatfield, pp. 181-184.

21. *NJA*, I, 156-157.

22. *Ibid.*, I, 167-170; *Calendar of Stevens Papers*, I, 3-4; Hatfield, pp. 135-136.

23. *Records of the Town of Newark*, p. 78; *NJA*, I, 292-294.

24. Danckaerts, pp. 347-352; *NJA*, I, 300-302.

25. *NJA*, 313-314, 322, 334-337.

Chapter Five

1. *NJA*, I, 437-438, XIII, 74.

2. John E. Pomfret, *The Province of East New Jersey* (Princeton, 1961), p. 156, 218; Leaming and Spicer, p. 198.

3. *NJA*, I, 437-438, XIII, 138; *A Bill in the Chancery of New Jersey*, pp. 55-56; *Minutes of the Board of Proprietors*, II, 131-132.

4. Hatfield, pp. 237-238.

5. Edsall, p. 92.

6. *NJA*, II, 124-129, 344-345.

7. *Ibid.*, II, 333-339.

8. Hatfield, pp. 248-249.

9. *A Bill in the Chancery of New Jersey*, pp. 46-47; *The Answer to the Bill in Chancery*, p. 32; The origin of the term Clinker Lot is unknown.

10. Peter Fauconncier Survey Book, 1715-1727. NYHS.

11. Hatfield, p. 317; *Minutes of the Board of Proprietors*, II, 13-15; Elizabethtown Records, p. 8, Princeton University Library.

12. *Minutes of the Board of Proprietors*, II, 41ff, 64-65; Elizabethtown

Records, p. 8, *op. cit.;* Hatfield, pp. 317-318; *A Bill in the Chancery of New Jersey,* p. 49; Historical MSS, 1664-1835, New Jersey, p. 45, HSP.

13. *Minutes of the Board of Proprietors,* II, 144; George J. Miller, *The Printing of the Elizabethtown Bill in Chancery,* p. 17.

14. A. Van Doren Honeyman, *History of Union County, New Jersey, 1664-1923* (New York, 1923), p. 115. For the text of the Charter see: Nicholas Murray, *Notes, Historical and Biographical, concerning Elizabethtown* (Elizabeth, 1844), pp. 28-43; Lloyd Smith MSS, #230-1, MNP.

15. Robert Ogden's Accounts, Rutgers University Library.

16. Historical MSS, 1664-1835, New Jersey, p. 145, 150, HSP; *Minutes of the Board of Proprietors,* II, 340-348; *A Bill in the Chancery of New Jersey,* p. 69; Hatfield, pp. 368-369.

17. *NJA,* VI, 426, 430-432, 455-462; Elisha Parker to William Alexander, Aug. 1, 1747, Lord Stirling MSS, I, NYHS; Robert Hunter Morris to James Alexander, Jan. 23, 1750, Stevens MSS, #7979.

18. *NJA,* XXIV, 112; Robert Hunter Morris to Cortlandt Skinner, June 17, 1760, Stevens MSS, #2797; John Stevens to W. Coxe, July 22, 1762, Stevens MSS #7731.

Chapter Six

1. Hatfield, pp. 281-288.

2. *Ibid.,* p. 256; Samuel A. Clark, *The History of St. John's Church* (Philadelphia, 1857), p. 33ff.

3. Ogden-Wheeler Collection, AM-13210, Princeton University Library.

4. Stephen Wickes, *History of Medicine in New Jersey and of its Medical Men* (Newark, N.J., 1879), p. 234.

5. Hatfield, pp. 339-342.

6. *Ibid.,* p. 350; *NJA,* XII, 354.

7. Wickes, pp. 16, 22-23, 33.

8. Hatfield, pp. 363-364.

9. *NJA,* XIX, 260.

10. *Ibid.,* XII, 389-390; Pyne-Henry, AM-9257, Princeton University Library.

11. Governor Belcher to Samuel Woodruff, March 17, 1751, Transcripts of the Belcher Correspondence, NJHS.

12. *NJA,* XIX, 115-116.

13. Peter Kalm, *Travels in North America* (New York, 1937), I, 181-182; Thomas Burnaby, *Travels Through the Middle Settlements of America, 1759-1760* (London, 1798), p. 56.

14. *NJA,* XI, 412-413.

15. *Ibid.,* XI, 175-176.

16. Hatfield, p. 381; M. W. Stanton, *History of Public Poor Relief in New Jersey* (New York, 1934), pp. 20-23; Elizabethtown MSS, #2, NJHS.

17. Belcher to Samuel Hazard, April 26, 1754, Hazard Family Papers, HSP.

18. Hatfield, p. 380.

19. "Diary of Jacob Spicer, 1755-1757," *Proc. NJHS.,* V. 63, p. 50.

20. See Dayton Papers, NJHS.

21. *NJA,* XX, 133-135.

22. Diary of Jacob Spicer, *op. cit.*

Chapter Seven

1. *NJA*, IX, 449-450.
2. *Ibid.*, IX, 524-525, 546-547; XXI, 671-672; Hatfield, p. 408; Clark, pp. 110-112.
3. *NJA*, XXIX, 444; XXV, 423-425.
4. Stephen Crane to the Whigs of Monmouth County, June 13, 1774, East Jersey Papers, NJHS; Hatfield, p. 411.
5. *NJA*, XXIX, 546.
6. *Ibid.*, XXXI, 42, 75-76.
7. *Ibid.*, XXXI, 89-91.
8. Emmet Collection, #751, NYHS; Peter Force, *American Archives*, 4th. Ser., II, 1674.
9. Matthew L. Davis, *Memoirs of Aaron Burr* (New York, 1836), I, 47-48.
10. Edmund Burnet, *Letters of the Members of the Continental Congress* (Washington, D.C., 1921) I, 382; Aaron Ogden's Account of the Capture of the Blue Mountain Valley, Ogden-Kennedy Papers, Princeton University Library; Hatfield, pp. 421-424; *NJA*, Sec. Ser., I, 68.
11. *NJA*, XXIV, 603-604.
12. *Ibid.*, XXVIII, 466; XXXI, 215.
13. *Ibid.*, XII, 418.
14. David Ross's Record Book, NJHS.
15. E. Kempshall, *Caldwell and the Revolution* (Elizabeth, 1880), pp. 10-11.
16. *NJA*, XX, 377; XXIV, 222; XXVII, 575; Carl Woodward, *Development of Agriculture in New Jersey* (New Brunswick, N.J., 1927), pp. 48-49.
17. *NJA*, XXXI, 161.
18. Inventory of William Peartree Smith's property destroyed by the British, State Library, Trenton.
19. Ledger, Graham's Tavern, NJHS.
20. Charles H. Sherrill, *French Memories of the Eighteenth Century America* (New York, 1915), pp. 79, 106.

Chapter Eight

1. Timothy Tuttle's Journal, NJHS.
2. Abraham Clark to Elias Dayton, July 4, 1776, Emmet Collection, #2861, NYPL.
3. A. Dunham to Provisional Congress, July 4, 1776, Provisional Congress Papers, #4, NJHS.
4. John C. Fitzpatrick, ed., *The Writings of George Washington* (Washington, D.C., 1932), V, 215-216.
5. *Proc. NJHS.*, New Ser., XIV, 452; *Minutes of the Council of Safety of the State of New Jersey* (Jersey City, 1872), II, 74.
6. *Pa. Mag. of Hist. and Biog.*, VII, 461.
7. *NJA*, Sec. Ser., I, 177.
8. Hannah Ogden to Francis Barber, Sept. 2, 1776. Copy at Rutgers University Library.
9. Letter of Robert Ogden, Oct. 6, 1776, Ogden-Kennedy Papers, Princeton University Library.

10. Jouet Memorial, July 30, 1783, AO-12713, Public Record Office, London; MSS, Box 16, State Library, Trenton.

11. Elias Boudinot's Views on Independence, June, 1776, De Coppat Collection, Princeton University Library.

12. Fitzpatrick, VI, 487.

13. *Ibid.*, VII, 61-62, 142.

14. *Papers of Alexander Hamilton* (New York, 1961), I, 226.

15. Fitzpatrick, VIII, 118-119.

16. *NJA*, Sec. Ser., I, 457-459; II, 45-46; *Selections from the Correspondence of the Executive of New Jersey from 1776 to 1786* (Newark, N.J., 1848), pp. 94-96.

17. George A. Boyd, *Elias Boudinot, Patriot and Statesman, 1740-1821* (Princeton, 1952), pp. 75-76. Contrary to tradition, Washington was not present at the wedding. At the time he was with the army at Fredericksburg, N.Y.

18. Dayton to A. Clark, Nov., 1778, Emmet Collection, NYPL.

19. Boudinot to Washington, March 2, 1778, Boudinot Papers, Princeton University Library; B. P. Smith to Elisha Boudinot, Feb. 20, 1780, Boudinot Family Papers, Rutgers University Library.

20. *NJA*, Sec. Ser., III, 160-161.

21. Hatfield, pp. 471-472.

22. Fitzpatrick, XIV, 153, 173n, 220; *NJA*, Sec. Ser., III, 106-109; Frank Moore, *Diary of the American Revolution* (New York, 1860), II, 135; Baurmeister places the invading force at 2,500. See Carl Baurmeister, *Journals* (New Brunswick, N.J., 1957), p. 257.

23. John W. Barber and Henry Howell, *Historical Collections of the State of New Jersey* (New York, 1845), p. 164.

24. Calendar N.J., State Lib. MSS, pp. 32-33; *N.J. Revolutionary Correspondence*, pp. 159-166.

25. *NJA*, Sec. Ser., III, 458-460, 491-493, 555-556.

26. Irvine Papers, II, 61, 92, HSP.

27. *NJA*, Sec. Ser., IV, 172.

28. Park Coll., #773-1,000, MNP.

29. Irvine Papers, II, 116, HSP; *NJA*, Sec. Ser., IV, 134-146.

30. Gates Papers, Box 14, NYHS; *Doc. Hist. of N.Y.*, VIII, 793.

31. *The Remembrancer* (London, 1789), Part II, 224-225.

32. *New Jersey Journal*, July 11, 1845, April 25, 1848 (hereafter cited as *NJJr.*). Hatfield's account is moderate in tone.

33. *NJA*, Sec. Ser., IV, 445-446, 453; Moore, II, 287-291.

34. *New Jersey Revolutionary Correspondence*, p. 227.

35. Maxwell to Livingston, June 14, 1780, Munsell, *History of Morris County, New Jersey* (New York, 1872), p. 33. Also consult Hans Mayer's translations of the Hessian diaries at the Morristown National Park Library.

36. See Hessian Diaries at MNPL.

37. Robertson to Germain, July 1, 1780, *Doc. Hist. of N.Y.*, VIII, 793.

38. *NJA*, Sec. Ser., IV, 498, 552; Theodore Sedgwick, *A Memoir of the Life of William Livingston* (New York, 1833), p. 351-352. One of the Hessian diaries mentions the rose incident.

39. *Proc. NJHS*, LXIII, 206; Greene to Washington, June 24, 1780, *NJA*, Sec. Ser., IV, 481-484; Hessian Diaries at MNPL; *The Trial of the Hon. Cosmo Gordon* (London, 1783).

40. *The Trial of the Hon. Cosmo Gordon,* pp. 8, 18, 67, 70, 102, 104; Hessian Diaries, MNPL.

41. J. J. Boudinot, *Life, Public Service, Addresses and Letters of Elias Boudinot* (Boston, 1896), p. 39; F. J. Marquis de Chastellux, *Travels in North America, 1780-1781* (Dublin, 1787), pp. 48-59.

42. W. O. Wheeler, *The Ogden Family, Elizabethtown Branch* (Phila., 1907), p. 133.

43. Scammel to Gilman, Aug. 24, 1781, Smith Coll., Box 36, MNPL; Sylvanus Seely's Diary, MNPL; Sherrill, p. 308-311.

44. Washington Irving, *Life of Washington* (New York, 1867), III, 612-613; Fitzpatrick, XXIV, 91n.

45. Barber and Howell, p. 169. Gallows Hill is in Westfield, N.J.

Chapter Nine

1. David Ross, Record Book, NJHS; David McGregor, *History of Free-masonry in New Jersey* (Grand Lodge Proc., XI, 1937), p. 51.

2. *NJJr.,* Aug. 7, 1793.

3. Richard P. McCormick, *Experiment in Independence in New Jersey in the Critical Period, 1781-1789* (New Brunswick, N.J., 1950), pp. 29-32.

4. *Proc. NJHS,* New Ser., XI, 329-332.

5. *NJJr.,* June 3, 1795.

6. *Ibid.,* Oct. 13, 1807.

7. Boudinot to Susan, Feb. 15, 1781, Boudinot Papers, Princeton University Library.

8. Sedgwick, p. 410; *Proc. NJHS,* New Ser., LXI, 31-46; H. Niles, *Principles and Acts of the Revolution in America* (Baltimore, 1822), pp. 200-201; Barber and Howe, p. 163.

9. See manuscript life of Count Niemcewicz written by Thomas Howard Kean at the Princeton University Library.

10. Sylvester S. Crosby, *The Early Coins of America* (Boston, 1873), pp. 278, 282, 287; *Proc. NJHS,* July, 1951, p. 275.

11. Memoir of Colonel William Edwards (1847), Grassmann Collection, Elizabeth, N.J.

12. *NJJr.,* Jan. 20, 1790.

13. Sedgwick, p. 400; L. Q. C. Elmer, *The Constitution and Government of the Province and State of New Jersey, etc.* (Newark, N.J., 1872), p. 73; Boudinot Papers, III, 58, HSP; *NJJr.,* July 9, 1805; Record H., Essex County Court House, Newark, N.J.

14. William Dunlap, *Diary* (New York, 1930), I, 95.

Chapter Ten

1. *NJJr.,* July 20, 1790, Sherrill, p. 42.

2. *NJJr.,* Sept. 25, 1793.

3. Wickes, pp. 435-436.

4. *NJJr.,* Feb. 19, 1799, Oct. 11, 1800.

5. Proc. of the Corporation of the Borough of Elizabethtown, 1790-1795, City Hall, Elizabeth; Minutes of the Corp. of Elizabeth, Rutgers University Library; *NJJr.,* April 26, 1806; Official Papers, 1801-1820, City Hall, Elizabeth.

6. *NJJr.*, Jan. 27, Feb. 2, 11, 1807.

7. Old Official Papers, City Hall, Elizabeth; Smith MSS, #601, MNPL; *NJJr.*, Aug. 13, 1793.

8. *NJJr.*, July 14, 1790, Sept. 1, 1801.

9. *Oration Delivered at Elizabethtown, 1793.* Printed by S. Kollock.

10. *I. W. Crane's Oration, 1794.* Printed by S. Kollock.

11. Papers Relating to the French Refugees, Dreer Collection, HSP.

12. *NJJr.*, April 21, 1797, March 2, 1802, Sept. 22, 1801, Oct. 4, 1804; Deeds, Essex County Court House, Newark, N.J.: BB125, C265-266, C429, D45, E119.

13. Mortgages C278, D16, D174-175, G494, Essex County Court House.

14. *Federal Republican*, May, 1803, Rutgers University Library.

15. *NJJr.*, April 21, 1801, June 8, 1802.

16. *Ibid.*, Dec. 4, 1804, July 2, 1805.

17. Howard Munford Jones, *America and French Culture, 1750-1848* (Chapel Hill, 1927); Sherrill, p. 267.

18. Elias D. Smith, *The School Interest of Elizabeth* (Elizabeth, N.J., 1911), pp. 38-40.

19. *NJJr.*, June 8, 1791.

20. *Ibid.*, Feb. 18, 1800.

21. Dunlap, I, 97.

22. Murray, p. 144-145.

23. Walter R. Fee, *The Transition from Aristocracy to Democracy in New Jersey, 1789-1829* (Somerville, N.J., 1933), pp. 105-106.

24. *Ibid.*, p. 35; *NJJr.*, Aug. 17, 1793.

25. Jonathan Dayton to Elias Dayton, Jan. 9, 1798, Signers of the Constitution, Morgan Library; *NJJr.*, June 7, 1797.

26. *NJJr.*, Jan. 21, 1795.

27. Fee, p. 92; *Proc. NJHS*, LVII, 90-96.

28. *NJJr.*, July 7, Sept. 29, 1807.

29. *Ibid.*, May 22, 1798.

30. *Ibid.*, Jan. 15, 1799; Fee, p. 187.

31. *Ibid.*, Dec. 8, 29, 1801; Jan. 5, 1802.

32. *Ibid.*, Dec. 30, 1800.

33. *Ibid.*, July 4, 1803.

34. *Ibid.*, Dec. 8, 1801.

35. *Annals of Congress* (7th Cong., 1st. Sess., 1800-1803), pp. 103, 171, 178.

36. *NJJr.*, July 14, 1803, Aug. 7, 1804.

37. *Ibid.*, March 10, 1817.

38. *Ibid.*, July 1, 1808.

39. *Ibid.*, Aug. 4, 1812.

40. *Ibid.*, Nov. 3, 1812.

41. *Ibid.*, Nov. 24, 1812.

42. *Ibid.*, Dec. 1, 8, 1812, Sept. 1, 1814.

43. *Ibid.*, Dec. 8, 1812.

44. *Ibid.*, Oct. 18, 1814.

Chapter Eleven

1. *NJJr.*, July 4, 1820.
2. Elizabethtown, Minutes of the Corp., 1822, 1833, Rutgers University Library.
3. *Ibid.*, 1826; *NJJr.*, Sept. 24, 1811.
4. Minutes of the Corp., 1828, 1841, *op. cit.*; *NJJr.*, Aug. 9, 1831.
5. *NJJr.*, July 11, 1854.
6. *Ibid.*, Aug. 19, 1800, July 30, 1811; Minutes of the Corp., 1811, *op. cit.*
7. Minutes of the Corp., 1822, 1845, *op. cit.*
8. *Ibid.*, 1845.
9. *Report of the Trial of Eunice Hall v. Robert Grant for Slander in June, 1821* (Elizabethtown, 1821).
10. *NJJr.*, Jan., March, Oct., 1830; Smith, pp. 32-33.
11. Minutes of the Elizabethtown Humane Society, Rutgers University Library.
12. *NJJr.*, Dec. 19, 1815, Dec. 1, 1819, Aug. 30, 1831.
13. *Ibid.*, Sept. 27, 1825; Town Meeting Records of the Township of Elizabeth, Rutgers University Library.
14. *NJJr.*, Sept. 13, 1830, June 9, 1846; Report of the Trustees of the School Fund, 1845, Rutgers University Library; Smith, pp. 47-51.
15. *NJJr.*, March 4, 1856; Smith, pp. 53-55, 64.
16. *NJJr.*, July 16, 1816.
17. *Ibid.*, May 2, 1854.
18. *Ibid.*, May 15, 1821.
19. *Ibid.*, Jan. 1, 1822, May 24, 1824, Jan. 14, 1833, Dec. 9, 1835.
20. *Ibid.*, June 26, 1821, Jan. 23, 1827, July 14, 1838.
21. *Ibid.*, Jan. 8, 1816.
22. *Ibid.*, Aug. 8, 1820, April 22, 1822.
23. *Ibid.*, Dec. 30, 1817.
24. *Ibid.*, April 26, 1808; Minutes of the Elizabethtown Philanthropic Literary Society, Rutgers University Library.
25. *Ibid.*, May 15, 1821.
26. *Ibid.*, June 8, 1847.
27. *Ibid.*, May 3, 1808.
28. *Ibid.*, June 24, 1823, July 12, 1823, July 21, 1835.
29. *Ibid.*, Feb. 16, 1836.
30. *Ibid.*, March 2, 1835.
31. *Ibid.*, April 13, 1847.
32. *Ibid.*, July 15, 1825.
33. See Philip L. Kleinhans, *Down Through the Years* (Elizabeth, N.J., 1937).
34. *NJJr.*, March 28, 1837; Gibbons Papers, Drew University.
35. *Ibid.*, May 18, 1819.
36. *Ibid.*, July 3, 1810, April 3, 1821.

Chapter Twelve

1. Letters and papers belonging to Edward J. Grassmann of Elizabeth, N.J., throw much light on this scandal.

2. Gibbons Papers, Drew University.

3. *NJJr.*, May 31, 1803, May 15, 1804, July 2, 1805, March 22, 1818.

4. *Ibid.*, Dec. 22, 1812; Daniel Dod to John Ward, Nov. 30, 1816, Grassmann Collection.

5. *Ibid.*, Nov. 3, 1812; Ogden's Petition, Oct. 29, 1813, State Library, Trenton.

6. Gibbons Papers, #336A, *op. cit.;* Stevens also ran a horse boat between New York and Hoboken at this time.

7. Gibbons Papers, May 5, 1815, *op. cit.*

8. Gibbons to Ogden, Aug. 4, 1815, *ibid.*

9. Gibbons Papers, Oct. 16, 1815, *ibid.*

10. *Ibid.*, Nov., 1815, Dec. 5, 1817; *NJJr.*, Feb. 27, 1816, July 1, Oct. 25, 1817.

11. Gibbons Papers, April 13, 1818, *ibid.*

12. Injunction against Gibbons, Oct. 20-21, 1818, *ibid.*

13. Brief for Gibbons by his lawyers, 1819, *ibid.*

14. *Ibid.*, #391; Ogden's Petition, *op. cit.; NJJr.*, Feb. 3, 1820.

15. Injunction, May 8, 1820, *ibid.*

16. Injunction, Sept. 30, 1820, *ibid.*

17. *NJJr.*, Aug. 14, 1821.

18. *Ibid.*, Nov. 20, 1821.

19. *Ibid.*, July 27, 1822.

20. Tax Rolls, State Library, Trenton.

21. *NJJr.*, May 19, 1829.

22. *Ibid.*, May 5, 1829.

23. *Ibid.*, Sept. 30, 1828.

24. Minutes of the Corp., June 5, 1833, *op. cit.*

25. *NJJr.*, Jan. 6, 1801; Gibbons Papers, Sept. 1, 1804, *op. cit.*

26. John Cunningham, *Railroading in New Jersey* (Newark Sunday News, Jan. 7-Apr. 19, 1951).

27. *NJJr.*, Feb. 15, Nov. 20, 1830, April 2, 1831.

28. *Ibid.*, Feb. 27, 1831; Contract for Building the Railroad, Feb. 25, 1836, Jersey Central Office, Jersey City, N.J.

29. *NJJr.*, July 26, Aug. 2, 1836.

30. *Ibid.*, Aug. 16, 1836.

31. See papers at the Jersey Central Office, Jersey City, N.J.

32. Emogene Van Sickle, *The Old York Road* (Flemington, N.J., 1936).

33. *NJJr.*, Jan. 5, 1836.

34. *Ibid.*, Jan. 10, Apr. 25, 1837.

35. Minutes of the Corp., 1847, *op. cit.*

36. *NJJr.*, May 6, Nov. 11, 1845.

37. *Ibid.*, April 25, 1848.

38. *Ibid.*, Jan. 9, 1849.

39. *Ibid.*, Jan. 13, 1849, Feb. 26, April 22, 1850.

Index

Scale 150 Chains to an Inch.

Chains.

the West Jersey Society's Purchase, made in 1711.

falls of Lamatunk

Indian Purchase, October 29th 1701.

the Line now claimed by the Elizabeth Town People as the Great

Indian April

Indian Purchase, Novemb. 10th 1714.

Indian Purchase June 24th 1717.

Indian Pur. March 16 1690 For.

Willocks Purchase made Octob. 13th 1709.

Cushitunk Hills

Holland Brook

The Lottery Purchase made June 20th 1700.

Indian Purchase Aug. 2th 1688.

Indian Purchase Octob. 9th 1685.

Indian Purchase Nov. 19th 1681.

Indian Purchase Nov. 19th 1681.

Malunick

Indian Purchase Nov. 19th 1681.

Indian Purchase May 12th 1681.

Indian purchase May 4th 1681.

Dead River

Indians Wigwam

Bound Brook

Managy O Pis.

Raritan River